Boring Formless Nonsense

Boring Formless Nonsense

Experimental Music and the Aesthetics of Failure

ELDRITCH PRIEST

B L O O M S B U R Y
NEW YORK • LONDON • NEW DELHI • SYDNEY

Bloomsbury Academic

An imprint of Bloomsbury Publishing Plc

175 Fifth Avenue 50 Bedford Square

New York   London

NY 10010   WC1B 3DP

USA   UK

www.bloomsbury.com

First published 2013

Library of Congress Cataloging-in-Publication Data
Priest, Eldritch.
Boring formless nonsense : experimental music and the aesthetics of failure / by eldritch Priest.
p. cm.
Includes bibliographical references and index.
ISBN 978-1-4411-2213-1 (pbk. : alk. paper)-- ISBN 978-1-4411-2475-3 (hardback : alk. paper) 1. Avant-garde (Music) 2. Music–Philosophy and aesthetics. I. Title.
ML3877.P75 2013
780.9'04–dc23
2012030063

ISBN: HB: 978-1-4411-2475-3
PB: 978-1-4411-2213-1

Typeset by Fakenham Prepress Solutions, Fakenham, Norfolk NR21 8NN

...so the other pirates don't see it.

Contents

Pretext

I am extremely grateful to Geraldine Finn whose support and counsel during the research of this work, as well as her commitment to the pure adventure of thought, helped make the morass of my own thinking, if not entirely clear (to me), then at least (partially) interesting. I am also grateful to the composers who were kind enough to discuss their work with me and to provide me scores, recordings, and images of these, which, for the most part, are not commercially available.

Thank you also to Timothy Murray and The Society for the Humanities at Cornell University, and to Brian Massumi for allowing me to crash his course and entertain my questions during a short stay in Ithaca, NY, while I was in the middle of writing this book. Paul Hegarty also deserves thanks for reading an earlier version of this work and accommodating the text's special blend of irreverence, sincerity, and auto-discombobulation.

Numerous friends and colleagues have also supported this work. Special thanks, however, must be made to David Cecchetto who takes things like this seriously (mostly), Marc Couroux for encouraging my dare and being part of its strange feedback loop, and John Mark Sherlock for his moments of therapeutic lucidity and staunch refusal to say "simulacrum" properly. My folks, of course, must be acknowledged, if not only for their boundless supply of emotional and financial support, then for having the courage to not completely understand what I've been up to all these years, yet love and encourage me anyways.

And while it's perhaps expected that friends, family, and colleagues will support, if not actively promote one's gambles, there is no such expectation that a stranger will. In this respect I have to give props to David Barker whose immediate enthusiasm for this work was not only unexpected but a sustaining device.

Thank you to Penelope whose wish is my command and unbridled success is my wish. And lastly, my immense gratitude to Claudette

Lauzon whom I shower with illimitable thanks for helping me to realize this project, but most of all, for the immeasurable love that I know I will spend my life failing to match.

Note: An earlier version of Chapter One appeared in *Postmodern Culture* 21, no. 2 (2011).

Introduction

A gamble

Right off I'll show you my cards: failure has no point. There won't be any more fussing here over the way failure and success spiral around each other. Even though it can be amusing to occupy oneself with the semantic loop that arises if one intends to fail and does so, whereupon one succeeds and therefore fails to fail, but in failing to fail one fails and therefore succeeds, and so fails again and succeeds again…I prefer not to. I don't suggest by this declination, this "Bartlebyism," that there are better things to do than ride this corkscrew of thought. I do, however, contend that there are fewer words to play with and fewer hands to reveal if all we want to do is solve this paradox. We can play a game of tag or we can play poker. While poker is probably not superior to tag when it comes to the point(lessness) of games, at least it has "straights" and "flushes," "flops" and "pocket kings," "folds" and "bluffs" by which the difference among the ranks of royals and suits is more variedly expressed. Failure, in other words, figures in what follows not as a paradox but as a gamble.

But let me also say that I have no intention of defining failure. Not only is the work of defining failure exactly the kind of thing that is *not* going on in the musical practices that comprise the remit of this study, but failure is itself a radically relational term that, despite its seeming finality and veiled fatalism, is easily overturned or inverted with the simplest change of context or relevance. Consider how easily Thelonious Monk's (relatively) awkward and somewhat clumsy playing style was reimagined as "inventive" and "imaginative," and how often film flops become cult favorites (like current rep cinema darling Tommy Wiseau's *The Room* of 2003).[1] In fact, the history of twentieth-century art can be seen as a continuous reversal of

---

[1] See Tom Bissell, "Cinema Crudité: The Mysterious Appeal of the Post-Camp Cult Film," *Harper's Magazine*, August 2010, 60.

failures: from fascist lunatic "noise" to visionary sound art (Luigi Russolo's *Gran Concerto Futuristico*), and from an ordinary pisser to an acute conceptual vector (Marcel Duchamp's *Fountain*).[2]

Secondly, failure as a term of art becomes, like Roland Barthes' *le neutre*, George Bataille's *informe*, or Derrida's "*différance*," a fugitive concept—one that evades those structures of thought and expression that impose themselves as obligatory, but which at the same time is only conceivable and sensible through those same structures. For instance, Barthes' concept of *le neutre* as an impossibly impartial position within discourse is undermined with every illustration of it, for as he himself notes, "to utter a word is immediately to affirm its referent."[3] To affirm something is to determine its position and thereby to say something about this "something" debars it from both "the perfection (the respite) of the negative"[4] and the indifference of the neutral. As such, Barthes can never unequivocally say what *le neutre* is. His only option is to confound language, to battle it. And Barthes does exactly this: He battles language not by refusing to speak, but by distracting and baffling it with *extemporizations* on subjects that hinge on ambivalence such as silence, Zen, negative theology, Pyrrhonic scepticism, affect, and androgyny. Essentially, what Barthes practices is a form of discursivity that respects discourse's capacity for digression and drift. By riffing on a thematic ambivalence, Barthes illuminates the sense of the neutral *in passing*, his improvisations each producing a peculiar angle that allows us to register what he calls the "twinklings" of *le neutre*. While this generates the impression that Barthes is merely practicing a form of free association, he is in fact creating an anamorphoric discourse, a discourse whose distorted form appears intelligible only when viewed from a particular gaze or at a particular angle. This kind of discourse is a way to "sidestep assertion,"[5] which itself is an expression of the way that *le neutre* must work to evade the authority of the "laws" that discourse generates by virtue of its habit of iteration.

---

[2] Both, perhaps coincidentally, from 1917.

[3] Roland Barthes, *The Neutral: Lecture Course at the Collège De France, 1977–1978*, trans. Rosalind Krauss and Denis Hollier (New York: Columbia University Press, 2005), 42.

[4] Ibid., 43.

[5] Ibid.

The "sidestepping" of assertion can itself be understood as an expression of failure insofar as the implicit explication of *le neutre* can go easily unnoticed. That is, the obliquity of Barthes' disquisitions on the neutral—a technique that *in*-folds rather than *un*-folds the many ways in which *le neutre*'s evasion (dis)locates a paradoxical (pro)position such that it asserts its own non-assertion—may fail to be perceived and appreciated. Failure rings through Barthes' notion of the neutral not so much as an analogous paradox of explicable inexplicability, but in the way that its figure, too, participates in the "implicarity" of its expression. If it is to avoid an explication that converts its dim twinklings into shining successes, the implication of failure must take a chance in not being registered or discerned. And it's in this respect that failure begins to resemble a gamble, for there is no certainty that failure's significance as a virtual or implicit cipher for the relevant beliefs, expectations, and goals of a culture or social group will be perceived in such a warped discursive hand. Yet it is perhaps in mistaking failure's implication for the lack of an explication that failure fails to be even a gamble. So opaque are its insinuations and suggestions that the allusive risk of failure, the very capacity to be otherwise than what's expected, is lost to its own digressions. But then again, maybe that's its interest, for failure can only ever succeed, and this success is failure's failure.

With this in mind, and before I lay out my own peculiar hand, I want to look at the different ways that failure has been theorized and thematized, and draw out some of the (in)felicities of these approaches. While the following commentary respects the digressive nature of discursive matter by surveying a broad range of failures, I nevertheless follow a certain drift that describes, somewhat circuitously, the arc of failure's increasing abstraction as it passes from the familiar halting of malfunction, through the wonder of naiveté and frustration of undecidability, to the sublimated ambivalence of absolute potential.

Failure

A country road. A tree. Evening. Estragon, sitting on a low mound, is trying to take off his boot. He pulls at it with both hands, panting. He gives up, exhausted, rests, tries again. As before. Enter Vladimir.

Estragon: (*giving up again*).
  Nothing to be done.
Vladimir: (*advancing with short, stiff strides, legs wide apart*).
  I'm beginning to come round to that opinion. All my life I've tried
  to put it from me, saying Vladimir, be reasonable, you haven't yet
  tried everything. And I resumed the struggle.
  (*He broods, musing on the struggle. Turning to Estragon.*)
  So there you are again.

As tired and worn as Estragon's boot, these opening lines of
Beckett's *Waiting for Godot* are the archetypal image of modern
failure: a struggle, a meditation, and nothing to be done. The passion
of the mystic and the clown, where holy resignation is a practical
joke. Most accounts that take failure as an explicit theme revolve
around just this kind of dialectical indecision, where a conflicted
existentiale spins and stalls on the coincidence of futility and
stubborn persistence. Take, for instance, a recent edited volume
on failure in contemporary art. Several of the collected writings,
from artist statements to critical essays, represent failure in relation
to terms that fixate on the way mutual negations paradoxically
affirm each other, from Søren Kierkegaard's take on irony ("it can
be just as ironic to pretend to know when one knows that one
does not know as to pretend not to know when one knows that
one knows")[6] to Julian Schnabel's description of his own art as "a
bouquet of mistakes" ("I am making a synonym for the truth with all
its falsehoods").[7] But perhaps the most prevalent image of failure,
in this same volume and in contemporary culture at large, is the
myth of Sisyphus: A king punished by the gods for his impudence is
infected with an interminable compulsion to repeatedly push, carry,
or roll an immense stone up a hill and then watch it tumble down.
What the expression "Sisyphean" captures is nothing less than the
sentiment and affection of an "eternal involvement"—existentialism's code for "life." Hence Beckett's equally resonant and affecting,
"*All of old. Nothing else ever. Ever tired. Ever failed. No matter. Try*

---

[6] Søren Kierkegaard, "The Concept of Irony," in *Failure*, ed. Lisa Le Feuvre (Cambridge, MA: MIT Press, 2010), 73.
[7] Julian Schnabel, "Statement," in *Failure*, 131.

again. Fail again. Fail better."[8] But there is something queer about these words: the rhythm extracts a sense of life from their entropic despair to suggest that something productive or generative lies within their downward spiral of miscarriages. And indeed, as writer-artist Emma Cocker contends, the Sisyphean task is "more than a model of endless or uninterrupted continuation of action…it is a punctuated performance."[9] While the sense of the task remains the same across every iteration of the "un-deed"—a goal, an action, an insufficient attempt—the Sisyphean gesture itself has the potential to be endlessly individuated. And this potential inheres in the punctuation, in the interval where the task rests and difference slips in to create "a *pause* for thought, a space for thinking."[10]

The pause, what Camus, in his *Le Mythe de Sisyphe* (1942) called a "breathing-space," is nestled in the circuit of failure as a splinter of heightened awareness that carries a potential for a difference which "produces an unexpected surplus, the residue or demonstration of wasted energy."[11] Surplus is where failure's specificity abides, a specificity that exposes a culture's limits and absurdities, its structures of desire and orders of the real. Much of the conceptual and post-conceptual art that emerged from the experiments of the 1960s and 1970s can be seen as attempts to isolate and express this surplus. For instance, John Baldessari's *Throwing four balls in the air to get a square (best of 36 tries)* (1974)—a sequence of eight photographs that capture a hand throwing four balls into the air, almost, but not quite forming a square—expresses an ocular surplus in the way an initially narrow demonstration of repeated failures can become seen as an inadvertent juggling act. More recently, Belgian artist Francis Alÿs' video work, *The Rehearsal (II)* (2001), which shows a burlesque dancer practicing her routine in parallel to a musical rehearsal on the soundtrack, expands the ordinary flow of desire by extending its feeling into the typically occulted time of production instead of limiting it to the time of the product—the performance. *The Rehearsal* is Sisyphean insofar as its intended results—i.e. a swifter

[8] Samuel Beckett, *Worstward Ho* (London: John Calder, 1983), 7.
[9] Emma Cocker, "Over and Over, Again and Again," in *Failure*, 154.
[10] Ibid., 155.
[11] Ibid., 156.

removal of the bra, a smoother transition from verse to chorus—can never be anything but "good enough," which is to say that practice has no end: it is excessive. Practice skews the concluding perfection of the perfect. To open practice to desire is to scar the verisimilitude of all performances, performances of gender, ownership, race, or even art, music, and thought, with the sense of their own ongoing imperfection. In chasing failure and its factious breathing space, these works, and presumably those who experience them, are led to new events, new ways of expressing the sense, or the nonsense as it were, of failing.

It is the expression of an incidental and immanent excess, the "silver lining" or the hidden grace of Sisyphus's plight that is the most common way in which art is thought to engage with failure. In fact, I would suggest that Cocker's view of failure as "a device for deferring closure or completion, or...a mode of resistance through which to challenge or even refuse the pressures of dominant goal-oriented doctrines,"[12] can be taken as a general definition of an aesthetics of failure. The problem with this definition, however, is not only that it's too broad, but it's also too satisfying, too sufficient. It suggests that the aesthetic practices it applies to are certain of their own project and their own effects, that power is so clear a target and its agents so feeble that a well-aimed failure can safely and securely "rupture or destabilize the authority of the rule while keeping it in place."[13] As such, this aesthetics of failure misses the point, which is my point: that failure has no particular point, that it is radically perspectival and, ultimately, despite the regularities that restrict its measure, radically indeterminate.

The obvious way to explain this indeterminacy is that failure is essentially an assertion of "judgement relative to certain *norms*."[14] But as historian of science and philosophy Koen Vermeir notes, norms are often vague, multiple, and part of a "broader framework

---

[12] Ibid.

[13] Ibid.

[14] Koen Vermeir, "The Reality of Failure: On the Interpretaion of Success and Failure in (the History and Philosophy of) Science and Technology," in *Variantology 2: On Deep Time Relations of Arts, Sciences and Technologies*, ed. Siegfried Zielinski and David Link (Köln: Buchhandlung Walther König, 2006), 343.

of beliefs, expectations and goals"[15] such that the judgement made in their regard is subject to perpetual revision. For instance, musician Kim Cascone's widely circulated essay about the aesthetics of failure in electronic music judges failure according to the conventional uses of digital technologies.[16] Vermeir calls this convention a "function on which the characterisation or meaning of the artefact crucially depends,"[17] such as the ability for a bicycle, whether fast, slow, safe, or stylish, to "go," or an mp3 player, whether an iPod or some cheap Chinese knock-off, to "play music." Cascone's expressions of failure—"glitches, bugs, application errors, system crashes, clipping, aliasing, distortion, quantization noise, and even the noise floor of computer sound cards"[18]—are judgements made according to the way they skew the assumed functionality of the digitally instrumentalized artefact, a functionality that in contemporary industrial cultures revolves around expressions of speed, connectivity (to other digital technologies), and simulation. Yet these "failures" are not naked failures. They are dressed in scare-quotes, which directs judgement towards something non-functional, something that creates an irresistible alliance with a network of significations that do not necessarily interfere with the "positivist and functionalist paradigm [of] our technological society."[19] From this perspective, a "glitch" is a dialectical attribute of digital technology's core function and is at once a technological failure and an aesthetic success.

This example of "failure" suggests that judgements which shift from assessing functional to non-functional norms, lets call these "aesthetic," entails a shift from the distinct to the indistinct. Said another way, failure's passage from a digital field—"it works 'this' way or it does not"—to an analogue field—"it works *well* 'this' way, *less* well 'that' way, but if you do 'that' over and over again and again, something wonderful happens" (maybe)—turns its event inside out. The discrete event of the glitch as a break in an artefact's practicable relays becomes a continuous event when the evaluation of its

---

[15] Ibid.
[16] See Kim Cascone, "The Aesthetics of Failure: 'Post-Digital' Tendencies in Contemporary Computer Music," *Computer Music Journal* 24, no. 4 (2000).
[17] Vermeir, "The Reality of Failure," 350.
[18] Cascone, "The Aesthetics of Failure," 13.
[19] Vermeir, "The Reality of Failure," 348.

occasion is caught up in its own duration, in its temporization. A point of fault becomes a faultline when its evaluation is prolonged, for the process of assessment, in effect, suffers a hitch that cannot help but accumulate expressive correspondences, an accumulation that intensifies the abstract potential of a fault by giving the derivative meanings that cling to its spurious barb the chance to tell another story. Aesthetic norms, besides being vague and multifarious, encourage this kind of serial or intensive engagement because their measure is an abstraction of how one relates to things rather than how one uses things. And this kind of measure is largely feeling-based, for feelings are embodied gauges of how organisms "abstractly see [or hear] potential."[20] As Brian Massumi argues, perception is not simply a matter of registering what is actually before us but a way of sensing the virtuality or event-ality that is implicated in an encounter between our body and objects. Every actual sight or sound is set off against an auratic flow of virtual movements or actions that poise the body for what may come. The feeling of beauty, for example, is not a registering of the harmony of parts to a whole, but a process of dwelling in the fluctuating intensity or principle of a promise that what-may-come will be apt and satisfying. While this latter point suggests that aesthetic norms house a dimension of use or purpose, such as Darwin's theory that music functions as an erotic lure,[21] this is largely eclipsed by the way certain forms, like a song or even a simple arabesque, for instance, foreground the abstract dynamics that inhere in perception. Aesthetic assessment is an ongoing affair whose findings are persistently self-modulating such that aesthetic success and failure play out their mutual indeterminacy as relative degrees of satisfaction.

The emphasis that aesthetic judgements place on relative satisfaction is what makes failure in terms of music so dodgy and disputable.

---

[20] Brian Massumi, *Semblance and Event: Activist Philosophy and the Occurrent Arts* (Cambridge, MA: MIT Press, 2011), 43.

[21] Darwin's take on the origin of music reflects what he sees as an order of sexual selection based on sensation, on the way that vibrations pass from a material phenomenon to an immaterial effect—desire. See Elizabeth Grosz's essay "Vibration. Animal, Sex, Music" in *Chaos, Territory, Art: Deleuze and the Framing of the Earth* (New York: Columbia University Press, 2008) for an unpacking of Darwin's theory of music as it is filtered through Deleuze and Guattari's concept of "the refrain."

Because a melody not only solicits comparison with a tradition of song or a convention of thematic development, but also proposes the contemplation of and/or identification with a type of mood that in turn plugs into the micro-politics of social affiliation, its satisfaction, even though polyvalent, is always more or less failing in one sense and succeeding in another. While common to all aesthetic judgement, this ambiguity of satisfactions is made particularly evident when considering the category of "outsider music." For example, The Shaggs. Hailing from Freemont, New Hampshire, The Shaggs (Dot, Betty, and Helen Wiggins) represent a wider field of musical culture that is "outside" by virtue of its originating beyond the pale of official culture.[22] Branded as outsider art, and characterized by a stunning absence of self-consciousness whose piercing sincerity can't help but make the non-outsider feel like a voyeur, the music of The Shaggs is pure incompetence. To the unprepared listener, The Shaggs' 1969 studio album, *Philosophy of the World*, comes off as what music critic Irwin Chusid's describes as a spectacle of "hacked-at chords, missed downbeats, out-of-socket transitions, blown accents, and accidental convergences."[23] Yet despite The Shaggs' excessive ineptitude and botched musicality, there is an irresistible charm that radiates from their performance. Chusid suggests that this is because *Philosophy of the World* is "100 percent authenticity and refreshingly guileless."[24] That is to say, the album's paroxysmal and convulsive grooves embody a kind of sincerity that official musical culture is incapable of achieving. As such, it purports to access a form of purity that, like all forms of sincerity, comically exposes the routine workings and conceits of what *should* be supple and elastic—like our definitions of "art" or "music." Because *Philosophy of the World* is presented as an unabashed album of pop songs, it sets up certain expectations and activates assumptions about musical phenomena that are utterly disappointed. But in failing to satisfy these, it remainders a certain bathos that reflects on the artificially stable categories of aesthetic success. By most accounts the songs on *Philosophy of the World* should fail

---

[22] In general, this means culture whose expressions are affiliated with some kind of social institution, whether conservatory, museum, gallery, record company, university, or even social club.

[23] Irwin Chusid, *Songs in the Key of Z: The Curious Universe of Outsider Music* (Chicago: A Cappella, 2000), 1–2.

[24] Ibid., 2.

as "music," especially as pop music, which by definition hews to an especially rigid expressive formulae. Although while the Wiggins sisters clearly fail with respect to the conventional norms of practicing an instrument, performing in a band, and writing songs, the impossible consistency of their gormless performance on *Philosophy of the World* has a way of mystifying expectations and subverting the usual set of expressive correspondences such that anyone who listens to this music for anything greater than the time it takes to dismiss it cannot help but feel a qualitative realignment in how things like competence and originality are satisfied. In this regard the aesthetics of outsider music, which revolves around a logic wherein the absolute failure to satisfy an already determined purpose coincides with the success to satisfy an unintentional objective, draws explicit attention to the ultimately indeterminate nature of failure.

In addition to intensifying the perceptual convolutions of evaluation, aesthetic judgements stress how failure's thematic representation is often oxymoronic. Despite being represented as a phenomenon constituent to progress and achievement, failure's entanglement with success is not so much essential as it is structural and expressive. To represent failure, which is to abstract its occasion from a wider event, is to articulate expressions of unintentionality with expressions that affirm intentionality, as for instance Bruce Nauman's double exposed photograph, *Failing to Levitate in the Studio* (1966), in which the artist's body is shown suspended and collapsed between two folding chairs, and Jonathan Monk's *Searching for the Centre of a Sheet of Paper (White on Black/Black on White)* (2003), an animated video depicting two people trying to place a dot in the centre of a sheet of paper, do. Both works thematize failure and so couple an involuntary event—*not* levitating, missing the centre of the paper—with a voluntary activity such that the outcome cannot but express itself as a negative event. Like Lewis Carroll's Snark, the expressions of failure in these works say their own sense, which is to say that "failure" (in scare-quotes or in the genitive case "aesthetics of failure" (also in thematizing scare-quotes)) is an "x" that radiates sense but is itself "never where it is sought and always where it cannot be found."[25] A thematic failure is a structural

---

[25] Ronald Bogue, *Deleuze and Guattari* (London; New York: Routledge, 1989), 75.

effect, an oxymoronic expression that resembles any other aesthetic expression to the extent that its expression foregrounds the way one always perceives relationally and processually, the way one feels an abstract potential for more or otherwise in every occasion of hearing or seeing, *etcetera*. However, the "failure effect" isolates the abstract potential of an event so thoroughly that unlike Mona Lisa's enigmatic smirk that actually satisfies some of its possible expressions of being amused, beguiled, or charmed, it obscures itself with the virtual satisfaction of everything that it is not. Thus, the singularity of failure is concealed by the coincidence of a purposeful mistake. Making a theme of failure is therefore an oxymoronic expression.

But so what if a thematic failure is oxymoronic? An oxymoron is not impassive, for its conjoined contraries produce a hermetic expression whose form enjoins "a definite mode and shading of association."[26] In *Infidel Poetics* (2009), Daniel Tiffany argues that a puzzling or cryptic expression such as that presented by a riddle "does not imply the absence of disclosure or sociability"; instead, its deliberate obscurity "serve[s] as the impetus and object of a guessing game—a social configuration which converts the sound bite of the oracle into a literary toy, improvised in contests of wit on convivial occasions."[27] More specifically, Tiffany contends that "lyric obscurity," the seemingly alienated and alienating effects of certain types of expressions (of which he suggests poetry is the most representative), stages a failure of meaning but nevertheless functions "as an expressive medium, or substance, harmonizing disparate phenomena, just as sociological obscurity defines the basic condition of countless subcultures and historical underworlds."[28] The failure of meaning does not then necessarily annul the relational power of obscurity. Instead, much like the counterfeit relations that sustain various social underworlds, obscurity facilitates "transactions…in the absence of ostensible relations,"[29] and so enjoys the status of what Tiffany, borrowing from Leibniz, calls a "courtesy substance": obscurity is "a 'semi-being' straddling the divide between sensible

---

[26] Daniel Tiffany, *Infidel Poetics: Riddles, Nightlife, Substance* (Chicago: University of Chicago Press, 2009), 5.

[27] Ibid., 4.

[28] Tiffany, *Infidel Poetics*, 10.

[29] Ibid., 9.

and insensible orders of existence."[30] Obscurity's failure to make its form transparent is, in this sense, a transversal medium that catalyzes the "expressive and reciprocal correspondences"[31] between hermetic forms.

Susan Stewart maps a similar kind of underground relationship in her 1979 work on the mutually contingent nature of sense and nonsense, suggesting that nonsense, a substance parallel to obscurity, has various pragmatic and social effects that extend its forms of failure into the domain of the real. For Stewart, sense and nonsense are byproducts of the interpretive procedures a social group employs to compose and accomplish a shared horizon of relevance. What is established as either sense or nonsense, and by extension as real or unreal, is not fixed or entirely opposed to modification or manipulation, for as Stewart writes, it is only "an assumption of consensus" that makes either profile effective.[32] However, a consensus does not have to revolve around positives: "It may be that this consensus is assumed through a pattern of acknowledged misunderstandings,"[33] which is to say that things like obscurity, error, peccadillos, false impressions, and fiascos, too, can provide a certain (if only a negative) definition to consensual reality.

But perhaps a more radical and much less assenting model of the oxymoronic—the openly obscure—and one that aligns more with the sentiment of this work, is Paul Mann's notion of contemporary subcultures that he names "stupid undergrounds." Unlike either Tiffany's or Stewart's analysis of the largely hidden structures that organize a culture's social sphere, Mann argues that the members of various "Apocalyptic cults and youth gangs, *colleges*, and phalansteries, espionage networks trading in vaporous facts and networks of home shoppers for illicit goods; monastic, penological, mutant-biomorphic, and anarcho-terrorist cells..."[34] are hyper-aware

---

[30] Ibid., 10.

[31] Ibid., 12.

[32] Susan Stewart, *Nonsense: Aspects of Intertextuality in Folklore and Literature* (Baltimore: Johns Hopkins University Press, 1979), 49.

[33] Ibid.

[34] "...quasiscientific research units, paranoid think tanks, unregistered political parties, subemployed workers' councils, endo-exile colonies, glossolaliac fan clubs, acned

of the complicity and indirect collusion that is endemic to modern society's structures of centre/margin, power/resistance. Whereas for Tiffany's and Stewart's infidels and interpreters, membership in a community relies on a form of willful ignorance, Mann's undergrounders are not so much ignorant as they are willfully indifferent to their ineluctable participation in the cultural power/knowledge structures that they agitate. This indifference is further marked by a brazen apathy or morbid fascination that does not pretend to enact a higher ethics, redouble the critical gesture, or produce a greater kind of novelty. Instead, stupid indifference is simply a way to "get off" on the symptoms of difference excreted by a self-aware culture's compulsive need to organize, catalogue, and capitalize on (commodify) experience. As Mann writes,

> The energy released by the stupid underground is never anything more than an effect of its very morbidity. It is marketed as novelty, but that is not its truth. Nor will it ever constitute a base for opposition: it cannot be yoked to any program of reform, nor serve any longer the heroic myth of transgression. It is merely a symptom of order itself.[35]

Importantly for Mann, because his is a post-Baudrillard reality of simulation, the delightful misery of the stupid undergrounds belongs not only to the marginal and disenfranchised but is shared by the cultural critic who feels driven to examine the simulacral cadavers that festoon the desert of the real. Mann suggests that like the undergrounds themselves, there is justification for this critical drive

---

anorexic primal hordes; zombie revenants, neo-fakirs, defrocked priests and detoxing prophets, psychedelic snake-oil shills, masseurs of overdiagnosed symptoms, bitter excommunicants, faceless narcissists, ideological drag queens, mystical technophiles, subentrepreneurial dealers, derivative *dérivistes*, tireless archivists of phantom conspiracies, alien abductees, dupe factota, tardy primitives, vermin of abandoned factories, hermits, cranks, opportunists, users, connections, outriders, outpatients, wannabes, wanna-not-bes, hackers, thieves, squatters, parasites, saboteurs; wings, wards, warehouses, arcades, hells, hives, dens, burrows, lofts, flocks, swamis, viruses, tribes, movements, groupuscules, cenacles, isms, and the endlessly multiplied hybridization of variant combinations of all these, and more." Paul Mann, *Masocriticism* (Albany: State University of New York Press, 1999), 127.
[35] Ibid., 139.

besides "an unendurable habit of attention, a meager fascination [that is] no more or less commanding than that hypnosis one enters in the face of television."[36] In this regard, the stupid undergrounds and cultural criticism are both masochistic gestures that reflect a self-fulfilling trend in contemporary culture to manage its addiction to difference by intensifying the expression of that difference. In this model then, the stupid intelligence of both critic and undergrounder draw out the oxymoronic as a way to "complicate cultural space for a moment or two...to thicken it and slow one's passage through it... to render criticism [and expression] itself as painful and difficult as possible."[37]

Except perhaps for Mann's analytical suicides, what all these figures of failure and the oxymoronic seem to construe are the mechanics of an unacknowledged potentiality, what might be characterized as the potential of potentiality. But while this doubleness of potential is merely implicit in the preceding figures, it is something that Giorgio Agamben attempts to foreground in his essay on contingency with respect to Herman Melville's *Bartleby, the Scrivener*. For Agamben, Bartleby's formula—"I prefer not to"—is an expression of absolute potentiality that "destroys all possibility of constructing a relation between being able and being willing."[38] It is potentiality's capture by what Agamben calls our "ethical tradition" and its emphasis on expressions of the will—"what you *want* to do or *must* do"—that elides capacity with necessity and so exempts from potentiality the concurrence of "to do" *and* "not to do." "I prefer not to" is an experimental event in the sense that its utterance, which suspends negation, doubt, and contradiction, expresses the full potential of potentiality and designates "an experience characterized by the disappearance of all relation to truth."[39] That is to say, "I prefer not to" questions what is possible; it "call[s] into question Being itself, before or beyond its determination as true or false" so that "whoever submits himself to these experiments jeopardizes not so much the truth of his own statements as the very mode of his

---

[36] Ibid., 128.
[37] Ibid., 129.
[38] Giorgio Agamben, "Bartleby, or on Contingency," in *Potentialities: Collected Essays in Philosophy*, ed. Daniel Heller-Roazen (Stanford: Stanford University Press, 1993), 255.
[39] Ibid., 259–60.

existence."[40] Here, Agamben's tone reveals that Bartleby's formula is not only an experiment but also a kind of existential analytic, and that the failure in which it is always implicated is an affair of being, of Being-in-the-world.

From the perspective of potentiality, the mechanics of failure have little to do with actual cases of malfunction or deficiency and more to do with the contours of existence. The paradox that failure articulates in this respect is not a dialectical conundrum as much as a category of being, a category that while no less real than, say, "minds," "classes," "properties," "events," or "relations," cannot be lived *out* but only lived *in*—being lived in the occasion of its self-abstraction. In other words, paradox characterizes a mode of being that is virtual. Michael Marder draws out this line of thought with regard to Martin Heidegger's analysis of experience in *Being and Time*, suggesting that from failure springs forth "Both too much and too little: not things in their actuality, but being in its possibility, in the futurity of its future."[41] For Marder, Heidegger's existential analytic divorces the question of failure from "the ideals of actuality and actualization"[42] because his phenomenological method emphasizes the "possibilization of *Dasein*" over the essentialization of being. Being (*Dasein*), in this analytic, is nothing but "ecstatic"—standing out. But *Dasein* is not *a* standing-out-from-some-thing, which would make it just another thing among things, but the *activity* of standing out, the "standing out-ness" itself whose expressions are essentially expressions of involvement, concern, and fascination. To be more precise, the ecstatic nature of Being is its *potential* to stand out and this can only be expressed in terms of what Heidegger calls *Dasein*'s "falling" (*Verfallen*), its way of caring for and belonging to the everyday. As such, the ecstasies that express Being are also the ecstasies that perplex it; in Heidegger's terms, standing out articulates the "authentic" stillness or virtuality of *Dasein* with the "inauthentic" turbulence or noise of being-with (*Mit-Dasein*). What this amounts to is that *Dasein* can only express itself, its potential to

---

[40] Ibid., 260.
[41] Michael Marder, "Heidegger's 'Phenomenology of Failure' in *Sein Und Zeit*," *Philosophy Today* 51, no. 1 (2007): 77.
[42] Ibid., 70.

stand out, by failing to be itself, to be only and fully this potential (to stand out). It is here, in the existential comportment where *Dasein* dis/articulates itself from its own potential, that Marder argues failure is uncoupled from actuality and comes "to be associated with the realm of possibility, if not the very possibility of possibility."[43] The virtual fissure that cleaves *Dasein* is a structural necessity of the existential analytic that elaborates a convoluted awakening wherein *Dasein* (loses and)[44] finds itself, first in the din of its sociality where it "*fails to hear* [*überhört*] its own self in listening to the they-self," and then as "something which failed to hear itself, and which fails to hear that it *listens away* to the they."[45] Or as Marder writes,

> The ecstatic constitution of *Dasein* renders failure itself ecstatic, given that the failure of hearing the call of conscience is measured against the "success" of placing the call by "one's own *Dasein*" who fails. Failure fails ecstatically.[46]

Dasein's *ekstasis*, which is its "authentic potentiality-for-being" that by necessity is "always already [socially] inflected or convolute," is the "modalization of failure."[47] In other words, how one finds oneself feeling about the type of situation that one (already) finds oneself in is always a mood of *Dasein*'s originary failure. Strictly speaking then, existence is a series of moody failures.

Music

From the outset, I said that I would refrain from defining failure and instead illuminate its "twinklings." By far the brightest twinkle is that failure is not a point as much as it is a potential or an intensive measure of relative satisfaction. And music, too, insofar as it is

---

[43] Ibid.
[44] This has to be placed in parentheses, for the matter of Being's being "lost" is a matter that is retrojected in how it finds itself (*Befindlichkeit*).
[45] Martin Heidegger, *Being and Time*, trans. John Macquarrie and Edward Robinson (Oxford: Blackwell, 1978), 315–16.
[46] Marder, "Heidegger's 'Phenomenology of Failure'," 72.
[47] Ibid., 73.

as a place holder for the potential to compose, perform, or listen, yet also a potential to practice, to study, dance, shop to, protest or pray with, and most especially, to feel (to), resembles failure in its elusive satisfaction. As such, music, like failure, is point-less. Music's productive inconstancy models the kind of polymorphous perversity that makes failure so supple and multivalent, so evasive and so frustrating.

Of course, not all musical expressions reflect on or exploit the way music's own polymorphism untidies a culture's sense of reality and itself. Pop and film music, for example, function on an industry myth that music's social and emotional cues are reducible to a set of formulae and therefore representative of a well-ordered system of cause and effect. India's classical music, which classifies its *rāgas* (melodic formula) according to their appropriateness to a particular time of a day or season, and the traditional work songs of Sub-Saharan Africa whose rhythms are used to coordinate the body's movement with the timings of a task, explicitly emphasize music as an organizing force. However, when music's ambiguous or indeterminate nature is emphasized, even though its forms may still be embedded in distinct social practices with their own set of norms and conventions, it loses its status as an existential appliance and tends to fall into the category of the "experimental," a category like nonsense "that gives us a place to store any mysterious gaps in our systems of order."[48] For this study, however, I will use "experimental" in a more precise way to refer to music that takes the self-conscious and deliberate confusion which is characteristic of post-Cagean aesthetics as an expressive norm.

"How and what shall I listen to?" "Why is this music?" "What am I supposed to do with these sounds?" These are expressions that register the experimental occasion's ambiguity and refer to musical works that fail to affirm a ready-to-hand reality, for what is foregrounded by such an "experimental comportment" is music's event-hood. Rather than affirm a world whose terms and relations are fixed, the experimental designates the way and the degree to which a musical occasion traces an adventure through time and space, bringing disparate phenomena to interaction and invention. Thus, what makes

---

[48] Stewart, *Nonsense*, 5.

music experimental and truly pointless—a failure of sorts—is not how it ruptures the totality of our involvements (i.e. everyday reality) so as to be mutely present-at-hand, but how it emphasizes the way multiple and incompatible views and demands can subsist indeterminately in its occasion as a vague fringe or aura of potential aesthetic effects.

This sense of indeterminacy would seem to suggest that the experimental overlaps with some of the more daring practices of improvised music. While there is little doubt that Anthony Braxton's *Composition No. 247* (2000), with its minimalist-like para-unison melody[49] written for no instrument in particular that, like many of Braxton's works, carries the additional instruction for performers to spontaneously insert any other of Braxton's works into *247*, shares a sensibility with the priorities of Will Redman's *Book* (2006), a work comprising, as Redman describes, "ninety-eight graphic extrapolations of conventional music notation for interpretation (however radical) by any performer(s) in any place at any time in any part for any duration,"[50] I want to suggest that the latter has a slightly higher degree of failure than the former owing to the contradiction that inheres in its "intentional unintentionality." To act on this contradiction, which is what soi-disant "experimental" composers do, is to add a measure of internal inconsistency to the process(es) that composition embodies. And for the most part, because the musical results of an improvisation so closely align with an improviser's will as to make his/her intended or unintended profiles indistinguishable from each other, improvisation is exempt from this inconsistency. This of course does not mean that improvised music can't be experimental or can't fail; it just means that composed music's discrepant dealings with intention and inadvertence makes its failure shine a little brighter.

* * *

If this work has a point (which, if it's faithful to its thesis then it shouldn't), it is this: Experimental composition has no point, or at

---

[49] Braxton uses in this work what he calls a "diamond clef'" to indicate that pitches may be read in any clef (treble, alto, tenor, bass). The "para-unison" that describes *247*'s spontaneously harmonized melody is an effect conditioned by Braxton's leveraging an instrument's transposing conventions so that performers may read the same melodic material while sounding different pitches.

[50] Redman's *Book* is freely available at bookmusic.org.

least its post-Cagean variety has no particular point. But having no particular point doesn't exempt this music's expressions from having an effect. Music that swerves towards the experimental comportment of intentional unintentionality still affects us. As Aden Evens writes,

> Stripped of intention, sound no longer triggers responses from the standard catalog of emotions, no longer refers to the human activities of manufacture, performance, etc... [but] one still hears difference, sound is still pointed, but now out-of-joint, no longer pointing along a two-dimensional line with a universal history and a determinate future.[51]

Having no particular point is having too many points, just as that which opposes the absence of sense is not no-sense but too much sense—a presence opposing the lack of presence. Yet, as Sartre illustrated in *Nausea*, the revelation of this excess or superfluity does not necessarily come across as entirely pleasant, which is why Roquentin, when sitting by the Masqueret Fountain with its bubbling sound in his ears, a putrid odor in his nose, and the image of a chestnut tree's black and swollen bark in his eyes, declares, "Existence is a deflection," the displacement of a cloying abundance—*dépenses*. Sounds stripped of intention do not cease to signify, but neither do they say anything in particular. Instead, they imply or connote so much about so little in much the same way that affections like "sadness" or "love" evince only indistinct impressions of extremely complex sensations. A "de-intended" musical event, like the kind that Cage tried to manage, has an excessively charged vagueness to it by virtue of the way its "accidental" advent expands the margin of uncertainty informing its event to 100 per cent. This is why such formally remote works like Cornelius Cardew's *Treatise* (1963–7) or Christian Wolff's *Burdocks* (1970–1), both examples of what is called an "open work," give the sense of being swarmed by unarticulated signifiers and incipient movements: they are infused with an absolute vagueness that is "the way in which potential

---

[51] Aden Evens, *Sound Ideas: Music, Machines, and Experience* (Minneapolis: University of Minnesota Press, 2005), 49.

presents itself in the unfolding of experience."[52] It is what *sheer relation* sounds like in action, but with nowhere to go, no cynosure to guide it or transcendental signified to conduct it. As such, experimental composition tends to be boring, formless, and nonsensical (and sometimes nauseating). To that end, this study considers recent musical practices that express failure in these terms and in the way that they articulate an unintentional im-particularity by formulating expressions of waiting, insufficiency, distraction, dissatisfaction, bullshit, duplicity, and pain.

Manner

While this work appears to be composed of three distinct and independent chapters, they are, in fact, linked by more than simply how the consecution of their titles reads like a dopplering judgement. As modes of failure, boredom, formlessness, and nonsense have an internal correspondence in which the sense of each echoes within the others as a potential line of expression. Thus, boredom can be expressed by encounters with formless and senseless phenomena, and similarly, nonsense can be characterized by the tedious deformation of what passes for sense. This, however, is not made explicit in any of the chapters; rather, it is implied by the way many of the works that illustrate the expressions of one mode can be used to illuminate another, albeit from a different angle that emphasizes different properties and qualities of the musical work. Yet, despite this interpenetrability, I have retained the order of the chapters precisely because of the effect that their being read one after the other generates.

I begin this study by considering what is perhaps the most common trope of aesthetically fashioned failure: boredom. In this chapter, I challenge the received sense that boredom is an inchoate form of interest and suggest instead that the mood no longer affects the contemporary subject in a way that directs attention to the overlooked, a place where a splendor of intensities lay concealed

---

[52] Brian Massumi, *Parables for the Virtual: Movement, Affect, Sensation* (Durham, NC: Duke University Press, 2002), 232.

in the folds of infra-ordinary awareness. Considering first how boredom has become an ordinary affect of contemporary art and then examining the history of the malaise as a specifically modern mood, I contend that aesthetically articulated boredom is now more ambivalent in its effects in that it is more difficult to distinguish its hollowing sink from the low-level dullness that pervades activities such as watching television, continually checking one's email, or monitoring various twitter feeds. Drawing on Sianne Ngai's notion of the "stuplime," a stilted and undecidable response to expressions of an infinitely iterated finitude, and evoking alternative ways of suffering the passion of waiting, I use recent compositions to focus the scattered rays of monotony on a wider set of logics that can be found in numerous other aspects of contemporary culture. While heir to a well-defined tradition of anti-art represented in music primarily by the so-called "New York School" and by Fluxus, I argue that many composers who are now writing long, quiet, repetitive, and slow-moving music of the kind that is intended to be experienced without (external) interruption, express a sense of boredom that articulates with contemporary culture's dimensions of depression and simulation in a way that connects ambient feelings of uncertainty and being unjustified with neoliberal norms of independence which insist an individual take initiative and responsibility for his/her own identity.

Although my intentions in this chapter are directed primarily at adjusting the terms and stakes of what I see as boredom's stand-ardized justification in art and music as a way to delegate a work's meaning or value to the recipient—a gesture that is not without its merits—it is also a first attempt to baffle or outplay (*déjouer*) the discursive paradigm that frames so much criticism and analysis of avant-garde music. This means that I draw my argument crookedly, which entails making conceptual detours, drifting in and out of remote subjects, and, occasionally, running into a dead-end. Basically, in this chapter I try to enact an essayistic kind of "shunpiking," a way of writing that avoids major paths and toll roads for more "bucolic" and "scenic" interludes. Admittedly, this is only my initial attempt, and the roads only get windier from here.

In the second chapter, the focus shifts from the simulated and depressing refrains of having to choose one's "self" for oneself, to the conundrum that contemporary culture's norms of self-invention are enforced from within a field of continuous distraction. Whereas boredom's disaffection expresses the poverty of our culture's curiosity, formlessness characterizes how this same culture has developed habits of inattention in response to ubiquitous media forms (i.e. records, television, internet, *etcetera*). Audio technology, which not only historically leads the way in the escalation of mechanical reproduction's tendency to become smaller, more portable, and increasingly invisible, disarticulates sound from its site of production in a way that gives the listener permission to disregard the material cradle of sound. Music, which survives its own "live" death by becoming a recording (which is arguably less a death than a reincarnation of sorts), has been indirectly affected by this capacity for dis-articulation in that individuals in contemporary industrial societies have effectively learned how to listen away from or "unlisten" to musical sounds that are always, to some degree, drifting in the background. I suggest that listening away effects an aural anamorphosis by emphasizing music's background elements, elements which turn out to be the sloppy and imprecise qualities—affective and social qualities—that, in its obsession with structure and form, the tradition of Western concert music consigns to a non-conscious register of perception.

From the perspective of this art music tradition, the unconsciously acquired habits of listening away and under-hearing music offend its defining principle of structural listening, not by overturning its purview, but by turning it inside out. Whereas structural listening is based upon a set of historically developed techniques for immobilizing the body and sequestering its faculty of hearing in order to restrict perception to the active reception-interpretation of a work's immanent formal relations, the unintentional cultivation of distraction, in a sense, reverses this process and expands the field of immanence indefinitely, making the body sensitive to everything that is not structurally significant, even to things that it cannot hear. But listening away is ultimately a soft offense, for it is expressed not in a confrontational manner that characterizes the anti-aesthetics of Fluxus or the abject aesthetics of bands like Throbbing Gristle and Cabaret Voltaire, but in the incidental way that slipping on ice offends the balance of the body or the way in which puns offend language as a fixed and predictable set of correspondences. In this respect, I enlist Georges Bataille's idea of *informe* to address how certain contemporary experimental compositions exploit the drifts and digressions of distraction in a way that paradoxically draws attention to the "black noise" and "allure" radiating from musical sounds that have become something to be "unfocused on." Arguing that this murky allure elicits a strangely inaccessible sincerity, one that seduces the piqued listener into peculiar hermetic or "toy involvements," I conclude this chapter by suggesting certain composers suffer from what Rei Terada calls "phenomenophilia," an attraction to "off-beat perceptions" that deals with cultures of distraction by converting fragmented in/attention into a series of incipits to keep one's interests in-going rather than ongoing.

The final chapter, "Nonsense," can be considered a response to the speculations of the two previous chapters. Taking its cues from Chapter One's discussion of norms of self-invention and Chapter Two's discovery of a charm in distraction and a desire for outré perceptions, this phase of the study literally creates a metaphor that speaks to the way that music cannot speak for itself. This perhaps makes Chapter Three the most challenging section of the book, for it requires a dual awareness to follow the constant double-speak that allows one to say two things at once. "Nonsense" therefore requires more explanation than the other two chapters, for its form of address, by virtue of its topic, is highly reflexive and self-divided. You might expect then that a chapter on musical nonsense would take the kind of modernist twaddle of Kurt Schwitters' *Ursonata* or the virtuosic bilge of Frank Zappa's *Gregory Peccary* as its exemplary cases. And if not these, then perhaps something seemingly less mannered or refined such as the cochlear threshing of Lou Reed's *Metal Machine Music* or the electric squawk of Belgian musician Wim van Gelder (aka Portable Noise Kremator)'s cracklebox album. You might think that, but then you would be thinking about a chapter that is not this one.

To treat nonsense as simply a matter of non-understanding or unintelligible gobbledygook betrays a presupposition that nonsense is "simply." As Susan Stewart notes, nonsense is anything but "simply." "The nature of nonsense," she writes, "will always be contingent upon the nature of its corresponding common sense, and since common sense is always emergent in social processes, including nonsense activities, that category 'nonsense' will never have a stable content."[53] The forms that nonsense takes will always be "determined by the generic system available to the given set of members"[54] so that its expression, its manifestation as a type of failure, is dependent on how a situation is given a unique orientation with respect to some seemingly transcendental operator such as "God," "society," "truth," or even "use." Nonsense is not merely a relational term that is conterminous with sense, but, as I will explain, like sense, nonsense is something to creatively move on. Nonsense is in fact closer in form and effect to what we may identify as "indirection," or more slangy-like, as "bullshit." Like these forms of expression, nonsense is characterized by a failure to respect the firmity and transcendence of "truth" and/or "meaning" and thereby shows reality to be a plastic and inventive thing.

I try in this final part of the study to demonstrate this sense of nonsense in a manner that doesn't just enumerate the familiar operations of reversal, inversion, simultaneity, infinity, and boundary-blurring that characterizes how nonsense is made.[55] Instead, I attempt to create a situation that is problematic in the sense that a problem is not something to be solved so much as it is something to be creatively accosted. Specifically, I target a paradox that John Shepherd identifies in the way symbolic processes allow us to manipulate our environment while exhibiting a certain independence from it. Out of this paradox, around which the practice and discourse of music revolves, I invent a fictional line of enquiry that loses itself in the deictic quagmire in which the non/sense of music is constituted, developing the idea of music as an effect that has a peculiar capacity to migrate between bodies—virtual and actual. I do this by exploiting the indirection inherent to the kinds of words that music's discursive constitution relies on, words such as "it," "this, "that," "I," "he," "then," and "now." These terms, which

---

[53] Stewart, *Nonsense*, 51.

[54] Ibid.

[55] A host of other studies explicitly interrogate this anatomy of nonsense. See, for instance, Elizabeth Sewell, *The Field of Nonsense* (London: Chatto and Windus, 1952); Wim Tigges, *Explorations in the Field of Nonsense* (Amsterdam: Rodopi, 1987); and Jean-Jacques Lecercle, *Philosophy of Nonsense: The Intuitions of Victorian Nonsense Literature* (London: Routledge, 1994).

Roman Jakobson calls "shifters," have a duplex structure that allows them to express both a conventional and existential relationship to the object(s) they represent.[56] Insofar as music is an inherently ambiguous quasi-object where, as theorist Ian Cross suggests, "one and the same musical activity might, at one and the same time, be about the trajectory of a body in space, the dynamic emergence or signification of an affective state, the achievement of a goal and the unfolding of an embodied perspective,"[57] it can be said to be duplicitous, double dealing, for "it" always refers both to a material and a set of relations whose correspondence, as Shepherd notes, is self-conflicted.

Like the "I" that associates with myself by convention, yet also stands existentially contiguous to my I, I am trying to say two things at once. This can be confusing at the best of times, and, considering that I exploit this feature of shifters throughout the chapter to move between voices who not only take up the issue of nonsense in different ways, but do so in a reflexive manner that replicates the already duplicated structure of shifters and the free indirect style that I use here less than sparingly, it can be downright mystifying. In this chapter I not only consider pseudonymic and "meta" practices as ways in which a duplicitous nonsense circulates in art music, I also employ them. As such, this essay should be read with the understanding that the surtext (the main body) is metaphorical while the subtext (footnotes/endnotes) is literal. This of course does not make the "sur" is any less real than the "sub." It just makes the former less direct than the latter. The form of the chapter thereby reflects the kind of duplicity (duplexity) that is at work in the music I examine (invent) by transposing it to a meta- and even hyper-level where the bond between symbol and material that the construct of Music (note the capital "M") problematizes starts to unravel in the face of its own artifice, its own bullshit. In this chapter then, I play my hand at

---

[56] Jakobson actually borrows the term "shifter" from the Danish linguist Otto Jespersen who introduced the term in 1923, but it was Jakobson who instigated its common use in linguistics with his 1956 essay "Shifters, Verbal Categories, and the Russian Verb." For the portion of his essay on shifters see Roman Jakobson, "Shifters and Verbal Categories," in On Language, ed. Linda Waugh and Monique Monville-Burston (Cambridge, MA: Harvard University Press, 1990), 386–92.

[57] Ian Cross, "Music, Cognition, Culture, and Evolution," Annals of the New York Academy of Sciences 930 (2001): 38.

making nonsense, not by being absurd but in making a theoretical straight from a fictional suit that will justify the gambit I have now made in telling you that I am going to bluff.

An immi/anent concern...

"What matter who's speaking? I would answer that it matters, for example, to women who have lost and still routinely lose their proper name in marriage, and whose signature—not merely their voice—has not been worth the paper it was written on; women for whom the signature—by virtue of its power in the world of circulation—is *not* immaterial. Only those who have it can play with not having it."[58]

With a few exceptions, almost all of the examples that I have drawn on to illuminate contemporary aesthetic failure are works produced by men. Not all these men are straight, however, but they are all university educated, middle-class, and white—a predictable homogeneity that undoubtedly generates a feeling of disquiet around the tacit assumption that "anyone" can play with failure. True, everybody can fail, but not anybody can play with failing. The above passage by Nancy Miller speaks to what I would call the "anybody-fallacy" that is remaindered by post-structuralism's discursively contrived decentring of "man." Miller argues that the "metalogically 'correct' position" advocated by post-structuralist theories—that signification of gender is an archaic practice—is "too confident that non-discursive practices will respond correctly to the correct theory of discursive practice."[59] For example, the "indifference" towards the origin of a text that Michel Foucault imagines he hears in a world after the death of the author is, "one of the masks... behind which phallocentrism hides its fiction."[60] In other words, practice lags behind theory,

---

[58] Nancy K. Miller, "The Text's Heroine: A Feminist Critic and Her Fictions," *Diacritics* 12, no. 2 (1982): 53.

[59] Ibid.: 49, 50.

[60] Peggy Kampf quoted in Miller, "The Text's Heroine, " 50. See also Michel Foucault, "What Is an Author?," in *The Foucault Reader*, ed. Paul Rabinow (New York: Pantheon Books, 1984), 101–20.

or, theory exceeds the social and institutional structures that make its claims effective.

While Foucault can imagine an authorial indifference and rationalize the conditions under which it would be immaterial whether the producer of a text is a man or women, in practice it is anything but immaterial. In fact, his capacity to think this results from a privilege that he has *not* to have to account for or justify his own voice. The "sovereign indifference"[61] of the theoretically impersonal text is something that can only be thought by one whose own voice already assumes its sovereignty, and advocating for the death of the author is a privilege of a suicidal "man" who has always had a life to lose and the right to end it. That is to say, only a subject whose agency is always (already) secure can put the potential of its own annulment into practice. Likewise, while in theory "everybody" has the potential to fail, in practice only those who have (always) already succeeded as social agents can play with failing, and in Western culture this has traditionally been the prerogative of men, particularly white, straight, and university-educated men. To practice failure and play with its potential is not for "anyone," it is for *some*. And this study is itself evidence of that. As a white, university-educated, heterosexual male, I am not only permitted to produce a study on the aesthetics of failure, I am permitted to write something that is aware of its privilege but does not *have* to question how this contributes to its production. Thus, to the extent that I prefer not to interrogate this text's privilege, I do so with full knowledge of the defect that it circulates. However, I submit that this defect is itself an affection of the failure that informs and animates this study, and as such, it embodies and enacts the concurrence of "to do" *and* "not to do" that, as Agamben notes, is typically exempted from potentiality.[62]

---

[61] Miller, "The Text's Heroine," 53.

[62] This gendered politics of aesthetic failure is something that remains to be explored, and as far as I can tell its interrogation revolves around the issue of a right to fail or to be indifferent to expectations, whether they are articulated as normative structures or relational standards. At stake in this right to fail is the value of aesthetic negativity, the value to pursue practices that seek intensity rather than a purpose in experience. As Christoph Menke argues, this value translates into art as a matter of sovereignty and a concern for forms of "non-understanding," a concern for a mode of experience that is not satisfied by realizing specified aims. For Menke,

It should be kept in mind, then, that throughout this study I give privilege to those impressions of failure which exhibit a sense of their own contingency and demonstrate a reliance on belief. And it is perhaps for these reasons that my attempt to scrutinize failure may prove to be too big a wager and that it may end up becoming just another successful expression of the discourse that it is trying *not* to be, which will make it the failure that it was all along. I propose, then, that this work advances awkwardly in its own contingency to express a failure that it knows it can never believe in. If this sounds a little too utopian, then allow me to appropriate a line from the poet and theorist Craig Dworkin who believes a fierce politics lies behind seemingly impossible tasks: "I would rather maroon myself nowhere than surrender to a status quo with which I am not content."[63]

*　*　*

Lastly, experimental music, my ostensible subject, finds its way into this failing scheme through tactics of duration, distraction, and duplicity; devices of (dis)engagement that characterize the operational purview of a post-Cagean experimental music community whose members have the peculiar privilege to toy with the intensity

---

where understanding entails conventional and automatic processes of perception "that selectively transform undefined material into interrelated and meaning-related signifiers,"[†] non-understanding is a way of suspending the habits of interpretation by continually returning perception and thought to the process of selection where each taking account of the undefined is backgrounded with more unselected material. And access to the right (but also the political and economic fortitude) to *not* be understood, access, that is, to what Jean-François Lyotard identifies as the "libidinal" or "figural" over the discursive dimensions of art,[‡] is by no means equal. Further to this point is the very validity of the right to the sovereignty of failure as it is premised on a discourse that not only favours certain expressions of aesthetic experience that presuppose the universality of the imagination, but one whose notion of sovereignty has gendered implications.

[†] Christoph Menke, *The Sovereignty of Art: Aesthetic Negativity in Adorno and Derrida*, trans. Neil Solomon (Cambridge, MA: MIT Press,1999), 43.

[‡] See Jean-François Lyotard, Libidinal Economy, trans. Iain Hamilton Grant (Bloomington: Indiana University Press, 1993) and *Discourse, Figure*, trans. Antony Hudek and Mary Lydon (Minneapolis, MN: University of Minnesota Press, 2011).

[63] Craig Dworkin, *Reading the Illegible* (Evanston, IL: Northwestern University Press, 2003), xxi.

of failure, and as such, to draw insights and observations about failure from "failure." In this sense, as a member of this same community, the failure ascribed to the music that I discuss here is a failure that describes my own discussion of the music. Its failure is my failure, a strange loop that lets me be both knight and knave, right and wrong, sincere and full of shit. It is a way to show how failure lives *out* the way one lives *in* contradictions: the way one finds interest in boredom, form in formlessness, and sense in nonsense.

But before moving on to the study proper, I want to consider the risk that's involved with living in failure's contradictions. Living in contradiction is exceptional. Basically, to live in contradiction is to enjoy an abnormal disconnect between knowledge and action. This is how Melville's scrivener, Bartleby, lives when he dwells in the prorogating effects of his formula, "I prefer not to." However, only ascetics and sybarites have either the spiritual mettle or the material convenience to "prefer not to." These are extreme positions and would seem to be beyond the ken of most individuals. Yet, as political and social critic Chris Hedges argues, contemporary Western liberalism has shown that it, too, "prefers not to." As a response to the authority of feudalism and religion, classical liberalism defines its ideals in a conviction to the rule of law. However, only the myth of liberalism now remains and, as Hedges writes, this myth "is used by corporate power elites and their apologists to justify the subjugation and manipulation of other nations in the name of national self-interest and democratic values."[64] The liberal class has ignored the fact that the legal system, which manages the law that they appeal to as guarantor of equality and individual autonomy, has been influenced by corporate powers as much as electoral politics and legislative debate has. The consequence is thus:

> The inability of the liberal class to acknowledge that corpora-
> tions have wrested power from the hands of citizens, that the
> [US] Constitution and its guarantees of personal liberty have
> become irrelevant, and that the phrase *consent of the governed* is

---

[64] Chris Hedges, *Death of the Liberal Class* (New York: Nation Books, 2010), 8.

meaningless, has left it speaking and acting in ways that no longer correspond to reality.[65]

The failure of the liberal class to act on its ideals of reasoned betterment and individual egalitarianism has effected a disconnect from knowledge and action, which has made the working and middle class that it purports to speak for vulnerable to a virulent strain of what Hedges calls "magical thinking."

The message that one can make things happen by thinking about the desired results rather than taking the steps required to accomplish these results is a message, writes Hedges, that is "peddled to us by all aspects of culture, from Oprah to the Christian Right."[66] Magical thinking essentially encourages faith in the preposterous and "permits societies to transfer their emotional allegiance to the absurd,"[67] which in turn converts portions of society's dispossessed into a lunatic fringe who also "prefer not to" face real problems.

Both the liberal class and the lunatic fringe of society "prefer not to," and so both are living *out* the effects of living *in* contradictions: The liberal class's staunch belief in the ideals of reason makes it increasingly irrelevant in a world that is made by design and fabrication, while the lunatic fringe's reasons for belief in the direction that its anger and rage take it make it like a child with a loaded revolver. And because the way that I approach failure in this study is "trans-rational," its "preferring not to" threatens to correspond with the liberal class's ineffectual fulminations and the lunatic fringe's absurd investment in the "reality" of pseudo-events (i.e., simulations of celebrity and sports culture).

The indulgence of living in failure's contradictions is a gamble that risks both exile into its own emptiness, and annihilation by its own excesses. Like Dostoyevsky's Underground Man, whose vain attachment to reasonable ideals sends him into utter obscurity, those who "prefer not to," who prefer to play with failure, risk living life in a corner, taunting themselves "with the spiteful and useless consolation that an intelligent man cannot seriously become

---

[65] Ibid., 9.
[66] Ibid., 200.
[67] Ibid.

anything seriously, and it is only a fool who becomes anything."[68] But "preferring not to" also hazards the intemperance of Michel Houellebecq's character, Michel, from his 2001 novel *Platform* who aspires to a state of permanent tourism where leisure tactics and morning blow-jobs substitute for the edification of the self and the well-being of society. Lotus-eaters or subterranean hermits, both place equal wagers on failure's promise. Thus, if my study of failure promises anything, it too must risk emptiness and annihilation. And to the extent that boring formless nonsense fulfills this promise, it will become exactly that which it names.

---

[68] Fyodor Dostoyevsky, *Notes from Underground*, trans. Constance Garnett (New York: Dover Publications, 1992), 3.

1

Boring

*It turns out that bliss—a second-by-second joy + gratitude
at the gift of being alive, conscious—lies on the other
side of crushing, crushing boredom. Pay close attention
to the most tedious thing you can find … and, in waves, a
boredom like you've never known will wash over you and
just about kill you. Ride these out, and it's like stepping
from black and white into color. Like water after days in
the desert. Constant bliss in every atom.*

DAVID FOSTER WALLACE
THE PALE KING (2011)

Introduction

I heard a string quartet a while ago by Los Angeles composer Art Jarvinen titled *100 cadences with four melodies, a chorale, and coda ("with bells on!")*. As the title suggests, the piece keeps ending, over and over again, each time promising to conclude a musical adventure that never was. Over forty-eight minutes, the consecution of endings, punctuated by solos and glimmering silences, draw out an irritatingly radiant array of mock-perorations. And I am always more or less aware of this: More aware when the sheer materiality of these several endings intrude upon my sense of contemplation, and less aware when, like Swann listening to Vinteuil's sonata, I am taken away by time passed. I am alternately *with* the music, my attention buoyed by a procession of simulated extinctions and untimely non-events, and *beside* the music, dreaming counterfactuals, shifting backward, forward, side-to-side in fantasies of otherwise. Sustained in the messy immanence of a perpetual conclusion, my attention floats on nothing in particular, nothing but a series of loose intensities that are now and again interesting, or boring, or both.

Listening to Jarvinen's piece, I hear David Foster Wallace's summons: Ride out the waves of boredom, Wallace insists, and "it's like stepping from black and white into color." Maybe once upon a time, when there was a patience to let the swells and breaks slowly teach us to ride its current, one could learn to surf the waves of boredom. But being bored is not the ride it once was. Through the second half of the twentieth century, boredom bored so many holes in the body of every genre, every medium, every performance, and every criticism, that it bled its promise of bliss into ever-narrower furrows of distraction. The problem with boredom now is that the rituals of bloodletting that go by the name "boring art" are largely indistinguishable from the practices of everyday life such that our interests have, in a sense, hemorrhaged. Bored to death, post-industrial culture is dying by a thousand little interests. Boredom no longer compresses into a tight bundle of bliss; now it just splays out—the pullulating temper of postmodernity's bad or "sensuous infinity."[1]

While characterizing the nihilism some associate with the postmodern, this sensuous infinity (a concept I borrow from Hegel who used it to describe a situation of perpetual alternation between

---

[1] The "sensuous infinity" that I refer to in this chapter is the sense one has of a perpetually receding end-point, or, a continually dividing mid-point. This can be represented in two ways using the familiar example of a number series (m, n, o...). An *extensive* infinity describes a series in which one can always count one more term beyond the last. This is represented by the formula (m, n, o...)+1. An *intensive* infinitude, however, describes a situation wherein between any two terms of a series lies a third term. The formula for this infinity is $\frac{1}{2}(m+n)$. Infinity has a curiously rich conceptual history that extends from the ancient Greek notion of *apeiron* (roughly translated as "primordial chaos"), to Aristotle's ontologically ambiguous "potential infinity," to the nineteenth-century mathematician Georg Cantor's mind-bendingly bizarre theory of "transfinite numbers," which introduces the idea of cardinality—a number of elements in a set—and the hypothesis that infinite sets can have different sizes, represented by the Hebrew *Aleph*: $\aleph_0 \aleph_1 \aleph_2$.

the determination of x and not-x) more accurately captures the affective scope of what it's like to endure the pressure of finding oneself a finite subject addressed by seemingly infinite demands. Boredom in this sense is a coping mechanism that cradles us from the madness of the infinite, but, insofar as there is no end to being bored, its cradle reduplicates the summons of infinity. Boredom's sprawl is therefore the propagation of an ambivalent event that shelters the subject from the loss of its practicable horizon with a homeless mood.

It is this ambivalence that I consider in the pages that follow in order to update the capacity, or incapacity, as it were, of boredom (in music) to articulate the feeling of being a subject in contemporary culture. While experimental composition is the primary aesthetic practice that I use to explore this concern, I deploy it more as a lens by which to focus the scattered rays of monotony on a wider set of logics that can be found in numerous other aspects of contemporary culture.[2] I suggest that composers, specifically those informed by a post-Cagean sensibility regarding the way boredom's intensity modulates itself over time, and who are writing long, quiet, repetitive, and slow-moving music intended to be experienced without (external) interruption, express a sense of boredom characterizing a more general feeling of being unjustified. This feeling is engine to a neoliberal injunction demanding constant self-invention. In other words, the transcendental satisfaction promised by a work such as Charlemagne Palestine's *Strumming Music* (1974), a fulfillment that discriminates aesthetic boredom from mundane *ennui* and *spleen*, is no longer operative. There is no water in the desert, but only a parallel series of fatigue and regeneration that split infinity in two: "I can't go on, I'll go on." In contrast to the certitudes of artists like Dick Higgins, who give boredom a euphoric aura, and Andy Warhol, whose repetitions suggest that boredom is the affective corollary of commodity culture's delight in simulated novelty, the contemporary compo-

---

[2] While repetition, slowness, and suspension are not exclusive to experimental composition, I emphasize the Cagean tradition of composition here, for a certain conviction and celebration of boredom is fundamental to the aesthetics of post-Cagean composition in a way that the drone doom metal of SunnO))) or the numbingly pensive groove of British dubstep never is.

sitional practices that I consider in this chapter exemplify a type of ambivalent boredom that manifests symptoms of what Sianne Ngai describes as an aesthetic "stuplime," an aesthetic category she suggests "introduces into contemporary aesthetic figurations of boredom an important acknowledgement of what Marx and Engels referred to as the "everlasting uncertainty and agitation" of modernity.[3]

As expressions of this everlasting uncertainty, I argue that recent musical complexes of stuplimity can be understood to condition a practice of waiting, or an art of witnessing events in their eventality. In a sense, an art of waiting is something of a vanity whose quasi-passive enactment is one of the only spaces left for a cultural practice whose hyperreflexive proclivities and suicidal tendencies estrange it from both popular and academic consideration. This, however, is precisely *not* to attribute to the art of waiting a subversive intent, but to suggest that waiting is a form of "acting out" the ambivalence inhering in contemporary neoliberal culture's promise of endless self-invention. As such, current aesthetic boredom does not undermine habits of reception, but simply and sincerely fails to be (potentially) interesting, and thus, as William James would suggest, to meet the minimal conditions for experience. However, this form of failure puts the art of waiting perilously close to those practices of what Paul Mann calls "stupid undergrounds"—contemporary vanguards that "feign stupidity" or simulate a "posture of indifference"[4] as a way to get off on the symptoms of difference excreted by a self-aware culture's compulsive need to catalogue and capitalize on (commodify) experience. Yet, because an art of waiting is an art in which even the activity of judgement has to be suspended, contemporary aesthetic expressions of boredom avoid endorsing the "inane energy"[5] that sheer stupidity generates in abundance. If anything, aesthetic boredom and the art of waiting empties itself of both the irrational force inherent in conspicuous demonstrations of stupidity as well as the obscure energy generated by the execution of its own morbid curiosity.

---

[3] Sianne Ngai, *Ugly Feelings* (Cambridge, MA: Harvard University Press, 2005), 277.
[4] Paul Mann, *Masocriticism* (Albany: State University of New York Press, 1999), 139.
[5] Ibid.

On being bored

Traditionally, boredom is understood in relation to a lack of meaning. But I propose instead to describe it as a lessening of one's capacity to affect and be affected—a diminishing of our potential engagement with the world and its population of things. If we follow Brian Massumi in thinking of affect as the intensive measure of what "escapes confinement in the particular body whose vitality, or potential for interaction, it is,"[6] then boredom is rightly a *dis*-affection, for it reveals a certain corporal engulfment that, by virtue of a constant tension, borders on the neighbourhood of pain. Too much body and not enough imagination becomes an affliction.[7] This is perhaps why our culture has developed so many ways to live beyond its fleshy limits—to reduce the burden of embodiment and relieve the labour of existence. I'm not, however, speaking only about the virtual realm of cyberspace, but about everything that capitalizes on the terror of our finitude: Television, film and the Internet (to a certain degree) relieve our sinews and joint of their practicable mission, but so do art galleries and concert halls, spaces where bodies are incarcerated and the senses mortified in order to dispose our being *not* towards nothing, or death as Heidegger would have it, but towards anything *but* nothing. But boredom is not nothing. It is something in the way that a hole is something, and as such it fulfills its etymological destiny: it "bores a hole" in us.

Now, why would artists want to intentionally bore? To diminish our affect, which is the very thing that an organism lives through, seems, if not cruel, then somehow callous, bordering even on a kind of torture.[8] Isn't art's purpose to enliven, to vitalize, and thus to

---

[6] Brian Massumi, *Parables for the Virtual: Movement, Affect, Sensation* (Durham, NC: Duke University Press, 2002), 35.

[7] Elaine Scarry presents this argument in her work *The Body in Pain* (1985), which proposes that sentience lies along a spectrum hemmed by complementary extremes: At one end is the imagination, wherein the act of imagining coincides with the object imagined, and at the other end is pain, in which the act of perception takes itself as its own object. Scarry's theory is taken up explicitly in Chapter Three.

[8] I don't mean to equate the compositional practices considered here with the employment of music as an actual torture device, as for instance the US government's 1990 invasion of Panama during which loud rock music was used to force Manuel Noriega from refuge in the Holy See's embassy, or the FBI siege of the

increase and multiply our ways of connecting and interacting with things? For example, one typically goes to a concert or listens to music in order to be affected, to be *moved* from one state to another, and thus, in a sense, to affirm one's own capacity to change, to become something otherwise. As Tia de Nora has argued, people normally listen to music in order to model their own vicissitudes on the music's highs and lows, to put themselves in another mood that hopefully makes their light shine brighter, their selves swell with a sense of well-being.[9] Musical sounds have a way of enveloping and folding us within an illusion of vital activity such that, particularly in its everyday use, music is treated as a modulation device, an affective simulacra if you will.

But consider *Mein Schatz* (2007) by Los Angeles-based composer Eric km Clark. It is a five-minute work for solo "simplified" violin[10] comprising several cells of slowly and quietly bowed or plucked natural harmonics that sound the microtonal ambit of its unique tuning—hardly a work that choreographs an escape from the refrains of boredom. In fact, *Mein Schatz* seems to do the opposite. Though not excessively long, the phlegmatic presentation of its isolated segments composed of very elementary gestures are constitutive of a self-emptying event, an event whose expressions, deprived of concert music's conventional immanences—its gestural and tonal relations that determine its movements—take the act of dissipation

---

Branch Davidian compound in Waco, Texas, in 1993. More recent cases of music as an instrument of torture have been documented in an FBI report which indicates that loud music was used at the US army's detention centre in Guantanamo Bay as an "enhanced interrogation" technique. See Guantanamo Bay Inquiry at http://vault.fbi.gov/Guantanamo%20 [accessed October 2012]. There has been a recent spate of writing on this subject: See Suzanne G. Cusick, "Music as Torture/Music as Weapon," *Transcultural Music Review* 10 (2006); Jonathan Pieslak, *Sound Targets: American Soldiers and Music in the Iraq War* (Bloomington: Indiana University Press, 2009); Suzanne G. Cusick and Branden Joseph, "Across an Invisible Line: A Conversation About Music and Torture," *Grey Room* 42 (2011).

[9] DeNora proposes that music in everyday life functions as an "affordance structure," defined as "a resource or template against which styles and temporal patterns of feeling, moving, and being come to be organized and produced in real time." Tia DeNora, *Music in Everyday Life* (Cambridge and New York: Cambridge University Press, 2000), 111.

[10] This is a violin in which all strings are tuned to a single pitch. (However, in this work the tuning is actually: I: E¼b, II: Eb, III: E, IV: E.)

as their object.[11] Keeping the mood consistently monotonous, the work radiates little of the inner intensity commonly expected from post-Cagean experimental music. You can hear within the first five seconds of the work the virtual totality of its form, its rate of change, its volume, and its intensive scope. This is not dissimilar to many of James Tenney's compositions of the 1960s and 1970s. *For Ann (rising)* (1969), an electronic piece whose entire duration is perceived as a continuously rising tone—the "barber pole-effect"—and the solo violin piece *Koan* (1970) in which the performer executes a continuous tremolo between adjacent strings while slowly sliding one finger along one of these strings, are compositions wherein everything about the piece's form and development (as it were) is given at the beginning, the idea being to undermine the conventions and obligations of dramatic narrative and thus allow listeners to "get on" with listening to their listening.[12] Like Tenney's pieces, *Mein Schatz*, too, presents a refrain of slow growth and minor variations. But like all refrains, which assimilates and crystalizes differences to catalyze and organize the kinds of interactions occurring within its remit, *Mein Schatz* is no less territorial. It conscripts the activities and intensities coursing through a listener's body, as well as those vibrating between the concert hall, performers, and instruments therein, to bring attention to its peculiar immanent order of dissipative sound events. However, the refrain of *Mein Schatz* does not easily modulate the negative valence of its un-dramatic insistence in the way that other forms and other uses of music are conventionally intended to do. As an aesthetic expression of the repetition of the difference that *is* each presented tone, there is no formal way of escaping the kind of exhausting mood that its tedium engenders. Such a slow and persistently constrained set of movements is so allied to enervated forms of feeling that it's not a matter of whether this work is tedious, but rather of how the intensity of this tedium is valenced. In other words, *Mein Schatz* does not pretend

---

[11] On the nature of a self-emptying event see Brian Massumi, "Animatedness," in *Semblance and Event: Activist Philosophy and the Occurrent Arts* (Cambridge, MA: MIT Press, 2011), 138–42.

[12] Tenney coined the phrase "ergodic music" to describe a type of musical-statistical form wherein every part of a system or process, given enough time, will exhibit statistical equivalency with every other part.

to be un-tedious the way that Wagner's fifteen-hour *Der Ring des Nibelungen* does. It therefore does not afford the listener a way of being (or at least the semblance of being) unbored. Instead, for reasons that I'll address below, *Mein Schatz* is a work that articulates a contemporary neurosis regarding the incapacity of post-Cagean aesthetics to transfigure the homogenizing indifference of being bored into, at minimum, the condition of being (minorly) interesting.

The twentieth century, of course, has seen and heard a vast number of artworks that use forms of slowness, tedium, and repetition as aesthetic strategies to explore the strangely multi-valent effects of aesthetic distortion, but because the contemporary expression of these forms occurs in a cultural space that has become self-evidently untotalizable, there is much less concern today with boredom's being interesting. Composer John Cage's oft repeated saying that if you attend long enough to what is boring you will find that what is boring is not boring after all, summarizes the latter sentiment, and suggests that within the experiential horizon of boredom is an occulted interest that promises a sublimation of Hegelian proportions. However, neither the stakes nor the forms of attention that would give boredom its import are the same now as they were in 1960s when its affect was being explicitly marshaled for aesthetic effect. After so many artworks like Satie's *Vexations* (1893), Gertrude Stein's *The Making of Americans* (1925), Andy Warhol's *Sleep* (1963), and *Empire* (1964), and recently Douglas Gordon's *24 Hour Psycho* (1993) and Kenneth Goldsmith's *Day* (2003), it's hard to imagine that the desert of boredom holds any more water. But the redoubling of tedium in contemporary art and music might suggest something other than a redundancy. In contemporary Western culture, which is arguably characterized by excessive expressions of irony and multiple layers of metareferential discourse, the mood takes on a different life, a life that in fact resembles a kind of death, a stillborn death.

If this is the case, then the continued use of tedium in art and music can be viewed in a number of different ways. One way, and perhaps the easiest to conceptualize, is that aesthetic boredom has become redundant. An hour-long presentation of all the 8178 possible chords within an octave, which is the conceit behind composer Tom Johnson's *The Chord Catalogue* (1986), is no longer an anti-music,

Eric km Clark, *Mein Schatz* (2007). Courtesy Eric km Clark.

but, as Baudrillard says, an "art of simulation" that aims to efface the scene of reality while at the same time preserving the image of its disappearance.[13] Another way to consider contemporary tedium is to treat it as symptomatic of the postmodern habit to transpose the banalities of life into aesthetic fetishes that dazzle with the vertigo of their de- and re-natured appearance. A stronger view might be that boredom is being articulated to show the withering of its productive potential. This resembles a thesis advanced by art historian Christine Ross, who argues that the traditional models of melancholy and other despondent tempers as productive forms of subjectivity are being subsumed by a clinical discourse of depression that figures the individual as a more or less insufficient subject whose capacities are measured according to models of optimal cognitive-perceptual capacities and neoliberal norms of self-definition.[14] A contemporary aesthetic of boredom in this case would signal the present insufficiency for tedium to perform the role of anti-art that, at least since Cage, has tried to smuggle the aesthetic expectations and *Mehrwert*—"pay-off"—of its contrary in through the backdoor.[15] Boredom as an artistic device doesn't affect a postmodern culture that has, in words that echo Fredric Jameson's,[16] forgotten that there ever was a history of beauty to be lost, challenged, defied, or

---

[13] See Jean Baudrillard, *The Conspiracy of Art: Manifestos, Interviews, Essays*, trans. Sylvère Lotringer (New York: Semiotext(e), 2005).

[14] Christine Ross, *The Aesthetics of Disengagement: Contemporary Art and Depression* (Minneapolis: University of Minnesota Press, 2006). Below I discuss how boredom relates to what Ross sees as a depressive paradigm that characterizes recent art practices represented by artists like Ugo Rondinone, Vanessa Beecroft and Rosemarie Trockel.

[15] Diedrich Diederichsen applies the German "*Mehrwert*" (literally "surplus value") to contemporary attitudes towards art to indicate "an additional value that can be realized in return for a special effort or in connection with an exceptional situation." Diedrich Diederichsen, *On (Surplus) Value in Art* (Rotterdam: Witte de With, 2008), 21.

[16] For Jameson, a major theme of postmodernism revolves around what he calls "historical amnesia":

The disappearance of a sense of history, the way in which our entire contemporary social system has little by little begun to lose its capacity to retain its own past, has begun to live in a perpetual present and in a perpetual change that obliterates traditions of the kind which all earlier social formations have had in one way or another to preserve.

Fredric Jameson, "Theories of the Postmodern," in *The Cultural Turn: Selected Writings on the Postmodern, 1983–98* (London: Verso, 1998), 20.

conserved. Boredom is now just one more mode/mood among any number of existential motifs.

Another interesting, though not necessarily truer perspective, would be to see the current use of tedium as an expression of contemporary culture's chronic incantation of the same difference; that is, the desire for desire. Boredom is often described as a disaffection, an inability to form attachments or develop affection for the things of life. In a way, to desire desire is to experience and suffer the extreme success of our distractions, which is another way to say that it has become difficult to focus on the task of being oneself, of being driven by an elementary impulse to do something. The affective ambivalence of wanting nothing in particular that gives contemporary states of boredom their distinctive spirit can therefore be distinguished from Jean-François Lyotard's postmodern sublime that, despite its celebration of works which demonstrate the conceptual finitude of human being, retains a Kantian promise of a subject who wants to narrative itself out of an encounter with something that overwhelms.[17] Ngai's concept of the stuplime, however, evokes a hobbled or lame astonishment that captures the dubiety of being drawn to nothing in particular.

Each of these points are addressed in different ways throughout the chapter, though neither in order nor in isolation from one another, for it's the nature of boredom to be multiply expressed: as alternately shocking and exhausting, as a long-term investment with eventual pay-off, as commenting on our insipid fascination with ourselves, and revealing our general lack of imagination. I contextualize the contemporary interest in musical boredom, which I also refer to provisionally in terms of musical "extendedness," by considering antecedents in the experimental art and music of the 1960s and 1970s. Drawing on Ngai's notion of the stuplime and employing discursive tactics that take me from boredom avoidance training in office culture, to Michel de Certeau's polemological theory of the everyday, to the psychodynamics of absent object relations, to the libidinal flows of Lyotard's meaningless "events," I argue that contemporary boredom is a way

---

[17] See Jean-François Lyotard, *Lessons on the Analytic of the Sublime: Kant's Critique of Judgment, §§ 23–29*, trans. Elizabeth Rottenberg (Stanford, CA: Stanford University Press, 1994).

of paying attention to our culture's fixation on nothing in particular/ everything in general and that contemporary music engineers this by staging an encounter with a sensuous infinity. I begin, however, with a survey of the philosophical dimensions of boredom as it has been theorized since the eighteenth century, in order to construct a narrative that supports the idea that ours is not merely a bored culture, but a culture in waiting. After this we will be in position to unravel the ways in which contemporary musical tedium and monotony, through its own studied failure to separate itself from the spins and stalls of everyday life, becomes, to cite Paul Mann, something occasional that "complicate[s] cultural space, for a moment or two, for a reader or two, to thicken it and slow one's passage through it, and, as always, to render criticism itself as painful and difficult as possible."[18]

A boring history

The major studies of boredom trace the appearance of the mood to the mid-eighteenth century and attribute its emergence and prolif- eration to a modern crisis of meaning wrought by the metaphysical ambiguity and social anomie ushered in by the material processes of modernization and the egalitarian distribution of enlightened scepti- cism's paradoxical epistemological claims that render subjective experience in objective terms and categories. The effects and theories of boredom as a symptom of modernity began to appear in the nineteenth century with writers like Søren Kierkegaard, Charles Baudelaire, and Friedrich Nietzsche. Though not the first to address the emergence of the mood in modern Western culture, Kierkegaard articulated what he perceived to be a void consuming modernity's increasingly self-aware and self-affected sense of reality. Positing that "boredom depends on the nothingness that pervades reality; it causes a dizziness like that produced by looking down into a yawning chasm,"[19] he imagines that a mode of existence organized around the growing aesthetic affectation of human interests leads to an immoral

---

[18] Mann, *Masocriticism*, 129.
[19] Søren Kierkegaard, *Either/Or*, trans. Howard V. Hong and Edna H. Hong (Princeton: Princeton University Press, 1988), 287.

and ultimately bankrupt existence. Baudelaire, writing around the same time as Kierkegaard, gives boredom a more lyrical figure in his work *Les Fleurs du mal* wherein he describes "*l'ennui moderne*" as a distinctly modern malaise—"spleen"—whose mercurial pathos is expressed by an individual's alternation of disaffection and exasperation.[20] Echoing Baudelaire's diagnosis of modern life, Friedrich Nietzsche bestows the nihilism of boredom, what he calls its "calm wind," with an eschatological function, seeing humankind end not with the fiery judgement of absolute self-knowledge but the stupefying irony that humanity's essence is ultimately an elaborate performance of fleeing from boredom.[21]

Boredom has also been represented dramatically in the twentieth-century existentialist fiction of Albert Camus (*L'Etranger*), Jean-Paul Sartre (*Nausea*), and Samuel Beckett (*Waiting for Godot, Happy Days*), where it is depicted as an expression of life's finitude and contingency, and by implication, its insignificance. More sociological and policical studies of boredom are represented in the writing George Simmel, Walter Benjamin, and Siegfried Kracauer's examination of the malaise as symptomatic of an experiential atrophy due to processes of industrialization and urbanization, while boredom's philosophical profile is perhaps best known through Heidegger's examination of the mood as a modality of human existence whose characteristic detachment provides insight into the conditional circumstance of being.[22] For Heidegger, boredom, like anxiety,

---

[20] Charles Baudelaire, *Les Fleurs Du Mal*, trans. Richard Howard (Boston: David R. Godine, 1985).

[21] Friedrich Nietzsche, *Human, All Too Human*, trans. R. J. Hollingdale (Cambridge: Cambridge University Press, 1996).

[22] Heidegger treats the malaise as a disposition that reveals the way human being finds itself embedded in a world that matters to it. Boredom (as well as anxiety) is what Heidegger calls an "authentic mood" and is distinguished from "inauthentic" moods insofar as the former reveals the ontological strangeness of our radically contingent and provisional nature rather than the familiar forms of attachment that play out in everyday situations. For Heidegger, these moods are important for the way they attune us directly and forcefully to the enigma of being—namely, to the nothingness that underwrites being. While both anxiety and boredom compel us to face the groundlessness of being, their distinctive tones mark the way in which this matters differently to being: anxiety shows a way of being hyper-concerned at the prospect of having to perpetually secure onself in the world, while boredom, on the other hand, reveals an utter indifference to *Dasein*'s finding itself in the world's theatre of being. Heidegger's

awakens us to the radically contingent and therefore inessential nature of being, provided, that is, that one can withstand (or submit to?) the crushing force of being awakened to being-as-a-whole.[23] However, the humanistic traits of existentialism that were targeted and surpassed by (post)structuralism's critique of self-authored being,[24] and the increasingly central role that neuroscience and clinical discourse have come to play in defining human experience, have converted boredom into an epiphenomenon of the socio-psychic dynamics of contemporary information culture. Orrin Klapp's *Overload and Boredom* (1986), for example, contends that the excessive amount of information in contemporary culture functions as a site of excessive redundancy that increases semantic entropy, and thereby ushers in the onset of boredom.[25] Though all of these works look at boredom in slightly different ways, they each have in common the themes of modern meaninglessness and temporal homogeneity as factors contributing to the transformation of the present into an absolute, but empty, value.

Beginning with an outline of the history of diminishing affects that predate the category of boredom's somewhat sudden appearance in the mid-eighteenth century, Seán Desmond Healy's *Boredom, Self, and Culture* (1984) draws on each of the above authors' observations to argue that boredom is a consequence of a "growing metaphysical void at the centre of Western civilization."[26] Healy suggests that the

---

investigation into boredom is complex and comprehensive; however, because his project focuses largely on the mood's manifestation in the everyday, I'll only grapple with his theory to the extent that it helps articulates the connection between the way artists and everyday practices express the sense of the infinite by iterations of the finite. On Heidegger's analysis of moods and boredom see *The Fundamental Concepts of Metaphysics: World, Finitude, Solitude*, trans. William McNeill and Nicholas Walker (Indianapolis: Indiana University Press, 2001); and "What Is Metaphysics?" in *Basic Writings*, ed. David Farrell Krell (New York: Harper Perennial Modern Classics, 2008).

[23] "Profound boredom, drifting here and there in the abysses of our existence like a muffling fog, removes all things and men and oneself along with it into a remarkable indifference. This boredom reveals being as a whole." Heidegger, "What Is Metaphysics?" 99.

[24] Arising, curiously, at the same moment when the feminist and civil rights movements began to assert the agency of marginal identities.

[25] See Orrin Klapp, *Overload and Boredom* (New York: Greenwood Press, 1986).

[26] Seán Desmond Healy, *Boredom, Self, and Culture* (Rutherford; London: Fairleigh Dickinson University Press, 1984), 87.

mood developed from a minor to a major affliction through the gradual de-centring of tradition, culture, and ultimately self—social and historical structures affording the organization of one's conduct and experience into meaningful and practical events. Though the feeling of being bored was not without its antecedent afflictions—*daemon meridanus* ("noonday devil"), *accedia*, *tristitia*, melancholia, ennui— Healy contends that these were regarded as unusual maladies and "largely a theological concern, confined in its secular form to a mere handful of intellectuals."[27] Existing in some vague way before the term "boredom" appeared, it was not until the conditions and effects of the malaise "increased in such degree, incidence, and reflective awareness"[28] that a term was required to describe what seemed an indefinite indifference to things, an "affect without effectiveness in locating the source of trouble."[29] What Healy refers to as a waning sense of transcendence, an escape from the appetites of being, corresponds to the foundering idealism of Western European culture in the eighteenth century, spurred on by the advance of enlightened scepticism and its expression in the natural and physical sciences.[30] As the rhetoric of reflection on modern experience began to develop around materialist and rationalist explanations of experience, the idealization of meaning, "if by that is meant the urgent desire to search out and to pursue what is excellent and what is true," says Healy, "becomes increasingly incapable of being satisfied, or even of finding a credible object or direction, in a culture where Truth has been reduced to truth, or even more damagingly, to truths, or even to 'truths'."[31]

The ideologies and "truths" of myth, religion, and tradition that canalize the flow of desire to make sense of existence according to their respective modes of satisfaction became largely ineffective mediations in the wake of post-Enlightenment scepticism. Healy

---

[27] Ibid., 19.

[28] Ibid., 24.

[29] Ibid., 44. Healy notes the unknown etymology of the term but cites a philological study by Logan Pearsall Smith in which the term "bore" is identified as an eighteenth-century coinage. Curiously, this study also shows that "bore" was preceded two years earlier by the term "interesting."

[30] Ibid., 25.

[31] Ibid., 89.

writes, "Boredom is the inevitable accompaniment of the absence, or even serious uncertainty about the stability and reliability of values, purposes, meanings, and commitments."[32] If meaning can be understood as "the sense of a centre [that is not necessarily oneself but a "God" or a code which] endows [one's] existence with...a sense of the necessity of things,"[33] then what erodes the sense of a centre erodes also the necessity of things. To become unnecessary is to become contingent. Sartre, exploiting the French sense of sense (*sens*) to convey both meaning and direction, depicts this contingency viscerally when Roquentin, the protagonist of his 1938 novel *Nausea*, encounters a world that is radically indifferent to his existence. Perceiving the sheer un-necessity of any of his deeds or desires, Roquentin finds that he lives without sense, without meaning:

> It is the reflection of my face. Often in these lost days I study it. I can understand nothing of this face. The faces of others have some sense, some direction. Not mine.[34]

The death of God is only partially the concern here. As Healy suggests, boredom concerns more broadly the withering organizing principles of a society and its individuals. Thus, whether it is God, tradition, culture, or the fiction of a "self" that serves as the measure of meaning, the individual sense (*sens*) of things matters little, for boredom is an expression of the discrediting of *all* centring or grounding principles.

In a more recent work, *A Philosophy of Boredom* (2005), Lars Svendsen updates many of Healy's insights into boredom in order to align its conditions with the circumstances of postmodernity. More acute and insidious than the death of God or a diminishing sense of transcendence, is what Svendsen suggests is a growing inability for "us postmoderns" to fulfill a Romantic inheritance as "world-forming being[s]."[35] Drawing on Horkheimer and Adorno's critique of

---

[32] Ibid., 91.

[33] Ibid., 99.

[34] Jean-Paul Sartre, *Nausea*, trans. Lloyd Alexander (New York: New Directions Publishing Corporation, 1969), 16.

[35] Lars Svendsen, *A Philosophy of Boredom*, trans. John Irons (London: Reaktion Books, 2005), 32.

the culture industry and alluding to the logic of simulation explained in Baudrillard's analysis of contemporary culture, Svendsen argues that "as descendants of Romanticism [who] insist on a *personal* meaning,"[36] contemporary culture requires a sense of immanent mystique or opacity in order to make meaning. The human subject, Svendsen writes, is "a being that actively constitutes his own world, but when everything is always already fully coded, the active constitution of the world is made superfluous"[37]—*de trop* in Sartre's terms. In a world where "events, no matter how unimportant they may be... can be blown up to enormous proportions,"[38] everything becomes "potentially visible" and virtually transparent. Nothing is hidden from me, and my life—to the extent that I can still call what I experience "my" life—is, in all its splendid shortcomings and virtues, laid out before I become them. What's needed is not transcendence but a blind spot.

The transparency of contemporary culture's obsessive surveillance and transcription of itself, in aesthetic as well as epistemological forms, gives the impression that the world lacks secrets. Though this transparency is in a sense unreal, because it pertains more to the circulation of its own mediated forms of knowledge than any actual world existing apart from its representations, the postmodern subject is confronted with "a world" that appears not to require interpretation. Accordingly, "The world becomes boring when everything is transparent."[39] The Portuguese poet Fernando Pessoa expresses this sensibility at the beginning of the twentieth century, writing: "Tedium is not the disease of being bored because there is nothing to do, but the more serious disease of feeling that there is nothing worth doing."[40] Nearly fifty years later, this sentiment is echoed in 1968 by the conceptual artist Douglas Huebler who based his practice first on the observation that "the world is full of objects,

---

[36] Ibid., 31.

[37] Ibid., 32.

[38] Ibid., 37, 38. Svendsen is alluding specifically to technologies that can archive and treat virtually any dimension of experience as a specimen to be studied and thereby "interpreted."

[39] Ibid.

[40] Fernando Pessoa, *The Book of Disquiet*, trans. Richard Zenith (London: Penguin Classics, 2002), 365.

more or less interesting," and then on a resolve not to add to them: "I prefer, simply, to state the existence of things in terms of time and/ or place."[41] As if in direct response to Huebler's aesthetic strategy of (dis)engagement, Svendsen argues that the source of boredom is not a "growing metaphysical void," but an excessive reflexivity attributable to the Romantic neurosis that the self is "constantly in danger of acquiring a meaning deficiency."[42] This hyper-reflexivity, Svendsen concludes, is responsible for re-presenting the world as something already had, something exhausted of all its potential adventures and becomings.

While Svendsen's post-Baudrillardian vision of a radically mediated world extends Healy's premise that boredom emerges from the withering of traditional meaning structures, Elizabeth Goodstein's study of the discourse of boredom, in her work *Experience Without Qualities* (2005), suggests that the experience of boredom is "a lived metaphor for the dilemma of the modern subject."[43] She argues that the metaphorics of boredom, the way in which its expressions characterize the uniquely modern sense of disaffection, delineate an ambiguous experience that arises from the contest between a declining paradigm of faith and the emerging reflexive proclivities of modern epistemological scepticism. The rhetoric of this experience, "centered on [an] embodied subject struggling with the meaning and purpose of existence in a world increasingly bereft of both religious and worldly certainties,"[44] addresses boredom as a property of the world rather than an attribute of the self, while at the same time implying a "self" with no empirical purchase in the very world

---

[41] Huebler's aim is to merely document elements of the world through a motley assemblage of maps, drawings, photographs, and descriptive writings. However, he overlooks the fact that his very act of assembly is not simply stating the existence of things but changing the nature of the "things" that he is assembling. Thus, despite the sentiment, Huebler's practice is an enactment of the very processes of transcription that paradoxically show culture to itself by inventing new aesthetic configurations of its objects. See Douglas Huebler, "Untitled Statement," in *Theories and Documents of Contemporary Art*, ed. Kristine Stiles and Peter Selz (Berkeley: University of California Press, 1996), 840.

[42] Svendsen, *Boredom*, 33.

[43] Elizabeth S. Goodstein, *Experience without Qualities: Boredom and Modernity* (Stanford: Stanford University Press, 2005), 420.

[44] Ibid.

that its metaphorics constitute. Reflecting the reflexive capacities of (post)Kantian thought, the rhetoric of modern experience naturalizes its own metaphysical ambiguity and "evoke[s] the fatalistic generalization that life itself is a senseless series of momentary encounters with irrelevant objects."[45] Thus the *discourse* of boredom masquerades as a fundamental human mood because the *rhetoric* of modern experience, which draws its tropes from an "epistemological and ethical skepticism" regarding ways of "understanding and dwelling in the world,"[46] stirs the nihilism internal to boredom in such a way that the existential or practical insufficiency felt in being bored "eclipses the socio-critical dimension of the discourse."[47] Goodstein's basic argument then is that the metaphorics of boredom undercut its own ability to comment on the conditions that express what might be called the sense of senselessness.

Unlike Svendsen who sees a possible melioration, if not cessation, of boredom's urgency by accepting that life holds no great "Meaning" but only a series of fleeting "meanings,"[48] Goodstein sees no hope for boredom. Boredom for Goodstein has no redemption. The nihilistic impulse that composes its lived experience cannot reflect on the historical specificity of its *felt sense of senselessness*. That is why she is able to speak of an "experience without qualities," for without a language of reflection, experience remains unqualified and, in a sense, unjustified, unnecessary—*de trop*. As a "lived metaphor for the dilemma of the modern subject" who is unable to say or convey what ails him/her, the experience of boredom can only circulate in modern discourse on subjective experience as a mute performative, a paradoxically expressive non-expression of the dumb and unqualified way of being present to an objectified world that has lost its capacity to defer—to God, to tradition, to culture. In other words, boredom expresses the failure of modern reflexive discourse to account for its own culturally and historically determined conditions. As a lived metaphor that compares certain corporeal manners (weariness, fatigue, sloth) with a proliferating array of anomie,

---

[45] Goodstein, *Experience*, 408.
[46] Ibid., 413.
[47] Ibid., 408.
[48] Svendsen, *Boredom*, 154.

boredom entails a forgetting not only of its own metaphorics but of the general role that metaphor—understanding one thing in terms of another—plays in the discursive construction of experience and the expression of that experience.

Goodstein's diagnosis of boredom as the experiential side of a failed metaphorics is difficult to refute. Boredom is the expression of an experience that cannot be qualified, and as such is not something that can be overcome or resolved, for there is nothing to leverage hope or desire against. Instead, we leave boredom by dislocating and decoupling its metaphorics. But I'm not interested in this dislocation as much as I am in how boredom's failed metaphorics open the way to the felt sense of senselessness and how contemporary boring music stages the performance of being-unjustified.

This attention to boredom as an expression of failure is significant for at least two reasons. First, through the lens of failure, "boredom as a metaphor for the experiential predicament of the modern subject"[49] characterizes the plight of an ambivalent subject. This subject, in addition to coping with its essential ambiguity bestowed by modern scepticism, must manufacture its own interests or, following Félix Guattari's notion of subjectivity, "produce assemblages of enunciation capable of capturing the points of singularity of a situation."[50] Although boredom's metaphoricity is incapable of grasping its own historical contingency, the interruption in the habitual and therefore a-singular attachments to things, places, and times, can be read through Guattari's onto-aesthetic paradigm as "an activity of rupturing sense, of baroque proliferation or extreme impoverishment, which leads…to a recreation and a reinvention of the subject itself."[51] Boredom divests the contemporary subject of its certainties and at the same moment it grants this "larval subject," or subject in waiting, the power (the illusion?), if not the form, of self-invention. There are, however, a number of consequences that follow from this and I'll take them up in what follows, but before that

---

[49] Goodstein, *Experience*, 420.

[50] Félix Guattari, *Chaosmosis: An Ethico-Aesthetic Paradigm*, trans. Paul Baines and Jullian Penfais (Indianapolis: Indiana University Press, 1995), 128.

[51] Ibid., 131.

I want to address the second reason why the failure of boredom is significant.

The forgetting of boredom's metaphorics, though it sacrifices meaning, can be understood to occasion a productive situation in which, as Guattari's counterpart Gilles Deleuze argues in his work on time in cinema, "a different type of image can appear."[52] This "image"—whether a work of art or an everyday perception—is one whose capacity to stand for something else is impeded such that it "brings out the thing in itself, literally, in its excess of horror or beauty, in its radical or unjustifiable character."[53] Boredom has a way of unbinding expectations and responsive habits from their conventional assembly and customary valence; however, it does not give a superior view of being in the sense promoted by Sartre or Heidegger.[54] Instead, the inability to reflect meaningfully on subjective experience that characterizes boredom's failed metaphorics elaborates a situation—an "image"—that is both excessive and deficient, a situation whose senselessness (non-sens) expresses not the "thing itself," but the dumb refrains of nonsense. The "thing itself" is revealed in being bored as something that is essentially unjustified in itself, something radically supplemental, and, ironically, something that is perpetually interesting.

Cage, Fluxus, and inclusion

The predictable place to look for precedents to today's enactments of tedium is musical minimalism, particularly in the process pieces of minimalist composers such as Steve Reich, Phillip Glass, and Terry Riley. However, unlike more contemporary expressions of boredom that are constituted by an affective ambivalence, Glass, Reich, and

---

[52] Gilles Deleuze, *Cinema 2: The Time-Image*, trans. Hugh Tomlinson (Minneapolis: University of Minnesota, 1989), 20.

[53] Ibid.

[54] Sartre's position is that being is given entirely—without remainder—in its appearance. Thus the appearance of being bored is expressive of the ontology of the phenomenon of being as it manifests itself. See Jean-Paul Sartre, "The Phenomenon of Being and the Being of Phenomenon," in *Being and Nothingness*, trans. Hazel Estella Barnes (New York: Washinton Square Press, 1984), 7–9.

Riley's music is unabashedly affirmative. The pulsating hypnotic sameness of Reich's *Four Organs* (1970) or Riley's *In C* (1964) harness the perceptual and somatic effects of prolonged exposure to repetition in a way that hypnotizes the listener and keeps boredom out of mind. In this sense, musical minimalism escapes more than it articulates the sensuous infinity that I hear waiting in contemporary musical boredom.[55] An evidently more ambivalent boredom may, however, be traced through the less frenetic and rhythmical declaimed work of composers such as La Monte Young, Morton Feldman, Christian Wolff, and members of the 1970s British experimental scene including Cornelius Cardew, Gavin Bryars, and Howard Skempton.

The music of these composers can be immediately distinguished from that of American minimalism by its mensural or "floating" surfaces on which boredom is cultivated like the green patina that grows to tarnish and passivate bronze metals. La Monte Young's early piece *Trio for Strings* (1958), for instance, is a five-hour work in which long sustained tones alternate with spans of silence to create a static field of sounds whose timbral characteristics overtake the formal dimensions of the work.[56] From the late 1970s to his death in 1987,

---

[55] A case could be made for all of this music that repetition, not duration, is the salient factor in these works. In a sense this is true, but the dominant trope of repetition that characterizes these musics has to be understood to function not merely as a formal element but an ideological gesture whose execution serves as a type of aesthetic transgression, a sign of dis-obedience aimed at the prohibitions of high modernism. Moreover, repetition is not opposed to duration so much as each of its iterations is an expression of change as such. For this essay I prefer to focus on the figure of "duration" for two reasons: One, I find that "repetition" is still overburdened by its ideological function that keeps it shackled to an historical opposition; and two, despite disrupting teleological figures of time, repetition's affirmation of the eternal return of the same-difference (depending on your Nietzsche-Deleuze tastes) does not express the sense of a "bad" or "sensuous" infinity that is symbolized by the sheer extended-ness and slowness of the contemporary works which I consider in this chapter. Though much of the same phenomena that emerge in musical repetition apply to recent boring music's sense of infinity (such as a slackening of ego constancy and the replacement of tonal order for moments of varying intensity), the context in which these appear changes their expression such that the experience of "ego death" and "process" characteristic of repetitive music are refigured in light of boredom and as "insufficiency" and "waiting."

[56] But five hours is very little when compared to Young's later work. The numerous versions of which he captures under the rubric of *The Tortoise His Dreams And Journeys* (1964–present) are presented sometimes as day-long performances. However, perhaps *Longplayer*, a 1,000-year-long musical composition by Jem Finer that began sounding

Morton Feldman began to extend his characteristically asyndetic refrains (refrains that follow one from the other with no coordination but the momentum and contiguity of their appearance) beyond the hour mark to include the occasional six- or seven-hour piece such as his *string quartet II* (1982) and *For Philip Guston* (1983). Unlike the excited throbbing of minimalism, the slow and mannered unspooling of Young and Feldman's works never gather up the energies of attention enough to launch the imagination into the clutches of a higher interest. Instead, they allow attention to leak and settle into its own contemplation. The British experimentalists, too, took boredom in a route that did not necessarily lead to its dissipation. Gavin Bryars' *Jesus' Blood Never Failed Me Yet* (1971), a treacley orchestration of a loop of a homeless man's rendition of the English Hymn, though repetitive and drawn out, never quite drives boredom away, for its sentimental text and schmaltzy arrangement invoke the referential tendencies of musical sound to mire the listener in the nostalgia of 1950s Hollywood optimism. And the music of Cornelius Cardew, Michael Parsons, and Howard Skempton (a/k/a The Scratch Orchestra) used duration not to access a utopian dimension into which the energies of dissatisfaction would be sublimated, but to realize the principles of socialism in musical terms.

But even these studies in extendedness tend to avoid the rhetoric of boredom as an aesthetic category that attaches to contemporary experiments in tedium. A trajectory that follows visual and perfor-mance art practices of the 1960s and 1970s, particularly those informed by the assimilative principles of John Cage's putative non-intentionality, and the newly available plasticity and instanta-neous playback capacities of video, shows more explicitly an effort to express the multifaceted dimensions of an experience without qualities. While music audiences were actively blissing-out to Glass's four-hour *Music in Twelve Parts* (1970–4) and being aggressively politicized by the Scratch Orchestra's collective impulses, artists such as Nam June Paik, Bruce Nauman, and Vito Acconci can be

---

at midnight 31 December 1999, is an ever more exemplary case of extended musical durations. But unlike *The Tortoise*, whose duration, while protracted can in principle be experienced by an individual human organism, *Longplayer* cannot. And in this regard, *The Tortoise* and *Longplayer* differ in their presentation of what may be distinguished as a "secular duration" versus a "mythical duration," respectively. See longplayer.org.

seen situating viewers in a narcissistic and, as Rosalind Krauss writes, a "self-encapsulated" time.[57] Paik's *TV Buddha* (1974), for example, which consists of a Buddha statue facing and peering at its own televised projection, expresses a form of self-absorbed duration whose short-circuit between reception and projection effaces the sense of creative advance that a sensible flow difference cannot help but introduce into perception. Bruce Nauman's *Violin Tuned D.E.A.D.* (1969) or Vito Acconci's *Centers* (1971) likewise draw from video's mechanized duration the tedium of an indefatigable body. Preceding even these experiment in video, however, Dick Higgins, George Brecht, and Yoko Ono, members of the loosely knit neo-Dada movement Fluxus, produced "text scores" that invoked composition's implied imperative mood to critically redouble the normally sublimated boredom of the everyday.

In many ways, the works of these artists are indebted to the expansive gestures of John Cage's conceptual rhetoric. I don't want to spend much time wrestling with the contradictions and latent imperialism in Cage's thought, but since his work often stands as a synecdoche for a certain species of aesthetic vanguardism, one that touts its expressions and practices as radically inclusive (while at the same time disavowing its esoteric faith in the a-referential ideals of "absolute" music), it needs to be addressed not only for its contribution to the development of an aesthetics of boredom in composition, but also, and relatedly, for the complexity of ideas of spectatorial co-creation that pivot around its axis.

Although somewhat overextended, the axiom, derived from Zen Buddhism, that if you stay with something long enough you'll find that it's not boring at all, has come to represent Cage's attitude towards music, art, and life in general. How much Cage believed this wisdom is beside the point that it clearly served him as inspiration (justification?) for a way to broaden the terms of what can count as aesthetic material. Since the composers that I associate with contemporary boring music are themselves inheritors of this type of post-Cagean aesthetic disposition, Cage's neo-Dada praxis (and theorization of that praxis which takes for granted the implication of the addressee in the constitution of

---

[57] See Rosalind E. Krauss, "Video: The Aesthetics of Narcissism," *October* 1 (1976): 50–64.

an artwork) is not only salient, but indeed, crucial to the present study. But to be fair to Cage, he wasn't so much interested in being bored, or boring, per se—at least not in the way that Andy Warhol made boredom both a career and an alibi for his career.[58] Cage's project, I believe, was more generous and sincere in its intentional non-intentionality than our recently cultivated ironic reflex will permit. Whereas Warhol's boredom can be understood as a cynical embodiment of art and consumer culture's mutual implosion (itself arguably indebted to Cage's own aesthetic anarchism), Cage's boredom can be construed more honestly as the expression of a veiled ideology that assumes a continuity between the natural realm (the "real") and art.

For Cage, a sprawling "nothing"[59] stood in the way of his project to appropriate the totality of sounds to the category of music. But

---

[58] Warhol's notorious reputation for "being bored" can be illustrated in many ways, but perhaps his films *Sleep* and *Empire* are most representative of his sense of tedium. Both *Sleep* and *Empire* are eight-hour films that fixate on the passage of time by focusing the camera on a single event. In the case of the former, the film is a partially looped shot of a sleeping John Giorno, while the later is a continuous shot of the Empire State building as late afternoon dusk passes into evening darkness.

[59] This "nothing" is, for Cage, not a nihilistic "nothing" but a creative nothing that resembles the void of numerous eastern mystical traditions. But Cage validates this sense of nothing in a way that makes art servile to science. His argument is thus: Drawing its first premise from Ananda K. Coomaraswamy's assertion that "the traditional function of the artist is to imitate nature in her manner of operation," Cage posits a second premise, "Changes in science give artists different understandings of how nature works," to conclude that "art changes because science changes."[59a] For Cage, the science contemporary to his work was quantum mechanics' whose model of a fundamentally indeterminate reality validates Cage's argument and affirms the veracity of a chance-based art. The problem, however, is not the logic of syllogism, but the way that Cage obscures the fact that "nature" is a representation of, in this case, a scientific model. This is a fact that Cage himself introduces in his second premise, and one that he ignores when he admits to finding "nature far more interesting than any of man's control of nature."[59b] "Nature" as he infers it is no more natural than is his musical portrayal of its indeterminacy, and as I show above, this elision of an "indeterminate nature" as itself a representation leads Cage to mistakenly hypostatize his very artificial "chance operations." I don't actually have a problem with this circularity, for it generates all manner of fugitive phenomena that mess with the integrity of the musical field. In fact, Chapter Two and Three of this study examine the power and the effects that this type of thinking has for art.

[59a] Cage, *Silence: Lectures and Writings*, 194. Cage attributes this saying to Coomaraswamy; however, Douglas Kahn notes that Coomaraswamy himself borrowed the notion from St. Thomas Aquinas who wrote: Ars imitatur naturam in sua. See Douglas Kahn, *Noise, Water, Meat* (Cambridge, MA: MIT Press, 1999), 170.

[59b] Cage, *Silence*, 194.

"nothing" can be seen here as a convenient ideological construct that allowed Cage to extend his notions of chance to the domain of the real. Art historian Ina Blom argues that Cage's perspective on chance as the expression of an "infinitely heterogeneous reality where all things interpenetrate"[60] makes it appear as though his chance operations are not simply a compositional conceit, but a way of expressing the reality that they presume. Blom contends that chance functions within Cage's project "both as an ideology—a view of the world (or nature) as an indeterminate a-causal sphere of infinite changes—and a method through which to produce the work of art *as* reality."[61] Cage's belief in an indeterminate reality and his practice of an indeterminate music thus make sense of each other: the real as a purposeless domain coincides perfectly with its chance expressions.

Cage imagined a radically inclusive world of sound where any "audible, potentially audible, or mythically audible sounds" could be materialized as music.[62] However, nestled within this fantasy was, as Douglas Kahn argues, a strategy borrowed indirectly from Luigi Russolo's 1912 *Art of Noise*, which can be cited as the first treatise on musical inclusiveness, and directly (though in a distorted way) from Edgard Varèse, that would "let sounds be themselves" so long as they were interpolated within the purview of a very narrow musical sensibility (a sensibility that Kahn sees allied to the stipulations of absolute music—a-referentiality).[63] Though Cage's effort to open musical experience to a wider materiality was premised on a phenomenological account (I'm referring here to the oft-cited story of his experience in an anechoic chamber), it could only be made effective through a rhetorical maneuver that ciphered the semiotic remainders of sound first through the frame of duration and then through the supposed paradoxical intentionality of silence. Silence, as

---

[60] See Ina Blom, forthcoming manuscript awaiting publication based on pages 5–70 of Ina Blom, *The Cut Through Time: A Version of the Dada/Neo-Dada Repetition* (Oslo: Acta Humaniora/UniPub, 1999).

[61] Ibid.

[62] Kahn, *Noise, Water, Meat*, 164.

[63] Kahn's critique is decisive here. He contends that Cage's musicalization of sound-in-itself is carried out along the lines of a radically exclusive principle embodied in the nineteenth century as "absolute music" which predicated its terms on musical areferentiality. See Kahn, *Noise, Water, Meat*, 164–5.

Cage conceptualized it, was "all the sounds that we *don't* intend;"[64] therefore, its experience is a matter of intentionally *in-attending* to the sounds that populate the field of hearing. Any sound was musical so long as it was intentionally heard as music and *un-heard* in its worldliness. That is, sounds are musical to the extent that their being heard articulates the intentions that constitute the traditional horizon of listening musically while at the same time seeming to disarticulate those intentions that tradition places on the composer.

This rhetorical sleight of hand, aided perhaps by the schizophrenic condition inherent to modernism's hyper-reflexive discourses, and the procedural interventions of his "chance" operations, allowed Cage to shift the act of intentionality from composer onto the listener in such a way that the composer's ego-culpability would become, if not extinguished, then at least scattered in a hall of mirrors.[65] Cage is quoted as saying: "If you're non-intentional, then everything is permitted. If you're intentional, for instance if you want to murder someone, then it's not permitted."[66] For him it seems that what lies outside of intention is a nothingness that is in itself, if not beautifully harmonious, then effectively innocuous. But the benevolence of this was challenged by many of Cage's students who operated under the banner of Fluxus. In her 1998 essay "Boredom and Oblivion," Blom contends that Fluxus submitted Cage's structurally and formally neutral "field of endless heterogeneity and multiplicity" to the "kinds of marks that it would—in principle—be immune to: the marks of ownership, of singularities, of different subjectivities, intentions, and

---

[64] Michael Zerwin in Kahn, *Noise, Water, Meat*, 163.

[65] Cage's investment in the discursively constructed aptitude of a creative "nature" afforded him the conscience to colonize a broader territory for (absolute) music by proposing that sounds that appeared to self-manifest by means of chance could be intended, or attended to, as though free of semiotic impurities. In other words, by rolling dice Cage could keep his hands clean. What should be gleaned from this foray into Cage's aesthetics is the way he divests composition of its intentionality yet leaves the intentionality of listening, with all its appurtenant investments and interests, firmly in place. The sentiment was perhaps right but the way it relies on a hyper-reflexive approach makes its expression self-conscious, by which I mean awkward and insecure. This discomfiture is, perhaps, a result of the fact that intentionality was never really extinguished in Cage's scheme, but simply reallocated, by chance, to a subject traditionally considered marginal to the production of musical sounds.

[66] Cage in Richard Kostelanetz, *Conversing with Cage* (New York: Routledge, 2003), 213.

representations."[67] That is, Fluxus introduced the body and all of its potential relationships into Cage's abstract model of inclusivity. Dick Higgins' series of works titled *Danger Music* (1962), for example, represent an attempt to draw out the implications of these corporeal "marks" that Cage's inclusive system expels. *Danger Music #17, with its instructions:* "Scream! Scream! Scream! Scream! Scream! Scream!" or *Danger Music #9* that simply reads: "Volunteer to have your spine removed," pierce the conceptual veil of Cage's theory that purports to embrace everything. But Higgins does this not to negate the creed of inclusivity, but to disclose its potential limits and tolerances. Taking Cage's hypothesis for granted, Fluxus found that "the space of immersion could not be formulated without an engagement with, and through, borders and limits."[68]

Whereas Cage's inclusive gesture posits "an empty framework waiting to be filled, precluding any actual relation between the structure and its filling material,"[69] Fluxus showed that this inclusion could only be accomplished by making the elements traditionally disowned or "exscribed" by music proper—i.e. a concert performance's start-time, the exchange of money for entrance to the hall, coughing, sniffling, waiting—coincide with the processes of semiosis that delineate the framework's structure. Boredom was, in this respect, instrumental to Fluxus, for its metaphysical ambiguity that blurs the distinctions between subjective and objective experience serves as an exemplary expression of the irreducible relation between form (structure) and content. Dick Higgins' account of a piece by George Brecht performed in utter darkness such that it became impossible to discern when the events signifying the work's conclusion had occurred, exemplifies the way in which, as Blom notes, "boring art involves the surroundings in ways not apparent when stimuli appear as exciting along certain lines of expectation."[70] Unlike Cage, who as Kahn argues, gathers all sounds under a distorted postulate of absolute music (total a-referentiality), Fluxus' storied text-based "event-scores" articulate the abstract proposi-

---

[67] Ina Blom, "Boredom and Oblivion," in *The Fluxus Reader*, ed. Ken Friedman (West Sussex: Academy Editions, 1998), 64.
[68] Ibid., 65.
[69] Ibid., 76.
[70] Ibid., 65.

tions used in conventional musical performances and compositions with ordinary items and mundane actions in a way that opens a space between the purview of music proper and the domain of the everyday.

This "between" Higgins termed "Intermedia." Not to be confused with an unmediated event, Intermedia describes how a Fluxus event-score effects Cage's inclusive gesture using elements of the world in which the performer and listener are embedded to enframe how he or she is always already included or "immersed" in a universal embrace. The Fluxus event doesn't divest these mundane elements of their signification in the way Cage's parasitic anti-formalism does; rather than try to efface the ego and ascend to universal-immersive position outside the realm of discursive reality, Fluxus shows that the act of radical inclusion entails the matter of subjectivity, a matter of being continuously positioned within an intensively plastic world of signs and bodies. Inclusion therefore cannot take place beyond the lineaments of subjectivity (and its implicit politics, its "will to power"), but only within them. One is included in a world or event by enacting, more *and* less intensively, a subject position. Fluxus can be understood then to adjust Cage's inclusive ideal by inverting its transcendentalism, by attaching "art effects" to the particular intensities of (everyday) life rather than banishing the difference between them: "The semiotic remainders that [are] generally placed at [art and] music's margins"[71] become the components of the frame within which a listener can actually "get lost" by getting bored.

By disrupting the familiar lines of expectation in a way that allowed attention to light upon the discursive and intensive regularities that constitute that "residual category into which can be jettisoned all the irritating bits and pieces which do no fit into the orderly thought"[72]— i.e., the everyday—Fluxus' "aesthetics of boredom" marks the emergence of two significant developments in composition. One thing that boredom's articulation of art with the everyday did was to suggest a certain libertarian socialist politics that presaged the DIY sensibility of 1970s punk culture, but within the floundering category

---

[71] Ibid., 76.
[72] Mike Featherstone, *Undoing Culture: Globalization, Postmodernism and Identity* (London and Thousand Oaks, CA: Sage Publications, 1995), 55.

of "art" music as represented by Christian Wolff and Cornelius Cardew's pseudo-socialist schemes that would both define music by and use music to create a collective "situation in which sounds may occur."[73] The other direction in which boredom moved music was in relation to the nature of musical time. Corresponding to the temporal sprawl that expresses the time of being bored was the change in musical time from being merely a metronomic quantity to a chrononomic quality. That is, duration becomes something more than a measurable parameter, aligning itself with various vital processes whose powers or intensities wax and wane. It is this shift towards duration and its corresponding affects that I want to focus on in the next section in order to draw attention to the way in which boredom's aesthetic expression becomes an occasion for us to witness the time of events and practice the art of waiting.

Duration

Expressed in Steve Reich's noted essay on music as a gradual process, in Feldman's interest in the sublime effects of scale, and in Brian Eno's development of open or generative musical systems,[74] duration began to resemble Henri Bergson's notion of *dureé*, the lived experience of dilations and contractions that give time its qualitative character. Writing about his experience listening to Steve Reich's *It's Gonna Rain* (1964), Brian Eno describes the very concrete effect that duration has on perception.

What happens when you listen to it is that your listening brain becomes habituated in the same way that your eye does if you

---

[73] Michael Nyman, *Experimental Music: Cage and Beyond*, 2nd ed. (Cambridge and New York: Cambridge University Press, 1999), 62.
[74] The newest and perhaps most commercially accessible of Eno's generative music systems is the iPhone/iPad/iPod application "Bloom," which was developed in collaboration with software designer Peter Chilvers. Bloom is in essence a twenty-first-century music-box that allows the user to set slowly evolving patterns of sound in motion by tapping the screen in various places. The generic term for Eno's particular brand of minimalism, a minimalism that despite its formal differences functions much like Muzak, is "ambient music."

stare at something for a very long time. If you stare at something *for a very long time* your eye very quickly cancels the common information, stops seeing it, and only notices the differences.[75]

Though couched in psychological terms, the way in which the expressive elements are compounded with the elongated form of the work reveals that Eno is recounting how one perceives difference as that substance which impresses on our senses over time. Eno's observation that you only "notice the differences" describes the sentiment of composers in the 1970s that time is not an "empty hopper" but essentially a matter (material) of difference.

At this point it might be suggested that the variety conveyed by these works has nothing to do with being bored, and that boredom is articulated only as an un-perceived expression of difference. To an extent I think this is true. All of these composers, except perhaps for Tom Johnson, whose accompanying text to his *An Hour for Piano* (1971) actually describes the difficulty of listening to the hour-long precession of vagrant semiquaver melodic patterns around a G pedal, address the issue of tedium and extendedness by getting rid of it: Reich and Glass by effectively hypnotizing the listener and performer, Cardew by incorporating the messiness and inchoate droll of undisciplined activities into the artwork, and Feldman by restating form as a matter of scale which changes the stakes of a musical experience to supplant the potential boredom of listening with a less judgemental response like "fatigue" and "weariness." In this way, boredom is displaced onto the listener and becomes an alibi for the disaffections that the composer's negative aesthetics elicit. In other words, faith in an experience irreducible to anything other than what the assumed "autonomous" work of art evokes is sheltered from the vulgar moods and tempers of the society that structures its occasion. Boredom's indifference is saved here from its sympathies with the tedium of the everyday.

In a sense, these composers' works recuperate the affect that boredom's temporal stall introduces. Consider how each of Feldman's harmonies is presented as an exquisitely cut gem, or

---

[75] Brian Eno, "Evolving Metaphors, in my Opinion, is What Artists Do," *In Motion Magazine*, 7 July 1996, http://www.inmotionmagazine.com/eno1.html (my emphasis) [accessed October 2012].

how Glass's repetitions conjure a sargasso of hallucinated melodies, reinvesting the monotonous field of minimally changing forms with a value whose aesthetic import is re-cast along the familiar lines of the sublime. Subordinating its low-level and indeterminate intensity to these recognizable aesthetic categories, boredom's sluggardly torsion and slow burn is elided by the thrill of its relief, in moments of diversion, or the work's end. Furthermore, boredom's recently acquired aura (witness 2009's highly lauded and well attended revival of Beckett's *Waiting for Godot* on Broadway and West London or the cynical entertainment value of the proliferation of reality television) suggests that the mood has been made an acceptable experience so long as it has been, named, framed, contained, *etcetera*, in one way or another. Under these conditions, boredom keeps us waiting by holding its transports within itself and offering only sporadic wonders whose Cartesian poetics give way to a Spinozan paralysis[76] in momentary reflections on the ludicrous nature of how we individually and collectively submit ourselves to ever more subtle forms of suffering in the hope of either opening a vein of new amusements, or bleeding-out the last of desire. In short, by considering the multitude of devices and strategies that have been invented to keep individuals and communities diverted, or let's say, un-bored, then we can suppose that boredom is not the exception to, but instead the very principle of contemporary culture. Assuming this, we can also see its expression in contemporary musical practices as forming another "image" of boredom that interferes with or unsettles its common currency in art as what Higgins once described as "a station on the way to other experiences."[77] Having little access to the recent institutional

---

[76] This distinction is important for wonder is conceived by Descartes as the "first passion" that leads to a series of thoughts and experiences that end in the knowledge or explanation of the initial spark, wheras Spinoza, on the other hand, conceptualized wonder as a paralysis of the essentially active mind in the presence of an inassociable novelty (object, event). Because for Spinoza the mind *is* its movement between thoughts or sensation, wonder in this case indexes a defective mind. In contrast to the stalled mind Spinoza pairs with wonder the opposite passion, disdain, by which a novelty's inassociable characteristics keep the mind from engaging the contemptible event in an association of thoughts, continuing instead to think of everything else but it.
[77] Dick Higgins, "Boredom and Danger," in *Breaking the Sound Barrier: A Critical Anthology of the New Music*, ed. Gregory Battcock (New York: Dutton, 1982), 22.

endorsements that would give it *Godot*'s modernist aura, and lacking even the sensuous appeal by which a mass- market could grant it the alibi of being entertainment, the image of boredom enacted in certain contemporary musical practices eschews the earlier "successes" of musical minimalism by simply practicing the art of waiting.

The aesthetics of boredom and the art of waiting

Go back to David Foster Wallace's thoughts on boredom. Though crushing, he imagines that boredom can be a nostrum to what he perceives as America's addiction to entertainment. Wallace, who hanged himself in the fall of 2008, was working at the time on a novel about boredom that he titled *The Pale King*. In this work, his stated aim was to interrogate the merits and powers of concentration and mindfulness. But it is in the posthumous publication of what is essentially an unfinished work that Wallace wanted to catechize the full breadth of a malaise whose emotional burn feeds quietly off the ever-expanding patina of diversion. For Wallace, media culture disables an individual's ability to decide how and what he or she pays attention to. While we can imagine for a moment that one could actually pay attention to nothing, the saturation of media makes it impossible. An individual's ability to slow the dizzying flows of media imagery and "find himself" in the fog of boredom would thus seem to occasion something other than mindfulness and something more like what psychoanalyst Adam Phillips suggests is a confrontation with "the poverty of our curiosity."[78]

In *The Pale King*, a multifarious assembly of character and sensory sketches, kaleidoscopic dialogue, and the explication of certain cryptic dimensions of the US tax code, all of which revolve around the concerns and experiences of IRS employees during the mid-1980s, Wallace devotes a chapter (§33) depicting the tactics

---

[78] Adam Phillips, *On Kissing, Tickling, and Being Bored: Psychoanalytic Essays on the Unexamined Life* (Cambridge, MA: Harvard University Press, 1993), 75.

taught by IRS agents processing tax returns to combat the threat of
boredom:

> Lane Dean Jr. with his green rubber pinkie finger, sat at his Tingle
> table in his chalk's row in the Rotes Group's wiggle room and did
> two more returns, then another one, then flexed his buttocks and
> held to a count of ten and imagined a warm pretty beach with
> mellow surf, as instructed in orientation the previous month. Then
> he did two more returns, checked the clock real quick, then two
> more, then bore down and did three in a row, then flexed and
> visualized and bore way down and did four without looking up
> once, except to put the completed files and memos in the two
> Out trays side by side up in the top tier of trays, where the cart
> boys could get them when they came by.[79]

Though Wallace never concluded his diagnosis of the pale king, I
wouldn't claim that being bored is an antidote to either entertainment
or information overload. The effects of boredom are much too diffuse
and uneven to target and effectively counteract the systematic
distractions and amusements that contemporary culture contrives to
keep its loose threads of desire in tow. That is to say, while boredom
may be ubiquitous, its effects are local and unpredictable. I would
suggest instead that the boredom Wallace was after is a tactical one,
a downtime in the sense of *la perruque*, which Michel de Certeau
imagines as form of subterfuge whereby an individual poaches time
for other ends that are "free, creative, and precisely not directed
toward[s] profit."[80] The difficulty, however, in seeing boredom in this
way is that the time it takes is structured by no apparent "ends,"
creative or otherwise.

This guerrilla or banditry boredom is carried out in the work of
Brooklyn-based composer Devin Maxwell. In his piece *PH4* (2004),
for bass clarinet, contrabass, and marimba, the listener is made
simply to wait, not *for* something but *to* something. Over its nearly

---

[79] David Foster Wallace, *The Pale King: An Unfinished Novel* (New York: Little, Brown
and Co., 2011), 376.
[80] Michel de Certeau, *The Practice of Everyday Life*, trans. Steven Rendall (Berkeley:
University of California Press, 1984), 24.

14-minute duration is unfolded a series of slow permutations on what Maxwell calls a "crippled gesture," in this case expressed as two short notes and one long tone distributed among the three instruments (with an occasional tremolo for variety). This crippling is used, as Maxwell says, to "build momentum which can or cannot lead to something interesting."[81] Reminiscent of Morton Feldman's early work, but also of the British composer John White's "machine music" pieces of the 1970s,[82] *PH4* develops a form of waiting from within its refrain that shifts attention to the event of the moment's happening, taking time away from the *meaning* of our expectations and giving it to the *feeling* of anticipation. In *PH4* the listener is made to wait and to listen out for waiting, not for what follows waiting but for the event that (much like dying) is both something we do and something that happens to us. The listener is encouraged to witness *PH4*'s event not as an occasion *of* attention but as an occasion *for* attention, where waiting is what happens while it happens.

Summoning de Certeau again, we can understand the waiting encouraged by *PH-4*'s evocation of a musicological downtime as a "'remainder' constituted by the part of human experience [in this case, being bored] that has not been tamed and symbolized in language."[83] Though one can speak of "waiting" in the infinitive form, it's known best in its specific expressions of "waiting for" something—waiting *for* the subway...*for* the movie to begin...*for* a song to end. But in terms of de Certeau's analysis of everyday practices, waiting falls into a species of lived art or tactical know-how that is "composed of multiple but untamed operativities,"[84] which is to say that waiting is a non-discursive art of organizing human experience without a proper time or place outside of its own occur-

---

[81] Devin Maxwell, email message to the author. 30 May 2009.
[82] John White wrote what he calls "machine music" during the period 1967–72. For White, the "machine" describes "a consistent process governing a series of musical actions within a particular sound world, and, by extension, the listener's perception thereof." John White, Notes to *Machine Music: John White and Gavin Bryars*, LP Obscure OBS 8. One of White's better known machine pieces is *Drinking and Hooting Machine* (1971), a set of instructions indicating types of drinking actions and the number of "hoots" that are to ensue after these.
[83] Certeau, *Practice*, 61.
[84] Ibid., 65.

rence.[85] Waiting can happen anywhere, anywhen. How one waits is mandated by circumstances, but the capacity to wait is independent of any variation it may take. As such, "to wait" characterizes a bizarre inactive activity that "operates outside of the enlightened discourse which it lacks."[86] What makes the waiting in *PH4* strange is that it brings out the quality of the infinitive in a similar way that we might say Samuel Barber's *Adagio for Strings* (1938) brings out the "essence" of mourning, or Sergio Ortega's *¡El pueblo unido, jamás será vencido!* (The People United Will Never Be Defeated!) captures the spirit of a mobilized working class. Boredom in *PH4* brings something of the extra-discursive operativity of waiting to attention. Or, to put this into another perspective, recall Wallace's IRS agent, who, confined to his "tingle table," enacts a virtuosic display of the art of waiting:

Then he looked up, despite all best prior intentions. In four minutes, it would be another hour; a half hour after that was the ten-minute break. Lane Dean imagined himself running around on the break, waving his arms and shouting gibberish and holding ten cigarettes at once in his mouth, like a panpipe... Coffee wasn't allowed because of spills on the files, but on the break he'd have a big cup of coffee in each hand while he pictured himself running around the outside grounds, shouting. He knew what he'd really do on the break was sit facing the wall clock in the lounge and, despite prayers and effort, count the seconds tick off until he had to come back and do this again.... He thought of a circus strongman tearing a phone book; he was bald and had a handlebar mustache and wore a stripy all-body swimsuit like people wore in the distant past. Lane Dean summoned all his will and bore down

---

[85] "Event," in the sense that I am using it here, draws on Gilles Deleuze's idea of an event as unactualized potential that underlies whatever has occurred or will evidently occur. An event refers then not to the interruption of a continuous state, but to a potential for action (or inaction) subsisting within a particular confluence of processes. The event of waiting is therefore something like the event of the event, an event in its paradoxically manifest suspension.

[86] Certeau, *Practice*, 66.

and did three returns in a row, and began imagining different high places to jump off of.[87]

It's in the last line of this passage that we see how boredom introduces the inarticulate, yet highly effective, "know-how" or capacity of waiting into the *logos* and "productivist ideal" of the tax return.[88] And from this example we can extrapolate that boredom is expressing the sense of waiting apart from its varying occasions.

While the boredom of this IRS rote examiner brings to suicidal attention the range of his vocational and existential deprivation, we might suggest that the aesthetically conjured boredom of *PH4* exercises the very capacity to imagine by making us wait, by "return[ing] us to the scene of inquiry"[89] where the individual comes to experience the conditions that make desire conceivable. What expressions of boredom in works like *PH4* specify are the protocols of desire.[90] Waiting to find new desires, to find ways of becoming what one hasn't already become, describes an art of becoming-otherwise, becoming wise to the ubiquity of unimagined possibilities. As such, "the paradox of waiting that goes on in boredom is that the individual does not know what he was waiting for until he finds it, and that often he does not know that he is waiting."[91] It is this paradox of waiting for nothing—the uneventful event of waiting—that characterizes the contemporary sense of boredom. If, as we've heard so many times,

---

[87] Wallace, *The Pale King*, 379.

[88] Certeau, *Practice*, 67.

[89] Phillips, *On Kissing*, 75.

[90] A benevolent description would call compositions like Maxwell's *PH4* or Clark's *Mein Schatz* "meditative" in aims of characterizing what seems an artless march through a forest of placid variations whose only goal is to peacefully exhaust itself. But as anyone who has meditated knows, meditation is anything but placid. Meditation is full of turbulence; it is a wave of thoughts and impulses that break on shores of doubt, fear, desire; aches, itches, weariness; anger, lust, indifference, and occasionally, tranquility. The energies at play in meditation are not merely a byproduct of sitting still; they are always there, coursing through us, fugitive until captured by our discursive interests. Meditation doesn't quell these signs of life so much as it serves as a way to cultivate a form of disinterest. That is, meditation is a practiced disposition to refrain from chasing and capturing these fugitive energies, of qualifying and channeling their force towards specific ends that tend towards sustaining the apparatus of capture. Thus, as the Zen Buddhist says, by "sitting as you are" meditation attunes us to the underlying condition of being alive, of being vital organisms: chaos.

[91] Ibid., 77.

the world is already coded by multiple layers of simulation, including the repertory of our desires and responses, then to be bored is not to wait for *some-thing* (we already have those "things") but to wait for *no-thing*. And to wait for no-thing is to risk waiting for nothing, a risk that is itself charged with an ambivalent mixture of wonder and contempt, fixation and flight.

Perhaps it's the intensity of waiting for nothing that Cage wants us to experience when he says, "If something is boring after two minutes, try it for four. If still boring, then eight. Then sixteen. Then thirty-two. Eventually one discovers that it is not boring at all."[92] What Cage implies is that boredom's "hedonic tone," its positive or negative feeling qualification, must be practiced, rehearsed, and, in unexpected alliance with eighteenth-century German aesthetician Georg Friedrich Meier's notion of beautiful thinking (*ars pulchre cogitandi*), which he borrowed from his mentor Alexander Gottlieb Baumgarten, "perfected."

Lane Dean's effort to imagine himself elsewhere than the returns office is an exercise that resists the practice of waiting by refusing him permission to adopt the refrains of boredom that lie within his constrained and routinized existence. However, to the extent that boredom can be seen as a kind of Spinozan wonder, a wonder that stalls in the face of an inassociable novelty, it offers the opportunity to practice the art of waiting, but it does so only under the condition that one waits for the novelty of a "nothing" that must be brought to attention and allowed to flourish in *in*attention. What, for example, is Cage's *4'33"* but a model of attention, refined under the sign of concert culture, that performs a sacrament whereby the object(ive) of attention is inattention? Traditionally construed in terms that suggest some kind of aesthetic pay-off (*Mehrwert*), the contemporary expression of boredom in *4'33"* offers no such thing but instead encourages the listener to practice a type of waiting that relies on the failed promise of its so-called "musical" form so that in this failure the listener might experiment with his/her appetites in the presence of no-thing and, as Phillips suggests, "by doing so commit

---

[92] Cage, *Silence*, 93.

PH 4

for Kevin and Katie

Devin MAXWELL

EMSIS NO. 05-002 S

Devin Maxwell, *PH4* (2004). Éditions musique SISYPHE. Courtesy
GoodChild Music.

himself, or rather, entrust himself, to the inevitable elusiveness of that object."[93]

So, is this really the virtue that Wallace wants to put us in mind of, a concentration on "the principally open field of endless heterogeneity and multiplicity"[94] imagined by Cage as interestingly boring? Having ultimately chosen oblivion, I'm inclined to think that this is not exactly what Wallace was after. Judging by the way Wallace often represented his fragmented thinking through a sophisticated use of footnotes, and, later, a deft handling of stream-of-thought prose, he was likely advancing an immanent form of concentration and mindfulness rather than the kind that adorns itself in the esoteric trappings of perennial wisdom-cum-aesthetic insight. Like the patient variations of *PH4*, which conjure an implacable scene of waiting (for nothing) that strands us in the desert of wall-to-wall delay, Wallace leads us to speculate that it is more productive to imagine contemporary aesthetic tedium as a means of coping with the felt sense of senselessness that inheres in contemporary culture's poverty of curiosity.

Like it or not, there is literally *nothing* to wait for because everything is already at hand. The proliferation of boredom shows us to be a culture in waiting, a culture more attuned to the singular and pure time of its own happening—its event-hood—than to the mixed and impure time of an immediacy mediated by a deferred desire. However, without recourse to overarching narrative complexes that supplement the singularity of waiting, one can only deal with the dumb insistence of an event that attunes us to its virtual infinity. The question then is not whether *PH4*'s musicalized boredom allows the listener's "feelings to develop in the absence of an object,"[95] but rather, how does being bored these days take the time of its happening, its waiting, as something it does and undergoes? In short, it can't take it. It is a deponent force, which is to say that boredom is active in form but passive in meaning. The boredom of waiting does not describe but instead witnesses its happening. It, and those who wait, become, in Lyotard's lovely words, "good intensity-conducting

---

[93] Phillips, *On Kissing*, 78.
[94] Blom, "Boredom and Oblivion," 64.
[95] Phillips, *On Kissing*, 78.

bodies,"[96] bodies whose alternating expression of wonder and fatigue are testament to the radical ambi-valence of events.

The premises/promises of aesthetic boredom

The kind of emotional or affective illegibility that typifies the experience of the aesthetically induced boredom that I've been outlining is consistent with the reports by its champions who tend to depict a committed engagement with the mood as expressing a concealed virtue. While boredom's relationship with art has a rich history that extends back at least to Baudelaire, the history that I'm really dealing with here is the increasing appearance of boredom in art from the 1950s onward. Cage's *4'33"* is paradigmatic of a certain unacknowledged articulation of boredom (as are Robert Rauschenberg's 1951 *White Paintings* from which Cage supposedly drew insight), but looking a little afterwards we see more explicit and unequivocal expressions of boredom in Warhol's *Sleep* and *Empire* and in the procedural poetry of Jackson Mac Low; and in 1968, Dick Higgins published his essay "Boredom and Danger" in which he considers post-war art's increasing interest in boredom as an aesthetic aspiration. In "Boredom and Danger" Higgins draws a line backwards from Fluxus' mid-century experiments to Erik Satie's turn-of-the-century iconoclasm, suggesting that the latter's outlandish use of repetition in pieces like *Vexations* (1893) and *Vieux Sequins at Vieilles Cuirasses* (1913) reflects a modern concern and response to actually having to live with the possibility of an endless future promised by the multiplying wonders of technological innovation and scientific knowledge. Recounting his own experience of *Vexations*, Higgins writes that after the initial offense wears off, one has "a very strange, euphoric acceptance" and an eventual insight into the "dialectic [relationship] between boredom and intensity."[97] From this

---

[96] Jean-François Lyotard, *Libidinal Economy* (Bloomington: Indiana University Press, 1993), 262.
[97] Higgins, "Boredom and Danger," 21, 22.

Higgins concludes that the fascination with boredom in art lies in the way it functions as "an opposite to excitement and as a means of bringing emphasis to what it interrupts."[98] For Higgins then, boredom dialectically affirms the intensities that frame its occasion making it "a station on the way to other experiences."[99]

But after nearly fifty years of sincere, ironic, and iconoclastic elaborations of aesthetic boredom, boredom as "a station on the way to other experiences" has the ring of cliché. Furthermore, calling boredom a station obscures a metaphysical ambiguity that is expressed in boredom's way of being both a property of the objective world ("*That* song is boring") and a subjective state ("*I'm* bored"). That is, qualifying boredom as a dialectical passage between intensities obscures the mood's stranger way of being both objective *and* subjective, dull *and* interesting—ambivalent. However, as I suggested in the previous section, boredom is less dialectically operative and more tactically effective. There is no time of waiting for *an* event, there is only a syncopated time of waiting *as* event. And furthermore, as I will argue in what follows, the event of waiting has been absorbed by another paradigm that allies the premise of boredom's potential to be interesting with an individual's capacity and responsibility to realize his or her "self." My point is that aesthetic boredom no longer has the same dialectical leverage it did for Higgins et al. Whereas the outlandish repetition of *Vexations* once invoked boredom as a negative "structural factor,"[100] the contemporary simulation of its refrain, one that can be automated and more importantly, one can be ignored, evokes a response that is less certain, less transcendent and more perplexed. In short, boredom is less promising these days.

A less promising boredom

But if boredom has less to offer, if its disaffection fails to bore into blissful indifference, what's the point of art's being boring

---

[98] Ibid., 22.
[99] Ibid.
[100] Ibid., 22.

anymore? For Christine Ross, boredom is one of the conditions that conveys what she identifies as a "depressive" paradigm in contemporary art. In *The Aesthetics of Disengagement* (2006), Ross argues that recent art works stage symptoms of depression such as slow time, perceptual insufficiency, and the dementalization of subjectivity to show how art, while filching from science's varied portrayals of depression, works to challenge and alter these as it generates its own expressions of the affliction. Ross suggests that these renderings of depressive symptoms are productive insofar as they map their own affective sense of the disorder, particularly by showing concern for the depressed subject in a way that is exempted from depression's clinical definitions. Challenging and enriching the classification of depression as a form of insufficiency, art, says Ross, addresses depressed subjectivity at the level of sensory appreciation (*aesthesis*), which expands the sense of insufficiency as primarily a cognitive or hermeneutical deficiency to include somatic and affective failures, failures that are no less expressive in their representation of depressed subjectivity than impaired thinking is.

Ross details a number of ways in which contemporary artists deal with the symptoms of depression. In a series of video works by Ugo Rondinone, featuring clowns engulfed by a torpor of unknown origin, Ross sees the "withering of melancholia" in art as it has become subsumed by a contemporary depressive paradigm. However, in Douglas Gordon's *24 Hour Psycho* (1993) and Rosemarie Trockel's *Sleepingpill* (1999), two video pieces that depict an illegible form of (slow) motion, she sees how slow time in art suggests the way depression interrupts the hermeneutic impulse of perception and revalorizes the domain of sensory appreciation. Here Ross construes the staging of depressed behaviour in these and other cases to show that they "are not the symptoms of a disease but 'normal' configurations of contemporary subjectivity."[101] And insofar as boredom's disaffection signals a diminishment in one's capacity to do something, it too articulates the feeling of insufficiency that dominates the subject of "a society founded on individualistic

---

[101] Ross, *Disengagement*, 61.

independence and self-realization," a subject whose "self is always on the threshold of being inadequately itself." [102]

In this view, boredom no longer forms a dialectical relationship with intensity that Higgins took its contrast with excitement to mean. Where boredom once served "as a means of bringing emphasis to what it interrupts," [103] it now functions in this "culture of individualized independence" where individuals have the "right" (or the duty) to choose their own identity and interests, as a symptom reflecting the individual's failure "to meet the neoliberal demand for speed, flexibility, responsibility, motivation, communication, and initiative." [104] Drawing on Alain Ehrenberg's study of depression, [105] Ross argues that, since the 1970s, Western culture has experienced a "decline of norms of socialization based on discipline, obedience, and prohibition and the concomitant rise on norms of independence based on generalized individual initiative...and pluralism of values." [106] Depression might be seen then as the psychic fallout of postmodernism's discursive execution of ideological and normative prescriptions whose celebration of difference, while directing "the individual to be the sole agent of his or her subjectivity," established at the same time the perpetual risk of "failure to perform the self." [107] As such, I suggest that Ross's reading of depression as symptomatic of neoliberal ideals and its expanded field of potential failure shows how depression has taken over where boredom left off: modernity's trope of anomic distress has been replaced with postmodernity's "pathology of insufficiency." [108] Boredom, I contend, appears now as a failure for the (neoliberal) individual to secure a sufficient self, a view that contrasts markedly with the Cagean directive of "losing one's self" in the dissolution of the life-art divide. Failure here is a potential gained while depression is a state earned by the injunction "to be oneself," an optimal functioning self in a world that expects

---

[102] Ibid., 160.

[103] Higgins, "Boredom and Danger," 22.

[104] Ross, *Disengagement*, 92, 178.

[105] Alain Ehrenberg, *The Weariness of the Self: Diagnosing the History of Depression in the Contemporary Age* (Montreal and Kingston: McGill-Queen's University Press, 2010).

[106] Ross, *Disengagement*, 91–2.

[107] Ibid., 92.

[108] Ibid., 61.

and prohibits nothing but that you demonstrate your right, and/or your (in)capacity, to create/perform your "self."

The curious thing about this paradigm is that failure comes to serve a major role in the expression of contemporary subjectivity. To the extent that the contemporary self must continually perform and reiterate its independence (ironically, on already coded models of performance), its failure to obtain the perfection of the idealized performances of this independence along the lines of adaptability, ingenuity, or initiative figures the contemporary subject as what Ross calls a "coping machine." Borrowing the term from cognitive science, Ross cites artist Vanessa Beecroft's performance installations as exemplifying the dynamics of coping that express the failed self. Crudely put, Beecroft's works can be seen to stage a confrontation with the impossibilities of performing feminine ideals. Typically comprising a group of female models chosen for their svelte appearance and homogeneous features, features that can be easily appropriated to common clichés of femininity, Beecroft instructs these meagerly clad (or unclad) women, always in high-heeled shoes, to stand motionless or pose indifferently before an audience for a duration of two to four hours. Ross reads the flagging resolve and subsequent alterations that appear in the performers' attempt to fulfill this performance as behavioral actions, but actions that fail, actions that are "not merely failures but mostly modes of coping with failure."[109] In failing to perform the feminine ideal that is aesthetically framed and exaggerated by the array of uniformly anonymous performers, Ross contends that a coping machine's exhibition of "depressive affects become a strategy by which one shapes one's individuality."[110] Beecroft's exemplary machines affirm then a mode of contemporary subjectivity whose "self" is differentiated and expressed not by mastery or affirmation of a prefigured quantity of, in

---

[109] Ibid., 76. Specifically, Ross positions this failing individualism as gendering a depressed subjectivity. These women—models—are required to perform the idealized and homogenized femininity that they perform *as* models, but in this case, they perform this performance far longer than they are usually asked (required) to do so. After about ten minutes of standing still, the model's capacity to keep still wanes and she starts to adopt other poses in order to cope with the growing tension in her body and the boredom that gradually envelops her.
[110] Ibid., 83.

this case, "femininity," but rather by its manner of coping, by the way it expresses an array of depressive affects that make the depressed/ bored individual his/her own (positively flawed) subject.

Ross's take on the way depression articulates a mode of subjecthood along the lines of failure, or in her words, insufficiency, is instructive and helps to show how the "metaphysical ambiguity" at play in the discourse of boredom is being reworked in contemporary culture. We can see this attitude of neoliberal self-responsibility reflected in the way composers who work with various forms of tedium insist that their music isn't boring—or at least that it doesn't set out to bore. Take this statement from Canadian composer John Abram, whose 68-minute composition *Vinyl Mine* (1996) catalogues the sound of a single pass from the play-off groove of each album comprising the (then) whole of his record collection:

> It's a pet peeve of mine that people say "It's boring," when they really ought to say "I am bored by this." I really believe that anything at all can be engaging and fascinating if you examine it the right way, or for long enough. The viewer's inability or unwillingness to engage with the work is not the work's problem, nor its maker's.[111]

Or consider this, from G. Douglas Barrett, who says of his piece *Three Voices* (a work that I consider below):

> As square and strict as this score is, there is always something unexpected which arises in performance—in this case having to do with the sheer concentration and endurance needed to repeat an action 169 times in strict coordination with two other performers.[112]

Both composers give boredom no purchase on their work, either displacing it onto the listener or treating it as a surface effect of the piece's formal monotony that will (eventually) become marginalized

---

[111] John Abram, email message to author, 17 May 2009.
[112] G. Douglas Barrett, email message to author, 3 June 2009.

by the appearance of the unexpected—provided that one is capable of perceiving it in this way. These comments, obviously taking for granted a Cagean faith in boredom's promise, inadvertently evoke the contemporary sensibility of insufficiency that requires the listener to be the agent of his/her own interests. Here again is Adam Phillips' idea that boredom returns the individual to the scene of inquiry, only this time with the belief that, as Ross argues, one must "initiate one's own identity [desires] instead of being disciplined to do so."[113]

Yet as insightful as Ross's intervention into the construction of depressed subjectivity is, it overlooks that fact that the viewer is somehow expected to understand the hidden operativity of slowness, monotony, fatigue, without actually having to experience the lived reality of these corporeal states. Of course it's possible, to an extent, to understand depression without having suffered it; however, insofar as Ross contends that many of the works she discusses aim to revalue "the sensory and affective dimensions of aesthetics,"[114] it bears noting that almost no one watches the entirety of Gordon's *24 Hour Psycho*, or stands for the duration of the performance with Beecroft's models. It could be argued then that the audience inevitably misses something of the somatic and intensive dimension of failure that is being staged by these works. In this respect we can see how musical enactments of boredom actually *make* the time and space for the kind of sensory regeneration that is only symbolized by the sluggardly pace of these optically-based works. That is, the forms of embodiment that are only ever portrayed by Rondinone's and Gordon's work, and which are supposed to "create the beholder as depressed," are actually made effective by the concert and listening rituals of music that conjure a phantasmatic space-time which allows and indeed requires one to endure the intensities of insufficiency that take time to play out. Music's "concerted" expressions of boredom make the experience of suffering what literary theorist Sianne Ngai identifies as "ugly feelings" of contemporary subjectivity an effectively affective part of its aesthetic expression *and* reception.

---

[113] Ross, *Disengagement*, 92.
[114] Ibid., 152.

Uglier feelings of the stuplime

How aesthetic expressions of boredom have affected us differently over time outlines something of the history of modernity's preoccupation with "ugly feelings." Along with envy, paranoia, and irritation, Ngai identifies a feeling of modernity that characterizes the kind of "syncretism of excitation and enervation"[115] generated by encounters with mind-bendingly vast and excessively dull art. Addressing and unpacking the under-theorized ambi-valence of aestheticised tedium, Ngai draws attention to the way that uts experience resembles the sublime insofar as a listener's "faculties become strained to their limits in their effort to comprehend the work as a whole," but differs from the sublime in that "the revelation of this failure is conspicuously less dramatic."[116] Naming this feeling of ambivalence "stuplimity," Ngai argues that works like Beckett's *Stirrings Still* (1988) and Kenneth Goldsmith's *American Trilogy* (2005–8) (or even abstract systems like the one representing "justice" to K. in Kafka's *The Trial*) do not effect an encounter with the properly (Kantian) sublime. While the vastness of the sublime that threatens to crush the finite individual "ultimately refer[s] the self back to its capacity for reason" and its ability to "transcend the deficiencies of its own imagination,"[117] the excessive accretion of banalities that comprise *Stirrings Still* and *American Trilogy* keep us mired in our insufficiency and in touch with the sensuous infinity intimated by these works.

The difference between the sublime and stuplime can be clarified and its affect examined by looking at the Canadian composer Chedomir Barone's work *Piano Installation with Derangements* (2004). At first glance there is nothing intimidating or overwhelming about its material in the sense suggested by the sublime. Essentially, it is a deliberately obtuse presentation of 750 coupled derangements[118] of a C major scale that when performed (as it was in 2005 by

---

[115] Ngai, *Ugly Feelings*, 280.
[116] Ibid., 270.
[117] Ibid., 266.
[118] A derangement refers to a permutational mode in combinatorial mathematics whereby no element of a given set (i.e. C major: C D E F G A B) appears in its original place.

the composer who spent three hours slowly [ca. ♩ = 52] and quietly playing each paired derangement, while holding the *sostenuto* pedal throughout and treating each quarter rest as an unmeasured fermata) invokes the vertigo of the sublime *without* eliciting the (Kantian) promise of reason that will rescue the affected mind from the failing of its imagination.

Staged as an "installation" so that listeners ("non-performers" in Barone's words) might come and go as they wish, the piece, says Barone, is actually intended for the performer, whose encounter with boredom, because he or she "*must* pay attention or the piece collapses,"[119] does not have the luxury of being carried away from its monotony. Like Beecroft's models, the performer attempts to accomplish an ideal, which in this case is described by a slow, quiet, and steady sounding of seriated C Major derangements. But of course, the performance is festooned with errors and slips, expressive failures that usually pass as justification for the work's boredom. However, the discourse of musical experimentalism that converts these "failures" into aesthetic successes—a discourse premised on the idea that "An error is simply a failure to adjust immediately from a preconception to an actuality"[120]—has the effect of obscuring the affective conditions that engendered their expression. Here's how Barone describes his experience of performing *Piano Installations*:

> I was perhaps a little over half way through the piece when I had a series of revelations. First, I realized that I was no longer consciously controlling my hands, or even reading the music. It seemed at the time that I was only looking at the pages, and my hands were somehow working by their own accord. Next, it occurred to me that I didn't even know "how" to play the piano. (I started to feel the sort of giggly panic at this point that you get when you've taken magic mushrooms and are strolling about town trying not to look/act high). Finally, I realized that nothing much made sense. I was smacking some wooden box with my hands for reasons unknown, and somehow sounds were happening as a result of my actions. Everything—the music,

---

[119] Chedomir Barone, email message to author, 8 May 2009.
[120] John Cage qtd. in Nyman, *Experimental Music*, 62.

Piano Installation with Derangements

Chedomir Barone
(2004)

Piano Installation with Derangements
2

Chedomir Barone, from score for *Piano Installation with Derangements* (2004). Courtesy Chedomir Barone.

the piano, the concert, the people sitting there—seemed utterly foreign and utterly ludicrous.[121]

Note, Barone never says that the monotonous refrains of the piece transported him to some transcendent plateau or endowed his sense of self with some agreeable estimation of itself. The expressions of sublime transduction are clearly absent from his description. Instead, Barone recounts a senseless mixing of bodies and fugitive intensities whose familiar semantic crust and affective attachments have corroded—not exploded—under the slow decay of his capacity to sustain a focused attention. Throughout this performance, Barone is neither elated nor self-secure. He simply finds himself enduring a slow burn that alternately sears and numbs attention as his body encounters the sensuous infinity of the finite's iterability.

Although Barone is relating a performer's experience of the work, its presentation as "music" (despite its title and the invitation to exit) solicits a kind of attention that condemns one to suffer the duration of the performance and so to cope with a "series of fatigues or minor exhaustions, rather than a single, major blow to the imagination."[122] The halting awe of the stuplime, which more accurately describes an experience of Barone's work, expresses a paradox in a way that both recalls and challenges Cage's immersive ideal. It does this insofar as the concerted stuplime articulates the Cagean conceit that displaces intentionality onto the listener who is at the same time created as, in Ross's terms, an insufficient subject. That is, the musicalized stuplime solicits a subject who is expected to be responsible for witnessing his/her incapacity to adequately intend to nothing in particular. The ambivalence infusing this paradox, which in the 1960s was managed and qualified discursively by appealing to the rhetoric of Zen and other traditions of *coincidentia opposi-torum*, is in this case expressed in the affective terms of "coping" and "striving," terms that embody a contemporary "form of living related to a loss of self but inextricably tied to the development of the self."[123] Thus, whereas something like Kenneth Goldsmith's poem

---

[121] Barone, email message to author, 8 May 2009.
[122] Ngai, *Ugly Feelings*, 272.
[123] Ross, *Disengagement*, 68.

Fidget (2000), which is nothing/everything but a transcription of his bodily movements over a single day, simply *represents* the array of corporeal techniques that he suffered over 24 hours, the audience captured by the musical address of Barone's much more modest three-hour performance is given its own occasion to yawn, to loll, to ache and so to shape the individuality of its members through their alternately flagging/rebounding capacity to cope with the stuplimity of its derangements.

What differentiates the boredom of this situation from its Romantic expression is the articulation of a neoliberal and cognitivist model of subjectivity in which individuality is constituted, expressed, and strangely empowered by the transitive banalities, rogue affects, and uneven fatigues that assail him-her-it. In other words, whereas Romantic boredom promised an ecstatic, eventual, and indubitable (if inexpressible) self-presence, contemporary boredom makes no such promise, leaving one, for better or worse, to carve a selfhood out of an apparently uniform tedium by showing how one is uniquely affected by the pressures of contemporary culture's norms of independence. In the context of an experimental music culture that has made it compulsory to flaunt an iconoclasm and an ostensibly catholic taste, this pressure is felt and manifested in the imperative to meet the strikingly neoliberal policy of required creativity, of the constant need to display not a mastery, for that is impossible, but capacity to creatively cope with the uncertain, the unforeseen, and the ultimately "unknown unknowns" of life. Thus, the extent to which the stuplime expresses a contemporary ambivalence to aestheticized boredom, one that contrasts with the rhetorically attractive refrains of its Romantic escapes, can be seen by the way it addresses a subject who is persuaded that it is both a right and a chore to wait for one's own interests.

* * *

The ambivalence of stuplimity plays out a little differently in the work of G. Douglas Barrett. Barrett's interdisciplinary practice traverses the conventions of traditional composition and visual art, and skews Barone's affectedly doltish (over)abundance of minor variations[124] by its conceptually mannered conceit of simulation, or what Barrett calls "transcription." Transcription for Barrett turns less on the order of the real and the hyperreal than it does on the way of making expressive the distortions, the insufficiencies, and the overlooked in what Barrett says are "processes that have to do with documenting, replicating, recording, and repeating."[125] These processes, of course, nevertheless participate in the general economy of simulation, for each instance is a type of image that cannot help but articulate the logic of models and copies that both generate and undermine the notion of the real or original.[126] Barrett's practice of transcription, however, can be distinguished from the contemporary history of simulation by virtue of the way his work emphasizes rather than dissimulates the disfiguring properties intrinsic to its processes. Like the act of translation, transcription for Barrett entails a certain amount of interpretive activity that does not so much introduce as express the difference that occasions two or more instances of a thing-event. In other words, Barrett's transcriptions witness and delineate in musical terms the virtual multiplicity, or multivalence, of an event as it is figured in different mediums: audio recording, notated score, and live performance (and this discursive medium in which you're encountering it now). What makes Barrett's transcriptions and their exquisite monotony elicit a stuplime ambivalence has, however, less to do with the familiar dimensions of repetition and extendedness than it does with the way it treats every source as an insufficiently expressed event. Take for example his work *Derivation XI* (2008), or

---

[124] Almost all of Barone's work consists of spelling out cycles or permutations of some element, whether that element is acoustical, kinetic, or otherwise. For example, his four-hour *Progressions for String Quartet* (2003) is a series of four movements each of which elaborates in quartet notes all possible combinations of the C scale with sharps, flats, and naturals. His hour-and-a-half to two-hour piece *Golden* (2003), however, comprises simply the execution of two contrasting and alternating actions at a uniform tempo and dynamic. The performance Barone gave of this work on 17 February 2003 consisted of the two actions "climbing stairs" and "hitting a flower pot."

[125] G. Douglas Barrett, artist statement, http://synthia.caset.buffalo.edu/~gbarrett/bio.html [last accessed May 2009].

[126] For example, in addition to using common audio recorders and transposing the captured sounds into musical notation, Barrett has designed a piece of software capable of performing a spectral analysis of a recording whose results are converted into tones that are then mapped onto a specified instrument or ensemble.

Derivation[Derivation{Derivation(Derivation(Derivation[Derivation{Backyard [*Music*] – Vol. 4 *(or Derivation IV.)} (or Derivation VI.)] (or Derivation VII.)) (or Derivation VIII.)} (or Derivation X.)] (or Derivation XI.)*

The originary event for this "piece," or more accurately, the series of derivations executed by Barrett since 2006, is a recording of a performance of his piece Backyard [Music] (2006), which is itself the transcription of a recording made of the ambient sounds of a Hollywood street corner. *Derivation XI* can be thought of as the eighth generation of *Backyard [Music]*—as the collective expression of the recording, transcription and performance—or, if you want to discriminate a performance, from a recording from a transcription, then *Derivation XI* will be the 20-second iteration of *Backyard [Music]*. In Barrett's terms:

> *Derivation XI is a transcription of a recording of a performance of a transcription of a recording of a performance of a transcription of a recording of a performance of a transcription of a recording of a performance of a transcription of a recording of a transcription of a recording (of a performance).*

Each subsequent occasion (recording, transcription, performance) of this process implies that the previous iteration is, in a sense, in-attentive to something that can only be attended to in the following iteration. In other words, the actual specificity of each derivation that makes it just what it is, is composed equally of a surplus that escapes expression. This dimension of escape, which changes with each derivation, is what Barrett transcribes, each time expressing again the derivation's same potential difference. But the ingressive potential, the factor of escape, of an event is not, however, exclusive to Barrett's derivations. As Massumi writes, it is the character for "actually existing, structured things [to] live in and through that which escapes them."[127] The ambivalence of the tedium that Barrett crafts derives from the charged uncertainty that gives "actually existing, structured things" their felt sense of pure tendency, a vague and vital "moreness" that rubs shoulders with Cage's heterogeneous field

---

[127] Massumi, *Parables*, 35.

of multiplicity. However, because of the way that Barrett's transcriptions still participate in a logic of simulation, a logic that dislodges all signs from their relation to a "real" referent, and which, argues Baudrillard, is the dominant economy of our age, they also remind us that there is no outside or model derivation, no original or central edict to show us what, how, or who to be…except of course for the model of individual independence, a model joyfully simulated in the 1960s and 1970s, but tediously, and often insufficiently, feigned by today's bored subject.

While the seriality of all Barrett's *Derivations* takes on the impressive but ultimately impossible task of actualizing the totality of its constitutive difference, his piece *Three Voices* (2008) composes another series of simulations through the description of "every possible ordering of entrances and cut-offs of sounds or actions for three performers."[128] From left to right, three lines, three performers, each playing a single tone, sound, or action corresponding to the 169 graphic portrayals of relative beginnings and endings, Barrett composes an exhaustive picture of a particular form of time, of time written sideways. An hour-long performance from 2008 features two violins and flute articulating the diversity of entrances and cut-offs through a series of soft iterations of the sonority Eb4, D5, Db6.

On one level, *Three Voices* resembles the fetishization of presence associated with the compositions of Morton Feldman. Like Feldman's works, which elaborate a succession of varied instrumental events, Barrett's piece stages a uniform flow of variations of the same event. However, to the extent that it aims to elaborate a kind of action, *Three Voices* is more usefully compared to Gertrude Stein's *The Making of Americans* in the way that it attempts to exhaust the telling of its "kind," its "list[ing] of every ordering of starts and stops of three elements."[129] Like Stein's litany of "kinds" of Americans, *Three Voices'* attempt to exhaust its kinds engenders a stuplime encounter with beginnings and endings. The labour involved in this sort of inventory art, from writing, performing and listening to it, summons affects that force the subject back upon itself, not in the recuperative sense of Kant's sublime which sees reason exercise its

---

128 Barrett, email message to author, 3 June 2009.
129 Ibid.

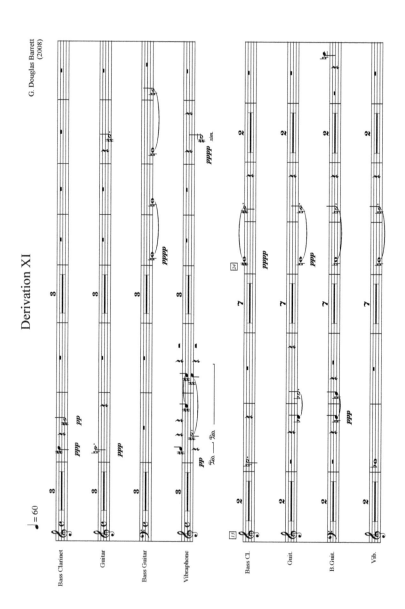

Derivation XI

G. Douglas Barrett
(2008)

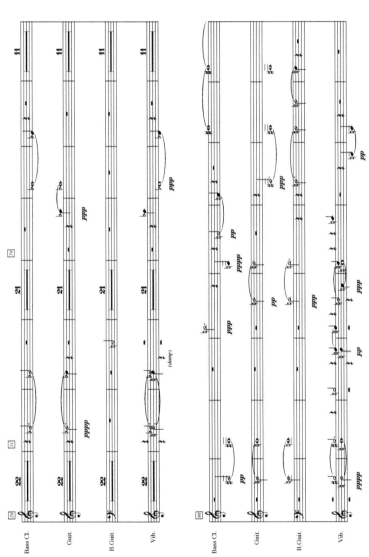

G. Douglas Barrett, from score for *Derivation XI* (2008). Courtesy G. Douglas Barrett.

limitations as a power relative to the imagination's unruly freedom, but in the sense that the imagination is made to continually reflect upon the vacuity of its reflexivity in a way that forces the listener to take responsibility for developing new ways and manners of listening.

Certainly one can imagine slips in intonation or uneven bowing and breathing as moments of "excitement" in the unfolding of *Three Voices*. But Ngai's description of *The Making of Americans* as a "labor of enumeration, differentiating, describing, dividing, sorting" tells us that this making involves very little excitement but instead "generally takes place as a painstakingly slow, tiring, seemingly endless 'puzzling' over differences and resemblances."[130] The instruction that *Three Voices* be played "soft, concentrated, for its own sake,"[131] indicates a making of kinds of beginnings and endings that are neither euphoric nor ironic, but unjustified multiples of kinds (of beginnings and endings) whose serialization promotes to absurdity their way of being an assembly of singular kinds whose strangeness breaks repeatedly upon the familiarity of their kinds of kinds. Works such as *Three Voices* and Barone's *Piano Installations* extract an affective response that is decidedly un-sublime. Both Barrett's and Barone's interrogations of the shockingly obtuse drift perilously close to the un-musical refrains of the everyday by unintentionally choreographing the contingencies and inexactitudes that inhere in and inform any program of embodied actions. While lacking the intensive magnitude of the sublime, like the buzz of everyday life, both *Three Voices* and *Piano Installation* are rich with hiccups that, because of their aesthetic making, lie on just this side of being boring.

* * *

As an affective category, the stuplime easily addresses itself to the kinds of affective engagement that one tends to form with objects given definition using a severely constrained set of rules and material. Barone's work is an example of a work generated using a severe constraint, but other examples could include George

---

[130] Ngai, *Ugly Feelings*, 292.
[131] Barrett, Performance notes to *Three Voices*.

Three Voices

G. Douglas Barrett
(2008)

1 ──────────────────────

2 ──────────────────────

3 ──────────────────────

──────────────────────

──────────────────────

────────────────

────────────────

──────────────────────

──────────────────────

──────────────────────

────────────────

──────────────────────

Three Voices   2

G. Douglas Barrett, form score for *Three Voices* (2008). Courtesy G. Douglas Barrett.

Perec's *La Disparition* (1969), a lipogram written as a novel entirely without the letter "e," and many of the films made under the rubric of Scandinavian directors Lars von Trier and Thomas Vinterberg's *Dogme 95*, which stipulates that filmmakers must, for example, film sound and visuals together, use only hand-held cameras, use only the items, spaces, and lighting available at the filming location, and refrain from invoking genre tropes. However, the presence of constraints does not a stuplime experience make. Musical serialism, which may be classified as an art of constraints, does not invoke the stuplime. Pieces such as Boulez's *Le marteau sans maître* (1955), though rigorously committed to its own constraints, tends to be carried out within the very self-aware context of European concert music whose expressive norms compel composers to qualify their work by recycling the history of musical affect.[132] The works that I've described here, however, put constraints to ends that refuse to qualify the effects they generate, preferring instead to maximize the difference of their idea(s). Thus, neither Barone's nor Barrett's work is beholden to the regime of difference that has historically and traditionally constituted and policed musical composition as a formalized array of tonal, rhythmical, and affective relations. Instead these works express the *difference* by which the regulated attributes of a qualified music—e.g., scales, chords, melodies, harmonies, timbre, dynamics—may be assembled, sounded, performed, and felt or not felt. Barone's work, for instance, contests the nature of neither the tonal scale nor the piano. These elements remain relatively intact; however, the manner in which these elements slowly and monotonously sound forth a series of scalar derangements tells a different story about music, not about what it should be, but about *how* it can be—even by *not* being music. Similarly, Barrett's *Three Voices* isn't concerned with its status as music: "These pieces are about actions and their overlappings, whether those actions produce sound or not."[133] Its graphical allusion to the musicalized timing of events show how "the ability to perform a sustained action, noise, or tone

---

[132] The exception to this may be La Monte Young's *Trio for Strings* (1958), which is exactingly serial. But you can also spy glimmers of stuplimity in serialist works like Jean Barraque's *Piano Sonata* (1950–2), which over its 50 continuous minutes, disposes of much of its obligatory expressivism.

[133] Barrett, email message to author, 3 June 2009.

coordinated among a group of three performers"[134] can provoke a response that needn't be drawn from the archive of properly musical feeling, by which I mean the archive of affective affectations developed throughout the nineteenth century to embody the crypto-sacred rhetoric of so-called absolute music.[135] It's in the way these particular composers "exaggeratedly submit to structural laws,"[136] and emphasize the senseless sense-making process of iterability subsisting within the most trivial musical parameter, that folds the affect of contemporary art's sensuous infinity into a process of bearing witness to the stuplimity of its happening.

Post...death...

Obviously, boredom today is not wholly distinct from the boredom of the 1960s and 1970s; the formal and conceptual similarities, as well as the discursive figures that are used by artists to describe and justify the boring things they do, are more than apparent. What is not so evident is the way in which the paradoxical "shock" of boredom now functions as a currency in what Paul Mann calls the "white economy of discourse." In his 1991 book, *Theory-Death of the Avant-Garde*, Mann argues that the devices of avant-garde or "oppositional" art, of which boredom is just one device along with "shock," "juxtaposition," "collage," and most importantly for Mann, "critique," are forms of currency in an economy that trades on expressions of conformity/resistance.[137] The avant-garde doesn't

---

[134] Ibid.

[135] Susan McClary discusses how the narrative conventions and affective codes of eighteenth and nineteenth century Europe inform the "standard sequence of dynamical events" of instrumental (art) music. In a way, this implies that the music's preservation, its very repeatability in the form of a score and performance tradition, is not only a conservation of the formal relations that composed its identity, but the affective scripts that its "sequence of dynamical events" encipher. Susan McClary, "Narrative Agendas in 'Absolute Music.'" *Musicology and Difference: Gender and Sexuality in Music Scholarship*, ed. Ruth A. Solie (Berkeley: University of California Press 1995), 330.

[136] Ngai, *Ugly Feelings*, 297.

[137] Mann argues that the avant-garde is essentially an expression of a system of radical recuperation, an expression wrought in aesthetic (artworks) and theoretical

occupy the latter term of this binary so much as its expressions mark the differential drift by which this pair is made sayable in a system of exchange. In essence, Mann is suggesting that the avant-garde's perpetual effort to differ makes it a discursive agent insofar as its expressions of difference produce the conditions of discourse. And as discourse is by its nature the scene of recuperation, the assimilation of difference to a white economy of exchange, the avant-garde is less a site of resistance and more "a system for instrumentalizing contradiction."[138] This insight into the avant-garde's complicity with a culture of exchange is supposed to be the death of the avant-garde; however, as Mann notes in pointing to the proliferation of "obituaries"—like his book and even this one too—the avant-garde's death makes it not less productive, but in many ways more productive: The death of the avant-garde is the n-state of the recuperation of its critical potential by a narrative of failure.[139] Here, Mann is saying that the avant-garde's critical posture is itself a commodity that can be used for purposes of exchange. While artworks continue to be made and sold, their real value lies in being placeholders or ingredients for the essays, books, conferences, and symposia that are like grimoires and séances for reanimating the dead. Within a discursive economy, every critical study of an avant-garde's death is like a type of necromancy. From this perspective, the current interest in aesthetic boredom would seem to lie not in how it affects someone, but in how a work's senseless drifts and empty feints persuade someone to talk or write about it. The catch here of course, one whose dialectical gesture is tautologically poised to collapse in an ever tightening spiral of immanence, is that art which is merely an interesting thing to write about—to discourse on—is boring, and being boring is merely interesting to write about. The bind for contemporary art and art criticism is that they each become unable to make a critical statement about their own situation without re-presenting the discursive mechanisms of their expressive distress. The only

(manifestos, essays) terms. The art and ideas venerated as "avant-garde" are instruments for simulating and expropriating difference (as it were). I speak more directly to this with respect to my own thesis at the end of the chapter. See Paul Mann, *The Theory-Death of the Avant-Garde* (Bloomington: Indiana University Press, 1991), 46.

138 Mann, *Theory-Death*, 46.
139 Ibid., 40.

way to escape this dilemma would be to dodge participation in the discursive economy altogether by imagining a place outside of discourse. And this, writes Mann, is "a place that, one is assured, does not exist."[140]

Or if "it" does exist, it exists in a way that cannot be articulated without being drawn into the wholly affirmative character of discourse, for "discourse has no negative force that is not reduced to dialectical systems-maintenance."[141] This means that if I am to do what I am about to, to suggest how contemporary boredom intimates an "escape" from discourse without actually dying the death of absolute silence, I should really stop writing and let a little nihilism loose on my own words. However, it is clear by this point that I won't. I have to at least suggest a conclusion, one whose even modest inference or speculation will compromise the chance of aesthetic boredom to be unjustified.

Well...I can't go on, I'll go on.

Perhaps the loss of an operational difference that makes the difference between aesthetic and mundane boredom effective, a loss diagnosed by Baudrillard as a consequence of media saturation that takes us beyond questions of representation, contemporary "aesthetic" boredom (which should by now be put under erasure), articulates the uncertainty of contemporary boredom. Unlike earlier artworks that focused on boredom's capacity to disturb conventions, to drum up differences in which discourse could be invested, contemporary boredom, in its stuplimity, seems to address the metaphysical ambiguity that has always been evident in boredom's rhetoric. Boredom, as the phrases I wrote above—"That song is boring" and "I'm bored"—reveal, a way of speaking about the felt sense of senselessness and the uncertainty affecting a subject caught between a withering paradigm of faith and the reflexive proclivities of modern epistemological scepticism. Thus, whereas a work like Steve Reich's *Four Organs* (1970) once promised to eliminate the uncertainty of being neither a faithful nor empirical "self" by annihilating this duality in an immersive gesture of extinction, Barrett's *Derivations*, all fourteen of them (from II to XV), transcribes and

---

[140] Ibid., 91.
[141] Ibid., 88.

simulates the ambivalence that has allowed boredom to spread beyond the desert of art into the wasteland of the mundane, where the intensity of being unjustified becomes indistinguishable from a day at the office. But this is no hard-won insight. It is the simulation of an insight into the fact that our waiting no longer pays off in the revelation of hitherto unknown interests, an insight into the theory-death that waiting tries to infinitely postpone. Waiting is stuplime: It is an uncertain witnessing of the time of events in their infinite eventuality and a way of listening to nothing in particular in order to imagine the impossible possibility of disappearing into an event that always never takes place.

Afterthought...

In 1971, John Baldessari produced his now-famous work *I Will Not Make Any More Boring Art*. Initially an installation commissioned by the Nova Scotia College of Art and Design, Baldessari, who couldn't make the trip to Halifax to install the work, had students write the pledge on the walls of the gallery. However, the better-known version of the piece is the 32 minute video of Baldessari himself writing the phrase over and over again.

In several ways, the composers whose works I have analyzed in this chapter blow open the liar's paradox at the heart of Baldessari's conceit. Baldessari's work, which articulates and comments on the nature of self-reflexivity that characterized so much conceptual and (post)minimalist art of the 1960s, is able to enjoy or at least amuse itself with a clever cynicism and irony that has come to charac-terize a certain species of postmodern aesthetics. Nearly 40 years later, however, this gesture lacks the critical edge that it once had. As Robert Goldman and Stephen Papson argue in examining the way contemporary "advertising practices try to turn self-reflexive awareness of advertising codes into an object of consumption,"[142] consumers in Western cultures have become (relatively) savvy to the

---

[142] Robert Goldman and Stephen Papson, "Advertising in the Age of Hypersignification," *Theory, Culture & Society* 11, no. 3 (1994): 43.

artifice of "the text" and the tricks of drawing attention to the meta-language that underwrites its codes and form of address.

But as it has become common practice in advertising (and so much contemporary art) "to create an empathetic relationship with the viewer by foregrounding the constructed nature of the text,"[143] the lie that Baldessari skirts, or rather, defers by continually shifting the viewer's attention between the aesthetic act and the place of meta-language, becomes another banal ploy to get us to buy something, be it a product, and image, or an idea of critique. This neutering of reflexivity as a critical tactic is precisely what Mann sees in the theory-death of the avant-garde. Contemporary artists who work with boredom can make no such promises not to bore. I don't suggest, however, that the composers that appear in this work allege to create an ugly feeling that really is interesting, even if only from an ironic point of view. At best, I think that the reflexive gestures, which conflate the tropes of advertising with aesthetic significance, are distracting.

> But distracting from what?...
>   ...Ways of mattering.

The vertiginous experience of self-reflexive uncertainty, scepticism, and depression that tend to caricaturize the malaise of postmodern anomie, seem in many ways to typify, if not a "real" breakdown (for the "real" has been exposed as just another "metaphor" and thus indistinguishable from a simulated or metaphorical breakdown), then a failure to form affective attachments to the task of sceptical reflection itself. Meditating on how one formulates values and how feeling and imagination play a role in these processes, philosopher Irving Singer suggests that above "inductive reasoning about the availability of satisfaction," which revolves around our self-interested concerns, is an imaginative activity that bestows, or treats the object of our attention "*as if* some appraisal found it to be excellent, even perfect, though no such appraisal has been made or can occur."[144] Singer contends that as it concerns developing various bonds with

---

[143] Ibid.
[144] Irving Singer, *Feeling and Imagination* (Lanham, MD: Rowman & Littlefield, 2001), 14.

the world and with others, appraisal, that is, reflection alone, is an insufficient mode of valuation. Ross's study of an aesthetics of disengagement is, in a sense, a study of reflection alone, a study of the pathology of wholly determining one's individual worth by appraising (reflecting on) the efficacy of one's own actions and conduct. Affectivity, argues Singer, is not merely an expressive response to external threats or fortune, but an active agent in the "making of importance."[145] For something to matter, "a person, thing or ideal must be treated as inherently meaningful, and not just instrumentally valuable."[146] Attachment, and thereby value, cannot develop under the strict regime of sceptical reflection.

Recent expressions of boredom, instead of persuading us that the world is really interesting after all (Cage), or that the expression of boredom as a cultural disposition is "un-boring" (Kenneth Goldsmith), present their somniferous refrains as a curious form of detachment or affective failure that models, or more correctly, that simulates a space of contemplation or composure from which the spectator can become sensitive to the minor intensities of everyday life and thereby reinvigorate his or her perception from within the vicissitudes of these (Ross). This is the redemptive ending that Ngai ultimately reserves for the ambivalence of the stuplime, an ending whose perplexing dysphoria entails the "slowing down of other emotional reactions" that leaves "a state of undifferentiated alertness or responsiveness—a kind of affective static, or noise" in its wake.[147] Ngai imagines that this "open feeling" makes possible an attention to a "kind of resistance,"[148] the kind of affective failure that Singer suggests "can result in a heightened and correlative reattachment to the very world from which one felt so painfully separated."[149]

Although I appreciate how Ngai and Singer address the problem and stubborn insistence of a negative affect, they both fail, it seems, to see the quandary that besets this project of affective re-attachment. Besides the debatable efficacy of the necromancy that is the actual practice of contemporary experimental art or avant-garde studies, the

---

[145] Ibid., 15.
[146] Ibid.
[147] Ngai, *Ugly Feelings*, 284, 83.
[148] Ibid., 284.
[149] Singer, *Feeling and Imagination*, 186.

state of undifferentiated alertness that stuplime events are meant to model is in this culture already being practiced and performed by that other sly form of stupefying delight—television. More stupefying than three hours of C major scale derangements is a marathon of *C.S.I.* (any of them: Vegas, Miami, New York), or better (worse?), one full day watching CNN repeat itself (and the multitudinous adverts by its host of pharmaceutical sponsors). Exceptional as these aesthetic crusades seem, they wage an ambivalent campaign, for the resistance or cool detachment they may conjure is no more or less interesting than the kind that watching *Seinfeld* stumble over nothing in particular simulates.

Or, as Paul Mann concludes,

No excuse, no justification: all one can put forward is an unendurable habit of attention, a meager fascination, no more or less commanding than that hypnosis one enters in the face of television; a rut that has always led downward and in the end always found itself stuck on the surface; a kind of drivenness, if not a drive.[150]

---

[150] Mann, *Masocriticism*, 128.

2

Formless

Pretext

This chapter is about shit.[1] It's about what shit sounds like and how one listens to it. Of course I'm not talking about actual shit. I'm talking figuratively about syncopated elements, the offbeat of a homogenizing groove that is called "music." In other words, I'm interested in the excretory phase of the process of making "music," in "the difference that must be expelled" from the process of its making "in order for the same to be the same"[2]—for another melody to be a tune like any other tune is a tune. Specifically, this chapter is about how habits of inattention, developed around the use of ubiquitous audio media forms, have become implicated in recent experimental composition, and in turn, how this music

---

[1] Scatology (a/k/a coprology) is the study of shit. Or more broadly, it's the study of shit that has happened. But let's not get too figurative just yet. Let's get our hands dirty. Let's review the various kinds of shit there are (avoiding for now that human kind): For that which comes in bulk we say "dung," while individually it's "droppings." When it belongs to cattle there's "tath," cows it's "bodewash," and of course (though this is flirting with the figurative) there's the ubiquitous "bullshit." Deer get a more refined term—"fewmets"—but it's nothing like the "frass" of insects, or even better, an otter's "spraint." Undomesticated carnivores leave "scat," stony shores gather the "guano" of seabirds, while foxes eject "billitting," hawks launch "mutes," and dogs, well they just "scumber." (It's worth mentioning here that playing with shit is the exclusive right of neither science nor lunacy but belongs, in addition to the realm of pure curiosity, to *spatilomancy*, a practice concerned less with things such as diet and behaviour than with divination.) For the names and other honorifics given to human shit and shitting I refer you to the exhaustive (and alphabetized) list provided at www.poopnames.com.

[2] Andrew Wernick, "Bataille's Columbine: The Sacred Space of Hate," *ctheory*, 1999, http://www.ctheory.net/articles.aspx?id=119.

replicates and warps the drifts and digressions that constitute those habits. That is, the essay takes an interest in the perceptual grotes-queries of distraction, especially those remaindered by a "world whose defining boundaries have been deformed by electric signal."[3] Thus, the kind of shit that I consider here is a shit that musical aesthetics took when recording technology became the veritable sewage system of sound.

As early as 1938, Theodor Adorno observed that the mechanical reproduction of music, via radio and phonograph, had fundamentally altered listening conditions by dissolving the intersubjective and absorptive space that allows one to focus on a work's structural relations. Essentially, Adorno is arguing that audio technology, AM radio transmission in particular, is not a neutral medium but comes with a dimension of sound or noise that alters one's relation to and perception of music. Specifically, these background sounds modulate the perception of music's import, which for Adorno pertains to the formal properties explicated through a language of tones.[4] Here, the sticky matter of music, which may be said to concern all that which is backgrounded in order to adjust perception to the elements that express music's "integral form," becomes less backgrounded. While Adorno's essay tends to lament the fact of this interference, it draws out the more important point that technologies entail the exclusion of certain vital dimensions from the perception of the events that they help realize, and the ubiquity of a technology cannot help but establish a regime of perception.[5] Like water then, whose own vital intensity is obscured by an elaborate subterranean system of distribution and drainage that makes it effortless to access, the contemporary omnipresence of effected by ubiquitous playback technologies musical sound affects the way music affects: if you barely notice musical sounds it's because you don't need to. Audio

---

[3] David Foster Wallace, *A Supposedly Fun Thing I'll Never Do Again: Essays and Arguments* (Boston: Little, Brown and Co., 1997), 51.

[4] See Theodor Adorno, "On the Fetish-Character in Music" (1938) and "The Radio Symphony" (1941), both in *Essays on Music*, ed. Richard Leppert, trans. Susan H. Gillespie (Berkeley: University of California Press, 2002).

[5] Of course Beethoven's Fifth Symphony, which in Adorno's essay is the compro-mised musical object par excellence, is it itself the realization of an elaborate social technology, namely the concert ritual with its attendant peremptory forms of sensory restraint and aural etiquette.

technology is thus a kind of sewerage of the ears: A system of wires, speakers, volume knobs, and playback devices are so many pipes, tanks, and valves. Turn this switch, insert that plug, and a supply of sonorities flow through social and economic conduits to pump refreshing vibrations through the cochlear labyrinth of our ears to our nervous system where they are "heard but not listened to." (Muzak's semi-official slogan for many years.) As the toilet does for water, playback technologies have taken listening underground. Musical ablutions that wash away the gooey residue of last night's mood and the film of everyday stress are performed unconsciously and without (intentionally) contemplating their sonic effluvium. As I will elaborate below, taking mechanically accomplished power over the emanation of musical sounds and making *these* managed expressions ubiquitous influences the way music is heard (or not) by converting a respect once paid to the restive effects of listening to music, particularly in the way Adorno recommends listening to "form,"[6] into a contempt or disgust. In this conversion, where process becomes product, as it does in a work like Alvin Lucier's *I am Sitting in a Room* (1969) in which the accretion of a recorded text spoken by the composer is transformed into an undulating mass of harmonic swells that express the acoustic resonance of the recording space, even the most recalcitrant music fails to express its "cultural negativity," a negativity that while expelled like shit acts more like the sacred.

But as I wrote above, this chapter is about shit, and so considers how, in becoming ubiquitous and generally "disposable" (a condition encouraged not only by the mediations introduced by audio technology but by an industry built around its dissemination), listening to music has become a disjointed and trivial affair. Specifically, I look at how certain contemporary experimental compositions respond to and exploit the effects of distraction that promote the simultaneous escape and capture of attention in order to carry out their own sort of "conversion," one that draws expressive potential from the way

---

[6] "A sense of form means: listening for the music and following it to where it wants to go; staying as far away from an imposed will, an imposed architecture, as an alien necessity in which for the most part an arbitrary subjectivity that has gone blind has become entrenched." Theodor Adorno, "Form in the New Music," *Music Analysis* 27, no. 2–3 (2008): 215.

in which musical sounds have become increasingly something to be "unfocused on," and, as a result, perceptually indistinct phenomena. To this end, I consider how different kinds of cultural shit—shit like "Muzak," the public shame of good taste—fertilize the wider field of listening with a farrago of attentional spores that sprout gnarled shoots of interest to seed new aesthetic sensibilities. Focusing on the unfocused, the picayune, and the dreamy qualities of listening as it takes place through distraction, I draw observations about and speculate on the way the formless appearance, that is, the amorphousness of particular experimental compositions, reflect and at the same time deform the depreciative and soporific effects generated by our culture's habit of putting listening aside. I'm suggesting then music that is "heard but not listened to"—a lovely catchphrase that with the right inflexion or sense of innuendo can evoke the cosseting qualities of luxury toilet paper—characterizes the aural and sensory shit-field in which contemporary notions of composition are left to go wild.

* * *

This talk about shit and sewerage, in addition to being generally provocative, is mobilized in order to focus my methodological lens, which despite the overtones, is not strictly scatological. "Shit" is evoked here largely to draw attention to the way music sluices certain expressions from its concept, whether this concept derives from specific theoretical axioms and societal praxes, or is invented to express the sense of an event in terms of the dynamic relations that prepare the conditions for its particular experiential occasion. Something is always ejected in order to homogenize, or at least to harmonize the set of perceptual acts within a musical practice's standard expression(s), even if this means prohibiting or simply ignoring certain fugitive sounds or ambiguous sensations. However, for a (musical) concept to consolidate its expressions, which its users (us) are compelled to do in order to validate its particular efficacy, it has to extend itself. But in doing so the concept encroaches upon the same renegade expressions that it precludes in order to compose itself. In the same way that the concept of hygiene has to cope with the variations of filth and varieties of shit that it creates, the concept of what is musical has to deal with the noise, the "not musical" that it remainders. This constant process of excretion, which never finally ejects or sublimates its inassimilable element but circuits it through a proliferating (as opposed to progressive) series of successes and failures, seems to address what I hear happening in the way composers like Martin Arnold, Warren Burt, and Christian Wolff are able to keep certain of Western music's normative niceties— e.g., melody, harmonic variation, rhythm, *etcetera*—in play, while at the same time letting this tradition's proscriptions flourish behind its back. Harmlessly schizophrenic and generally addled in character, this ambidextrous music is, I suggest, indicative of the way contemporary culture's condition of distraction imposes its addiction to "the now" (which is actually an addiction to "the next" that signifies the now (again)) upon a practice guided by rules of concentration that in turn develops expressive tactics for coping with an economy of intermittent attention. So in addition to the familiar strategy of defamiliarization that converts recognizably functional musical elements into deviant figures, a larger condition of distraction is at work in dividing attention between composition's historically developed praxes of reflection and its inveterate habit to indulge in the sensory gratification of those aural hallucinations that flicker and sweep over/alongside/about/around musical form.

To speak to the ambivalence of this divided aesthetic and to frame it within the context of failure's contortions, I've conscripted the commeasurably shifty notion of *informe*, or "formless," as imagined by the French writer Georges Bataille. As I'll explain, the idea of *informe* pivots on its own kind of conceptual pivot, one that matches the dithering of a music which tells us to take it as "art," and therefore to give it attention, yet, in its appearance, invites the kind of listening that tends to be brought to background music, or to music as it's heard (but not listened to in the structural sense) in everyday life. *Informe*, like the equivocal summons of this formless music, is self-defeating but strangely expressive of its own confoundedness. In effect, I'm poaching the conceptual valence of Bataille's *informe* in a way described by Brian Massumi, who writes, "A concept is by nature connectible to other concepts," and so "is defined less by its semantic content than by the regularities of connection that have been established between it and other concepts."[7] For Massumi, a concept is an expression of "the rhythm of arrival and departure in the flow of thought and language."[8] In this case, the obscenity of *informe* that Bataille draws out in writings like *Histoire de l'oeil* (1928) or the more abject *The Solar Anus* (1927), endows musical concepts, such as "virtuosity" and "structure," with a sense of offense that, rather than negating them, warps or "perverts" their manner of relating with other concepts like "competence" and "interpretation," "form" and "artistry." More thematically then, the relay that I stage between the concepts of *informe* and the event of distraction is one that expresses the non-confrontational creative offense that can be heard in pieces like Australian composer Warren Burt's *Another Noisy Lullaby* (2009) and Canadian composer Martin Arnold's *Burrow Out; Burrow In; Burrow Music* (1995), where attention, rather than compelled to gather its wanders around an omphaloskepsic negativity, is pulled in many directions at once by the formless charm of a multicephalous interest.

(Informe)

Before explaining how this chapter is laid out and how I think it works, I want to spend a few moments on the intellectual history of *informe* in order to tease out some of the relevant details that underwrite my thoughts on the concept as well as my own writing practice. Bataille introduced *informe* when he was editing the French journal *Documents*, a kind of alter-Surrealist periodical featuring a motley collection of essays on art and ethnography, as well as critical essays by folk such as Michel Leiris, André Masson, Carl Einstein, and himself, of course. In a number of issues was a section titled "Critical Dictionary." This part of the journal essentially comprised a series of short articles that were less definitions than quasi-literary interventions into the received ideas of things. Specifically, these entries were designed to disrupt the more conventional essays

---

[7] Brian Massumi, *Parables for the Virtual: Movement, Affect, Sensation* (Durham, NC: Duke University Press, 2002), 20.
[8] Ibid.

in the journal, but their blend of critique and creative irreverence, as well as their prescient interdisciplinary pseudo-methodology, gives them an intellectual purchase that extends well beyond the journal's original time of publication. The type of works included in the "dictionary" were those that promoted Bataille's notion of "heterology"[9] and "base materialism," a non- or anti-philosophy which took the disgusting and repulsive as its subject with aims to disturb the assumed stability of reason's categories. Entries like "Factory Chimney," "Big Toe," and "Spittle" not only work to unsettle the terms of what counts as a proper subject of study, but has the additional effect of exposing the integral role that filth and waste play in the composition of society. For example, contrasting the low and ignoble status of toes to the high and supple grace of fingers, Bataille writes,

fingers have come to signify useful action and firm character, the toes stupor and base idiocy. The vicissitudes of organs, the profusion of stomachs, larynxes, and brains traversing innumerable animal species and individuals, carries the imagination along in an ebb and flow it does not willingly follow, due to a hatred of the

---

[9] Bataille describes "heterology" as the study of what any homogenizing system of knowledge "excretes." For Bataille, a homogenizing system is an instrument of appropriation that works to make the sundry profiles of experience practicable, and as a consequence renders humans a servile species "fit only for the fabrication, rational consumption, and conservation of products." However, because the instrumentalization of experience automatically limits its process of appropriation, it produces "of its own accord its own waste product, thus liberating in a disordered way the heterogeneous excremental element." Importantly though, heterology is only a pseudo-science. It is not itself an organized or formal study of the heterogeneous—this would make it the kind of homogenizing endeavour that it opposes. Instead, heterology is a process of "consciously and resolutely" drawing attention to what is expelled. And this can only be a provisional task as its quasi-method entails a series of transitional moments that pass from observing first a "process of limitation" and then the "violently alternating reactions of antagonism (expulsion) and love (reabsorption) obtained by positing [showing] the heterogeneous element." Heterology is therefore never concerned with the "objectivity of heterogeneous elements," for by definition their occasion is utterly conditional. The objectivity of the heterogeneous is an abstraction derived from the same processes of limitation that makes the homogeneous an abstraction. Interestingly then, "only the subjective heterogeneity of particular elements is, in practice…concrete." Georges Bataille, *Visions of Excess*, ed. Allan Stoekl, trans. Allan Stoekl (Minneapolis: University of Minnesota Press, 1985), 97–8.

still painfully perceptible frenzy of the bloody palpitations of the body.[10]

While writing such as this generates an obvious polemical and critical effect, it is Bataille's entry on "*informe*" that makes the most radical intervention into modernity's "knowledge project," the enterprise of reason that he contends is what condemns human being to servility. Taking his own project—the Critical Dictionary—to task, Bataille writes in the entry on *informe* that a dictionary should not give meanings but *tasks*, or what might be called the performative operation of words. As such, he describes the task of *informe* as that which "lowers" (*déclasser*) or invalidates the significance or relevance of the thing(s) it classifies, including (maddeningly) the classification of its own operation-performance. At the heart of *informe* then is a thoroughgoing intolerance for any systematic elaboration of ideas.

This is something that Rosalind Krauss and Yve-Alain Bois play with in their 1997 work *Formless: A User's Guide*, where they attempt, as they put it, to "redeal modernism's cards."[11] By modernism, Bois and Krauss mean specifically Clement Greenberg's theory of modern art, which categorizes aesthetic modernism primarily in terms of a work's formal character, or more exactly, the way a work makes the display of its medium and the relations between its formal elements, its content. Though there are a host of theoretical problems with Krauss and Bois' project—particularly the charge that their re-dealing merely shuffles or switches the order of the same deck without changing the rules of the game—the way they go about putting *informe* to work, or rather, letting *informe* do its work by composing a book that enacts the non-systematic spirit of Bataille's dictionary, is enormously effective for it allows readers to make the same kind of erratic and informal moves between themes that characterize the inarticulate (dis-jointed) activity of *informe*. (That Krauss and Bois' book was so upbraided by critics speaks, I think, to the effect that expressions of *informe* have on thinking. For Bataille, both form

---

[10] Ibid., 22.

[11] Yve-Alain Bois and Rosalind Krauss, *Formless: A User's Guide* (Cambridge, MA: MIT Press, 1997), 21.

and formless are impure sorts; each category is always mixed and operating in the other's field in a way that damns the distinctness and clarity of either term ((which means that my project, too, can already glimpse its immanent failure)). As such, the bind embodied by Krauss and Bois' work, whereby everything about mainstream aesthetic modernism they try to undo is haunted by the fact that their book, with its cover and pages ((its "form")) has its own formalizing effects, and therefore is itself an instance of the fundamental instability that Bataille means to expose and operationalize in his own writing.)

Reflecting on Krauss and Bois' approach, one that displays a respectful disrespect for Bataille's own asseverations on the topic, and considering that my own engagement with the notion of formless/ness has been fragmented, frustrated, flitting, in short, distracted, it makes sense, conceptually and practically, for me to work in a similar manner. While there are of course other studies on Bataille's *informe* that I could model my own work on, such as art historian Georges Didi-Huberman's 1995 *La Ressemblance informe* or perhaps more relevantly, Paul Hegarty's recent writings on noise music.[12] But insofar as I am dealing with a contemporary musical practice whose compositional posture invokes the protocols of an avant-garde tradition that seeks to "justify its existence as the search for its own essence,"[13] my project resembles Krauss and Bois' in its attempt to destabilize a dominant understanding of musical modernism that emphasizes formal invention and the kind of attentive deference that this demands. Furthermore, this study also takes the insights and fallacies of someone like John Cage for granted, for while my invocation of *informe* has more modest aims than re-dealing the whole deck of musical modernism, or of overturning "Cageanism," there is a spirit of experiment in Krauss and Bois' thought that not only resonates with my own proclivities towards theory and writing, but actually animates my topic in a way that I think is faithful to the tactics of self-distraction employed by the

---

[12] See Georges Didi-Huberman, *La Ressemblance informe, ou, le gai savoir visuel selon Georges Bataille* (Paris: Editions Macula, 1995); and Patrick Crowley and Paul Hegarty, *Formless: Ways in and out of Form* (Bern: Peter Lang, 2005). See also Hegarty's website at: http://www.dotdotdotmusic.com [accessed October 2012].

[13] Bois and Krauss, *Formless*, 25.

music that I'm considering here. And, because I'm examining how cultures of distraction have come to inform the way music is listened to and the way music makers (specifically experimental composers) responds to this, it seems both productive, and ironically fitting, to perform this research in a way that puts its own claims under suspicion by trying to be both rigorous and slipshod.

What I propose is for the reader to consider this chapter a hyphenation of thoughts on how *informe* can be imagined to describe a distracted "form" of attention that develops musically expressive responses to the informational and affective atmospherics that characterize what David Foster Wallace called contemporary culture's "electric definition." That distraction is by nature an interruption in a felt continuity, the form/*informe* of this essay—comprising a series of interrogations on certain themes and practices of listening, scored with footnotes (notes that are in turn notched and scotched with their own set of asides)—reflects this situation. To this end I employ the "switchiness" that describes the mind of a multitasking subject and the bivalence of distraction's logic of escape and capture, not as a gimmick but as a way to simulate the effects that distraction has on listening habits and (to paraphrase what Hegarty wrote about the form of *Formless* in a review of Krauss and Bois' book) to illustrate *informe* working itself through the writing.[14]

---

[14] The subtext (which of course I place here in the footnotes) to this chapter's focus on distraction and its expression in contemporary composition, is the relation between form and content, or more accurately, *informe* and content. In drawing attention to a certain type of inattention, i.e., distraction, I'm not suggesting that the form-content formula is bunk. Rather, I'm suggesting that the proliferation of musical singularities generated by the general condition of distraction short-circuits the processes that make form significant. In a sense, the wholelessness that distraction compounds amplifies the valence of musical fragments in a way that, paradoxically, gives them an abundance of (in)content.[14a] Said another way, content becomes the effect of form's failure to serve as content. Said in yet another way, "What the drive to unity animating the process of propagation [distraction] achieves is less oneness than a controlled contagion of divergence."[14b]

[14a] This addresses the badly formed concept of "musical abstraction" in which acoustic gestalts—perceptual effects—are conflated with geometrical forms.

[14b] Brian Massumi and Kenneth Dean, *First and Last Emperors: The Absolute State and the Body of the Despot* (Brooklyn, NY: Autonomedia, 1992). Also available at: http://www.anu.edu.au/HRC/first_and_last/title_page.htm [accessed October 2012].

I recognize that this task risks failing, that it may only succeed at being a series of surface impressions that simply skim the film off the way distraction and *informe* articulate with the kind of musical poetry that constructs a self-contradictory "background concert" music. Perhaps there's no getting around this. The "hypertext" that a series of episodes and a scatteration of notes become seems inevitably to promote a reading velocity that, while encouraging increasingly supple forms of connection that multiply a text's associations, discourages a slower, more reflective engagement with the text.[15] But, I submit that this is an effect that reflects the habits of inattention, habits that we've contracted in response to the manifold and speedy summons our media-saturated environment generates. That is, a reading that "flits" over this chapter in a way that resembles how attention loses track of itself and its impression of a whole, a form, suffers the same kind of infinitization or "fractal deformation"[16] that I contend affects how music is perceived. Thus, while the epistolary form of the essay creates the kind of effects that I argue make the music that I'm writing about interesting and *informe*, an effect that Adorno, in his famous essay "On the Fetish-Character in Music" likens to a children's language "consist[ing] exclusively of fragments and distortions of the artistic language of music,"[17] it also makes *this* writing *informe*—fractally deformed. This means that by encouraging an intermittent reading, the "dis-integration" of my chapter is expressing something of the lived economy of *informe*.

How to read this chapter

Like *Formless* this chapter is sectioned into a number of broad themes around which a musical notion of *informe* articulates with

---

[15] Much of the difficulties of reading hypertext, whether it's expressed in HTML or in a more traditional format such as Laurence Sterne's *Tristam Shandy*, Jorge Luis Borges' *Garden of Forking Paths*, or Milorad Pavic's *Dictionary of the Khazars*, is the way that it encourages the reader to move rapidly between items and to forego assessment of relevance and/or gravity of the item/idea.

[16] Paul Mann, *Masocriticism* (Albany: State University of New York Press, 1999), 154. The "infinitization" of something is also its disintegration, its evacuation.

[17] Adorno, "Fetish," 307.

distraction. Unlike *Formless*, however, I don't perceive these sections as "key processes of *informe*/formless,"[18] but instead describe them as quasi-concepts which, following Deleuze and Guattari's view that concepts are inventions that draw forth an aspect of reality without these expressions being grounded in sense perception, articulate the effective relationships between variables that compose the circumstance of distracted listening and formless music. Thus my section headings are something like "probe-headings" in that they locate an escape from within the seductions of the "face," the white wall/blackhole of the text on/in which a reassuring meaning is inscribed/sunk. Here I suggest that while the organization is somewhat arbitrary, it's also necessary, but necessary only in the way that it reflects the kind of fragmented and ambient awareness that constitutes not only one's sense of distraction, but also how one listens to or away from music. As such, I recommend that you read through this chapter according to your own capacities, but ask that you be aware (as I am) of at least this:

> The problem for all who seek to show, bring or let be the formless, is transposition. For something to stay outside the world of form requires that an object remain a process, disabling the imposition of form at all stages. Arguably this is impossible, and that is its interest: the attempt can only ever fail, and this failing is formless/*informe* (the same could be said of attempts to theorise or demonstrate the formless).[19]

Story

My wife was leaving for Seville early one morning. We were having coffee before she passed through security. I don't recall the details of our conversation, but I believe it revolved around the art exhibition she was going to see and the recent protests that had been staged against its inadequate but nevertheless self-congratulatory gesture of aesthetic transnationalism. I have a few photographs of that

---

[18] Paul Hegarty, "Formal Insistence," *The Semiotic Review of Books* 13, no. 2 (2003): 7.
[19] Ibid.

morning that I took with my cellphone: The two of us, bleary-eyed, sitting at a table, paper coffee cups in hands hovering over emptied sugar packets. What's left out of these images (among other things) are the sounds from a speaker overhead, just below the volume of our conversation yet mingling nicely with the hissing espresso machine, the tolling cash register, and the pervasive airport murmur. Yet strangely, in being left out of the photograph, these supernal sounds have virtually the same presence, or non-presence, they did when I was drinking my coffee. That is, they hardly exist.

At some point during our conversation, I stopped hearing my wife and found myself drawn to the incessant pulsing of a saxophone and snare-drum duo playing a steady stream of staccato ♪♪♪♪♪♪ in unison at around 80bpm. Occasionally, the saxophone would accent a pulse or change pitch to form an erratic series of irregular phrases and note groupings. But, I couldn't quite hear everything that was going on in this piece. My attention was distributed among the pulsing rhythm, my wife's voice, the espresso machine, and other people's endless nattering. At seven in the morning, unshowered, and with a thin film of sleep clinging to me, I was dimly perceiving what I never expected to hear in a noisy airport coffee shop. Yet there it was (kind of) dividing my attention (or maybe gathering it): some kind of experimental music. Bemused, I interrupted my wife. "Do you hear that?" I asked. "Who'd put music like this on in a coffee shop?" Following a grimace that communicated her annoyance, she responded, "I wish they'd turn it off." "What? Why?" I balked. "It's great! When do you ever hear music like that in a place like this?" To which she replied, "What are you talking about? That's not experimental music, the CD's just skipping; it's been going on like that since we got here."

For a moment I thought she had no idea what she was talking about, and I continued to hear this unexpected minimalism for about another five seconds. But then, summoned from its wanders with susurrant coffee makers, the mild burn on my tongue of too-hot coffee, and the scatter of echoic boarding announcements, my full attention was given to the sounds above and I began to perceive that it was, indeed, the digital stutter of a CD passing glacially through a glitch on its surface. At this moment, I crossed a threshold and with that dispelled the illusion that so delighted me. I was no longer listening to the industrial resolve of American minimalism but the cloying sweet talk of Dave Koz, or someone/thing equally vapid.

The shock of this two-fold astonishment still sticks with me. First, hearing "experimental music" anywhere besides a concert hall, where its insult to taste can be easily corralled and halter-broken, was in itself thrilling.[20] But even more mind-bendingly enchanting was realizing that my perception was so wrong, so mistaken and utterly persuasive that I am now compelled to treat it as nothing less than pure sorcery. Call it an illusion if you will, but understand that what I heard was really experimental music. Skipping CD or not, I heard a saxophone and drum duet. That the sounds turned out to be the result of a malfunctioning CD doesn't negate the "reality" of this experience so much as it says something about the perspectival and plastic nature of perception.

This vignette is meant to draw attention not so much to the way that listening can be fooled, or put in error, but that listening, like other efforts of sensibility, produces "reality-effects" insofar as what emerges between the vibrating matter of sound and the nervous system organizes actions and certain forms of behaviours around its expressions. In this case, while the skipping CD was not actually a recording of an experimental saxophone and drum duet, the perception not of its malfunction but of its *dys*function—its functioning otherwise than intended—organized my sensibility in a way that seems almost magical, mesmeric even. Clearly, the partial obscurity of the sounds and my diffused attention contributed to this mis-perception. However, the way I mis-took these sounds was not incidental to their effect. Indeed, this mis-taking was absolutely integral to it. Though my perception was ultimately corrected, normalized, in relation to the din of so-called extra-musical sounds *and* non-sounds, this mis-take illustrates the weirdly creative effects that distraction has on perception. That distraction could be at all inspired may be contentious, but to the extent that its chronic

---

[20] It should be said, however, that the offense, or criticality, of experimental music is itself a bit of a conceit. The concert hall, or art gallery, or small "underground" club are so far under the radar of larger cultural trends that their expressions of the "cutting edge" are less than irrelevant. In other words, the concert hall is itself a pretense that conjures its own illusion of an offense, one that hardly registers even among its own underclass.

expression can be thought to "harmonize" scattered perceptions in a way that a skipping CD becomes an experimental composition, suggests that there is something unpredictably inventive and even charming to it.

Theodor Adorno makes a similar observation in an essay about how cafés function as environmental transducers by which music becomes "wholly appearance." Though referring specifically to salon orchestras and not "piped" music (or more generically the company name Muzak for whom those particularly saccharine instrumental versions of popular songs are named), he argues that café arrangements of (formerly) celebrated works tend to dissolve the structural autonomy that allowed the original version of the music to express its nature as "art." However, rather than completely liquefy the work, Adorno writes that the "splendidly shabby" sounds acquire "a second, strangely transparent form," a "netherworldly glow" that doesn't go unnoticed so much as it acts like "an acoustic light source."[21] Though he lays too much stress on the formal alterations exacted by café arrangements, that Adorno recognizes something "splendid" or "shiny" in the dim appearance of this half-veiled and half-forgotten music points to the way the field of distraction, constituted by the multifaceted demands of a café milieu, modulates a "passionate appearance into the cold comfort of reality."[22] Notwithstanding the backhanded compliment he pays to composers like Greig and Puccini, whose "true mastery" is revealed when their music finds itself perfectly suited to café listening, or the claim that a café arrangement falsifies a musical work, Adorno sees that without an insulating stillness surrounding them, musical sounds become a thing among others things: the too-hot coffee, the short bursts of laughter, a waiter's bad faith.

But maybe we should call this ensemble of background things "quasi-things," for in their mutual commotion none fully stands out as a complete object wholly open to scrutiny.[23] Instead they

---

[21] Adorno, "Music in the Background," 508–9.

[22] Ibid., 509.

[23] I'm drawing on Graham Harman's work here, but substituting the term "thing" for his more specific notion of "object." I find "thing," strangely, a more articulate capture of the relational-functional composition of perception. Harmon's emphasis on the primacy of objects founds a philosophical project know as object-oriented ontology (OOO).

withhold the full range of their expressive profiles, insinuating only certain aspects of the force that animates their qualities. In fact, this is how most "things" appear to our ordinary, plurivalent awareness that constitutes the expressions of everyday mind. But despite the fact that these things withhold dimensions of themselves from us, they continue to solicit our attention, asking us to participate, more or less insistently, in the local ontology of their apparition. A rhapsodic violin melody or a jangling teaspoon are, especially where their sensuous profiles are distributed among several objects that compete for our attention, grasped not by the matter of their form or structure, but by the *style* of their occasion, by the way their expressive signs entice or command us to explore their animating principle that, as metaphysician Graham Harman writes, "is never visibly present, but enters the world like a concealed emperor and dominates certain regions of our perception."[24] And as both my own and Adorno's example suggest, in the case of background music this principle of style is not negated so much as it is scrambled and obscured. Or as Harman puts it:

> Any noise exceeding the object of our attention is structured to as great a degree as the object itself. It is not a white noise of screeching chaotic qualities demanding to be shaped by the human mind, but rather, a *black noise* of muffled objects hovering at the fringes of our attention.[25]

Idle chatter, stirring spoons, car horns, and air conditioners are things with unifying styles of being and a need to be loved as much as John Adam's *Violin Concerto* (1994) is, or aspires to be. Distraction, however, interferes with the compelling unity of a thing's style and distributes its animating force throughout the field

---

Basically, Harman's OOO extends the traditional phenomenological notion of intentional objects to suggest that objects are not merely ideal principles of unity among a host of intentional acts, so much as real occulted things fissured by two strains of tensions that divide it from its plurality of expressive notes and the set of relations that compose it. See Graham Harman, *Guerrilla Metaphysics: Phenomenology and the Carpentry of Things* (Chicago: Open Court, 2005).

[24] Ibid., 55.
[25] Ibid., 183.

of sensible qualities that it shares with other objects. Thus, the style of a backgrounded music remains whether or not it's being listened to, and so participates in what Merleau-Ponty called "the flesh of the world" through the expressive correspondences that resound between its sensuous qualities and the other sensuous elements that are not strictly musical.

As Adorno's weird tribute to backgrounded music insinuates, this regard, or rather, this dis-regard suggests how the circumstances of listening to the side of music brings certain of its qualities to play on a wholly different level than if they were the sole object of attention. By withdrawing from the level of engagement defined as "foreground," one enters a sensory register whose style, or manner of drawing attention, hinges on the way sounds interact with other not necessarily musical qualities. Music's proper "object"—the dynamic unity it pleases us to call by that name—is absent at this distracted level; however, all of its sensual qualities are nevertheless aglow here.[26] And this may be the source of Adorno's fascination with café music and its "netherworldly glow." For Adorno, the customary relationship that obtains between a musical thing and its qualities concerns the way a work's structural logic is its own aesthetic object to the extent that it expresses something of the historical relation it bears to past customary relationships. In this relationship a work's sensuous qualities are said to fuse with its formal objectivity. But when the unity of a work's style and its multitude of qualities is severed or interrupted, as they are when listening is diverted from the cues that are meant to capture attention in this way, musical sounds become free-floating lures that attract and bind with other qualities to form new and unintended perceptions, "splendidly shabby" perceptions that become lures for attention.

This idea of musical sound as a "lure" has some resonance with Cage's notion of letting sounds be themselves, but is more familiar in the everyday way that attention draws somatic and psychic energies into carnal relations with a "shower of [musical] qualities freed from the elusive substances to which they presumably belong."[27] I'm referring here to the way a body finds itself involuntarily tapping its

---

[26] Ibid., 55–70.
[27] Ibid., 66.

toes or bobbing its head to a sound that it didn't know it was hearing, the body interacting with the qualities of rhythm, tone, and timbre apart from their relationship to any (formal) whole that exceeds their sensuous gratification. But this can also be expressed inversely, as, for instance, when one scans the radio dial. In this case one isn't listening for the way a sound points to a moment beyond itself, but for a fleeting sensory note loosed from its formal obligations so that it can commingle with the proprioceptive and kinetic tones of driving.

For ears trained to listen disinterestedly and to value the way musical sounds relay attractions and repulsions between one another, the carnal satisfaction of a sound event seems to caricaturize the sincerity of musical objects. And I would agree. However, I would contend that this "caricaturization" is an expression of allure, of how one is lured into the style of a thing by an irrational slackness that arises between this weird object—which for this study is a composition—and its familiar qualities. For Harman, allure is an effect of the way the sincerity of a thing is skewed by its encounter with other things. And phenomena such as humour and charm are expressive profiles of allure that attune the observer "to the inner ingenuousness of things," somehow managing "to put the very sincerity of a thing at issue."[28] At issue in what I am suggesting is "art" music's prolapse, its falling out of place as "art" and into the sensuous tumult of the background, is how distraction interferes with and caricaturizes a sincerity historically and culturally defined by its "form" or structure.

* * *

In short, I am saying that distraction does something to musical sounds. And what it does is to make them formless. But by this I don't mean that musical sounds become shapeless per se, so much as distraction disturbs the perception of music's formal structure in a way that makes "form" irrelevant to the experience. To make music's formal elements irrelevant is to tamper with its supposed sincerity, and this, paradoxically, is to give the musical "thing" a curious, almost perverse, charm. Specifically, distraction,

---

[28] Ibid., 141.

which means simply to draw or drag something away from one thing to another, attenuates the capacity for one musical event (a tone, a chord, phrase, or a whole section) to point to and make us expect another musical event, what theorist Leonard Meyer calls music's "embodied meaning."[29] Form, like all expressions of a thing's sincerity, has to do with the way something is "wrapped up right now in certain particular actions and no others."[30] Typically, form, musical or otherwise, is treated in perception studies as an emergent attribute, a "whole" of acoustic parts and dynamic patterns. But on a more philosophical level, a musical thing might be thought of as a measure of the degree to which its mannered and habitual routines of being remain concealed or unconscious, to it and to others. For someone like Adorno, this metaphysical principle of sincerity would be tied up with the complications of modern alienation that confound the capacity for a thing to simply be just what it is, a complication that is especially gnarly for modern art, which, as Adorno puts it, is defined by its congress of contradictions. As such, modern art's sincerity, which on Adorno's account would refer to its sincere self-inconsistency (which on another level is self-consistent), can only be conveyed ironically, cynically, or in some other reflexive manner that can't but hurl the thing and its qualities into a spiral of cascading negations. However, in a sense, this *is* the sincerity of a modern, alienated art whose destiny is to be just what it is—to be sincerely insincere. What gives access to what we may call an ironic mode of sincerity is an awkward style that articulates the effects of art's affected occasion, a style that shows itself as a formal rather than casual ("natural") occasion. Under this scheme, it becomes the task of the discourse to discern the elements and relations that delineate art's existence as a fabricated form. Adorno's notion of "structural listening" then would be reputed to access the (insincere) sincerity of a musical artwork by treating only those aspects of its appearing that attest to its alienated condition as relevant.

Though relevant chiefly to a certain class of nineteenth-century music practices, the notion of "structural listening" has nevertheless

---

[29] See Leonard B. Meyer, *Emotion and Meaning in Music* (Chicago: University of Chicago Press, 1956).
[30] Harman, *Guerrilla Metaphysics*, 135.

become a normative model not only for academic disciplines and institutions of appreciation, but for a general population inculcated with the notion that "an art object alone determines the qualities of aesthetic experience."[31] Rose Rosengard Subotnik advances an argument that this sensibility is an extension of late nineteenth-century European aestheticism wherein music is regarded as an autonomous object, an object whose value lay within the active reception-interpretation of immanent relations that are supposed to express something beyond their immediate sensory patterns. She argues that the adequacy and the rectitude for structural listening is grounded in the Enlightenment ideal of "a supposedly universal rational capacity"[32] that restricts listening to a (cognitive) level where only those elements which disclose the internal necessity of the thing's structure are relevant. In this view, which requires a concerted and sustained attention that presumes the existence of a continuous and rational awareness, structural listening remainders a host of fugitive auditory phenomena that interfere with the formal access to a work's supposed sincerity by siphoning off some of the attention required to satisfy its perception. But we only have to recall Adorno's fascination with the "shabbiness" of café music, and my own enchanting encounter with a dysfunctional CD, to note that listening is rarely drawn in structural terms and that contemporary conditions have made listening radically partial and precariously coherent. As such "the landscape of sincerity has changed."[33] The musical object has been liquefied and its swarm of sensual notes flung into "the drunken alchemy"[34] of contemporary attention—or lack thereof.

There are a number of ways to address how the deliquescence of musical form in contemporary listening brings out certain features that while "insincere" with regard to the ontological assumptions about form are nevertheless agents in their own right. Anahid Kassabian has approached the intermittent listening cultivated by a

---

[31] Ronald Radano, "Interpreting Muzak: Speculations on Musical Experience in Everyday Life," *American Music* 7, no. 4 (1989): 449.
[32] Rose Rosengard Subotnik, "On Deconstructing Structural Listening," in *Music, Culture, and Society: A Reader*, ed. Derek B. Scott (Oxford; New York: Oxford University Press, 2000), 170.
[33] Harman, *Guerrilla Metaphysics*, 178.
[34] Ibid., 170.

technologically produced musical omnipresence through a theory of ubiquitous listening whereby audition's being "always on" composes us as ambient subjects, nodes of transfer in the din of perpetual information exchange. More recently, Suzanne G. Cusick has written about the United States militarization of music as a torture device wherein the emphasis on the materiality of sound—i.e. volume, timbral quality, and its affective associations—renders the role of music's form utterly irrelevant. Steve Goodman, too, has extended the premise of a sonic materiality to show how sound, including music's intimacy with noise, participates in the general field of warfare and the wider ecology of dread.[35] While I engage to some extent with each of these models, I'm more interested in how contemporary (un)listening habits cleave to and pervert the normative comportments of concert listening in a way that sensitizes one to percepts that traffic in liminal and ephemeral experience. Furthermore, I am keen to consider how a concern, a love even, develops for these rogue events to become what Rei Terada calls "phenomenophilia." I focus later in this study on the attraction to "irregular, unstable, and very transient phenomena [over] the possible objects of aesthetic reflective judgments"[36] as it relates to the category of noise and a desire to evade "the perceived pressure of the given world and its natural laws on our potential endorsement."[37] For now, however, I want to use phenomenophilia as a figure for scrutinizing the rickety intimacy between attention and distraction, as well as a way to express something of the latter's overlooked charm. But before considering this further, I first want to ask what it could mean for music to be "formless," and how contemporary cultures of distraction redefine what counts as listening to music. Following this line of thought I then want to address how inattention realizes a form of musical autonomy that puts the sincerity of musical objects at issue.

---

[35] See Anahid Kassabian, "Ubisub: Ubiquitous Listening and Networked Subjectivity," *Echo* 3, no. 2 (2001), http://www.echo.ucla.edu/Volume3-issue2/kassabian/index.html [accessed October 2012]. Suzanne G. Cusick, "Music as Torture/Music as Weapon," *Transcultural Music Review* 10 (2006); Steve Goodman, *Sonic Warfare: Sound, Affect, and the Ecology of Fear* (Cambridge, MA: The MIT Press, 2010).

[36] Rei Terada, *Looking Away: Phenomenality and Dissatisfaction, Kant to Adorno* (Cambridge, MA: Harvard University Press, 2009), 23.

[37] Ibid., 16.

Becoming formless

Let's agree right now that there's no such thing as formless music per se, or for that matter, a formless "thing" as such. In the broadest sense, even the most amorphous thing has a minimum of form insofar as it expresses a limit in its very appearance as a thing rather than a weird and inaccessible non-thing. A color, for example, is bound to the contours of the surface it stains and the ambient light that modulates its hue. Even something as intangible as a mood has form in that it expresses a particular composition of effects that being a situated organism entails, situated in history, a culture, a crowd, *etcetera*. Practically speaking, formlessness in musical terms refers to a conspicuous lack or absence of the structural and/or semiotic cues given by the familiar elements of metre, cadence, harmony, theme-variation, melody, and so on. Typically, "music"[38] that is deficient in these cues is perceived somehow as failing to be musical, to be either aesthetically significant,[39] or, apart from its capacity to annoy, affectively moving. Generally speaking then, formless is not a good thing for "music" to be—to un-be.

But of course, within the avant-garde or experimental music, or even so-called "outsider" music communities, formlessness has had and continues to have a much less derogatory currency, functioning therein almost like a genre characteristic, a quality, or, paradoxically, a form—an un-form. For instance, reflecting on his first encounter with La Monte Young's music, Tony Conrad describes Young's work as "formless, expostulatory, meandering; vaguely modal, a-rhythmic, and very unusual; I found it exquisite."[40] John Cage's works, too, are obviously contemporary touchstones for the revaluation of what are considered musical criteria, as is the performance-project/lifestyle of the reclusive Texas musician/concept "Jandek," who for thirty years has been producing recordings of structureless songs sung

---

[38] Here, of course, is where classification begins to unravel, for how can we still call something music if by definition it lacks those salient attributes that distinguish music from sound, from noise, from speech?

[39] They don't possess what aesthetician Clive Bell calls "significant form"—a quality shared by all objects or events that elicits an aesthetic response. See Clive Bell, *Art* (London: Chatto and Windus, 1949).

[40] Tony Conrad, "LYssophobia: On FOUR VIOLINS," notes to *Early Minimalism Volume One Volume One* (Table of the Elements, 1997).

with a frail voice, accompanied only by distrait plucking on a guitar that seems tuned to no particular scheme.[41] But this sentiment for the formally obscure can extend back to include Nietzsche's claim that Wagner's music, owing what to our twenty-first century ears seems a rather quaint attack on very culturally and historically narrow conventions of structure and tonal harmony, is formless in its drunken or delirious effects.[42] But "formlessness" in any of these cases is structurally reliant on a notion of "form," a particular sense of form that the Italian composer Ferruccio Busoni, in his 1907 work *Sketch of a New Esthetic of Music*, asserts is in most cases an "architectonic," "symmetric," or "sectional" *style* that characterizes a particular historical approach to composition. While relevant and germane to the expressive problems and aesthetic values of a past era—chiefly nineteenth-century Western instrumental music—what can be called an architectonic or structural representation of form has over time become an apparently objective and necessary expression of music.[43] In this received sense of form, formlessness is taken as a negative attribute remaindered by the art music tradition's fixation (fetishization?) on past conventions. For Busoni, this obscures the real "truth" of music, which is to wrest expressions, what Deleuze and Guattari would call "percepts and affects," from reified or too consistent a plane of composition. In other words, Busoni's truth entails an ongoing realization of the inherently plastic nature of music. From a certain perspective, the history of aesthetic modernism and its "logic of offense" appears to have relieved formlessness of its pejorative quality, ultimately meliorating[44] its reputation to the effect

---

[41] In 2004 Jandek emerged (partially) from reclusion to begin collaborating with other musicians in live performances. For a guide to "Jandek" see Seth Tisue's website: http://tisue.net/jandek [accessed October 2012].

[42] See Friedrich Nietzsche, *The Birth of Tragedy and the Case of Wagner*, trans. Walter Kaufman (New York: Vintage, 1967).

[43] Ferruccio Busoni, *Sketch of a New Esthetic of Music*, trans. T.H. Baker (New York: G. Schrimer, 1911), 6–7.

[44] This improvement of formlessness is patently in line with aesthetic modernism's ideology of progress. But it is curiously resonant with the doctrine of meliorism which holds that the world is indefinitely improvable owing to a human ability to manipulate processes that would otherwise proceed and terminate without concern for its interests. For an overview of how meliorism is articulated by American Pragmatism see Colin Koopman, "Pragmatism as a Philosophy of Hope: Emerson, James, Dewey, Rorty," *The Journal of Speculative Philosophy* 20, no. 2 (2006).

that, as the example of Conrad's encounter with Young's music shows, a work's obscurity is no longer perceived as a shortcoming but a virtue. Hence Schönberg's wonderfully obtuse comment: "How the music sounds is not the point."[45]

However, despite the revaluation of formlessness, the above expressions are still given in terms bound to traditional protocols that see formlessness as an absence. Because something, no matter its incoherence, is still being given and had as "musical," and is still having an effect on one, it cannot be rendered in wholly negative terms. In other words, the experience of formlessness is positive while its sense is negative. Busoni hints at how we might understand the positivity of the formless within the domain of music when he writes, "All composers have drawn nearest the true nature of music *in preparatory and intermediary passages* (preludes and transitions), where they felt at liberty to disregard symmetrical proportions, and unconsciously drew free breath."[46] Though delivered with a touch of gooey Romanticism that bedims its utter sublunary nature, Busoni is directing attention to the overlooked occasions in music, particularly as it is heard, where the telic draw of a piece hesitates, where its unfurling gathers potential in the ongoingness-of-being-in-the-middle-of-itself. Busoni's "true nature of music" refers then to moments of suspense, moments in which, to take a traditional example, a sequence of notes have not yet crossed the threshold wherein they become a melody. We can think of this suspension between one experiential series and another—i.e., notes and melody—in a more contemporary sense as a *becoming* or an "event," which Deleuze describes as what "eludes the present" and "does not tolerate the separation or the distinction of before and after, or of past and future."[47] From this perspective, formless not only clinches a little wiggle room from its historical and structural reliance on form, but begins to have its own sense that follows a logic rife with paradoxes, a sense that goes in many directions at

---

[45] Arnold Schönberg quoted in Stephen Toulmin, *Cosmopolis: The Hidden Agenda of Modernity* (Chicago: University of Chicago Press, 1992), 185.
[46] Busoni, *Sketch*, 8, my emphasis.
[47] Gilles Deleuze, *The Logic of Sense* (New York: Columbia University Press, 1990), 3.

once to express a loss that is lost, a lostness that finds itself fully present to its being in uncertainty.

Toronto artist-composer Josh Thorpe's musical "ready-mades" are exemplary of formlessness as becoming, for their conceptual character, more than any actual sounding transition, isolates and embellishes the strange logic of becoming and the paradoxes of its eventuation that in ordinary circumstances are obscured by a determined emphasis on only one end of its occurrence. Openly signaling their debt to Marcel Duchamp's interventions (including their derivative character which redoubles their conceptual conceit), Thorpe's *Ready-made Aided #2* and *#3*, both for solo instrument that take works of JS Bach as source material, exhibit the bi-directionality that marks the logic of becoming by interfering in the customary relationship between an object's use and its ideas (its "sincerity"). These musical readymades have the effect of simultaneously pointing to and expressing the sense of what they are *and* what they are not. *Ready-made Aided #2* (2000), for example, takes Bach's first sonata for solo violin as its found object, its "found form," and scores (wounds) its traditional expression by asking the performer to 1) play the work slowly, and 2) do so wearing stiff, preferably suede, gardening gloves on both hands. When performed, the work divides in two, *becoming* more of what it is not (a mash of inarticulate notes, rhythms, and textures—a "platypus" as Thorpe calls it) and less of what it was (Bach's first violin sonata). In other words, the *expression* wrested from *Ready-made Aided #2* is formless in the sense that it is neither Bach nor a platypus but an event, a pinch point through which two musical series (i.e. notes|melody; Bach|platypus) divide from one another. Similarly, *Ready-made Aided #3 (for piano or harpsichord)* (2000) takes another piece by Bach, this time the *Goldberg Variations*, and intercedes in its form by literally cutting out every ornament from the score and pasting them, one after the other, in the order in which they appeared in the original. Additionally, Thorpe intuitively inserts silences between these naked ornaments and deletes any implying a cadence. In this piece, formless(ness) is articulated in the way ornaments, which are by definition "superfluous, non-components to the actual material of the music," become the "actual material of the music."[48] Ornaments here lose their decorative necessity (an internal contradiction that itself is already an expression of formless(ness)) and become a kind of almost-melody. However, the floridness of an ornament is such that it inclines to be heard as incomplete or partial so that in stringing these "rough pearls" (the original meaning of "baroque") together, one ends up with an ersatz melody, which in a way is maybe closer to the more common sense of baroque as "grotesque" or "whimsical." As such, *Ready-made Aided #3* oscillates, or better yet, hesitates between becoming ornament and/or structure.

Music noise

While I won't submit the above as exemplifying the "true nature of music," I will lean on the idea of becoming to address how the duplicity exhibited by Thorpe's readymades[49] articulate the way formless can designate a suspension or hesitation of the traditional sense of music as a succession of "felt probabilities." And to unpack this abeyance of formless I want to recruit the category of noise, for like becoming, the expression of noise as something that one is effectively listening *away* from while one is listening *to* music involves the kind of paradoxes and mutual determinations that show noise and music to have the same sense (more on this in the next chapter). In this context, the category of noise functions as a heuristic device that when paired with its negative attendant—"music"—does not settle the debts of either term but instead brings the sense of becoming into (the) ear.

In many respects, Paul Hegarty's work takes a similar approach to noise. In his *Noise/Music* (2007) Hegarty teases out the precession of music's and noise's two principal vectors: one is imperial, and is

---

[48] Josh Thorpe, "Here Hear: My Recent Compositions in a Context of Philosophy and 20th Century Experimental Music" (MA thesis, York University, 2000), 72.

[49] This duplicity is, incidentally, intensified by Thorpe's present disavowal of the works. By declaring them to be failures Thorpe reduplicates the logic of this very text, and so *Ready-made Aided #2* and *#3* become more of what they are (failures) while they become less of what they are not (failures).

Josh Thorpe, *Ready-made Aided* #2 (2000). Courtesy Josh Thorpe.

TABLE DES ORNEMENTS DE J. S. BACH
avec terminologie française courante

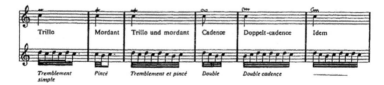

Josh Thorpe, from score for *Ready-made Aided #3* (for piano or harpsichord) (2000). Courtesy Josh Thorpe.

figured forth by various musical avant-gardes commanded first by Russolo's *Art of Noises* (1913) and then by John Cage's cry to "let sound be!", while other is a discursive effort to keep all expressions of either "music" or "noise" in suspension. Whereas the former charts the flight of music's empire across the entire spectrum of sound (one that maps nicely onto Western culture's expansionist economies), the latter is where the paradoxes multiply, for noise is only "noise"—a disturbance—when both it and music dwell within each other's field and thus constitute one another's threshold(s), mutually contaminating and/or modulating the limits of their respective affects. Noise in this regard is not opposed to music but is the other side of the same process that patterns both: coincident profiles of the same expressive event. Noise here is the becoming of the excluded, or what gets put out of the becoming of music. Said another way: Sound becomes more musical than it was and less noisy than it becomes. In a way, this fixes a region of remainders that immediately identifies them as elements of an anti-style. But to advance on these remainders is to continue the same process that remaindered them in the first place, and thereby to assimilate the difference that they expression. As Hegarty notes, "When noise is put to use," such as it is when it serves expressive ends—when it becomes noise music, "it can no longer be fully noise."[50] "Noise," he continues, "can never fully be—it is a transitional or temporary state."[51] In other words, noise is something that never *is* but ever *becomes*. The passage or transition that hasn't yet happened *qua* "transition" or "passage," but is still-forming, still working-out a potential *to become what it will have been*, is the sound of noise.[52]

Hegarty draws out this sense of noise (of its becoming) in terms that are highly resonant with Bataille's notion of *informe*, itself a noisy concept in that it denotes expressions of interference that are

---

[50] Paul Hegarty, "Residue- Margin- Other: Noise as Ethics of Excess," in *Argosfestival 2003*, ed. Paul Willemsen and Frie Depraetere (Brussels: Argo, 2003), http://www.dotdotdotmusic.com/seminars.html [accessed October 2012].

[51] Ibid.

[52] Again you'll notice that even here, I'm evoking aspects of form. The problem of dealing with becoming is that one has to talk about both profiles at once. Like the ambiguous duck-rabbit figure, this is seemingly impossible to do with language or to make apparent in perception.

immanent to the very attempt to make sense of things. In referring to types of Japanese noise music, as represented by the likes of Merzbow and Koji Tano's MSBR ("Molten Salt Breeder Reactor"), Hegarty writes,

> These forms of noise are *informe*, not free of form, not decon-structing it, not in a dialectical relationship to it, not against, but worked through, despite and outside, moving from inside (music) to out (sound) with the *noise the movement itself*—this is the "*besogne*" of noise—the enforced labour of noise—which neither wants to work, nor be merely noise, but becomes it through exclusion—an exclusion it reclaims, and through this, becomes music, which it fails to be.[53]

Hegarty is saying here that noise is a process. As a process noise marks something underway, the not-yet-finished, and this being-undone allows competing terms and relations to be co-present and active in the same dynamic event. Strictly speaking then, a noise-event suspends qualification and can only be expressed oxymoronically—i.e., noise-music. However, despite the paradoxical gyrations that affirm noise's affiliation with process and becoming, there is something inherently self-defeating about noise that is intentionally taken up or mobilized as an affront. The preparation of an offense includes an element of its own domestication insofar as planning an upset requires a certain amount of preconception regarding the kind of effects that will follow from its occasion. This is not only a semantic truth, wherein the meaning of noise is contaminated by the very thing it tries not to become—music—but it is also a matter of how noise's negative affect plays across bodily systems as variations on pain that work to fold the wretched superfluity of its "outside" into a rather predictable set of nervous responses: wincing, cringing, leaving, *etcetera*.

This is not to say that noise has no disturbing effects, clearly it does. But produced and consumed under the sign of music,

---

[53] Paul Hegarty, "General Ecology of Sound: Japanese Noise Music as Low Form," paper presented at Le travail de l'informe/functions of formless, University College Cork, July 2002. Also available at http://www.dotdotdotmusic.com/hegarty7.html [accessed October 2012].

no matter how bent or warped it may be, the theme of noise has no more access to the movement of *informe* as the theme of music does. To provoke the movement of *informe* noise does not have to be more noisy but more ambiguous. That is, noise must be equivocal. In some sense noise music accomplishes this equivocity. Through the conceit of being "music," a music of non-music, noise music troubles its own categorization. However, to the extent that this conceit becomes a proprietary condition, noise music reifies its equivocity and thereby specifies its form of *informe*, essentially undoing the undoing of formless. Unlike Hegarty, I don't believe that this failure to perform its own conceit is a sufficient expression of *informe*. Logically speaking it makes sense that it should, and that's why I've drawn noise into this discussion. But in practice and in effect, noise music exhibits such a rhetorical force that its manner of transgression, its prescribed form of failure, obscures the conditions that show its conceit to be coextensive with the conceits of music. In other words, noise music fails to fail its task of failing to determine itself through exclusion.

A less contented noise, which is to say a more equivocal and *informe* noise, would be a noise that does not thematize its abrasive figures but keeps certain of its intensities in play along the series of musical expressions from which it divides. Noise of this kind wouldn't flatter itself by repudiating the forms of music whose sense it shares. Instead it would aspire to pollute the purity of the latter's occasions in a way that makes the sense of a "musical" series—melody, dissonance and consonance, cadence, metre, euphony...—coincident with the sense of a noisy series—hiss, buzz, hum, screech, "essy"... .

The quiet rustling of Australian composer Warren Burt's *Another Noisy Lullaby* (2009) attempts to approach noise in this manner. An admitted conceit, Burt describes the piece as an overt riposte to Julian Knowles' (another Australian composer) objection over his (Burt's) being included in an essay on noise music. Paraphrasing Knowles' protest, Burt describes the issue as thus:

> I was too old, I didn't have a buzz cut, I didn't wear black leather, I didn't play in clubs in Europe, and the pub wasn't my main

venue of thinking…and I didn't have a bad attitude towards the audience.[54]

In *Another Noisy Lullaby*, Burt aims to subvert the militant and imperious tone of these conditions, asking: "If noise music is supposed to have an element of aggression and confrontation to it, how tender, how delicate, how nurturing can we make something, and still have it be noise?"[55] His response is a piece composed of what could be described as soft noise, sounds whose complexion of whispers evokes a mood that hovers somewhere between a tentative confidence and an insistent humility. Written for three to nine instruments[56] and "boomboxes," *Another Noisy Lullaby* draws its musical material from nonsense anagrams whose letters Burt uses to generate three categories of sound: simple diatonic melodies, whispered texts, and "noise-bands"[57] (contoured white noise). Immediately the work declares its difference from genre conventions in the way it sustains an atmosphere of muted and frail susurrations rather than the pressing viscerality typical of noise music. The text, for example, is executed "dramatically," a stage whisper in place of screams. The volume level of the boomboxes playing back the noise bands is set extremely low. And the instruments, explains Burt, particularly the wind and strings, play in such a slight and gentle manner "that compete control of the purity of sound is impossible."[58] Additionally, the element of immersion that is often taken for granted by noise music is in this work achieved spatially. In place of an encompassing might, the moony drifts of

[54] Warren Burt, "DECIBEL02: Warren Burt - Another Noisy Lullaby," Interview with Julian Day, Australian Music, Australian Broadcasting Corporation, http://www.abc.net.au/classic/australianmusic/stories/s2835399.htm [accessed October 2012].
[55] Warren Burt, Program notes, "Tape It!," Totally Huge New Music Festival, Perth, Australia, 10 September 2009. http://decibel.waapamusic.com/concert-1-tape-it/tape-it-program-notes [accessed October 2012].
[56] In the broadcast recording the work is performed by the Australian ensemble Decibel that comprises the instruments flute, bass clarinet, violin, and cello.
[57] You can get a sense of what these "noise bands" sound like by trying to make the following sounds: Trying saying the letter "K" but prolong the windy part of the phoneme and then change the shape of your mouth to shift the vowel sound to "k(o)—" then "k(ü)—" "k(aw)—" *etcetera*.
[58] Warren Burt, Performance notes to *Another Noisy Lullaby* (2009).

widely spaced boomboxes, faintly heard instruments, and breathy voices "merge into a sort of grey blur"[59] that in one sense captures the common sense of formlessness as amorphousness, but in a more interesting way deforms the typically repulsive force of noise into a lulling power.

Strangely, *Another Noisy Lullaby's* softness becomes formless (becomes but never *is* formless). It becomes *informe*, but in two ways at once: one, by the way its gentleness offends the more obstreperous conventions that are often taken as "facts" of noise music, and two, in that this same softness interferes with one's ability to discern those structural relations—art music's "facts"— that would constitute the work as a proper "aesthetic" object. What Burt's "tender noise" achieves is a hesitation similar to that expressed by Thorpe's readymades. Its veiled and obscure use of elements recognizable as either/both noise and/or musical occasions stalls the more pugnacious conventions that declaim noise as music. Additionally it frustrates the structural and affective expectations that yield musical events. But more importantly it suspends the taking up of either term, directing attention instead to a certain nonsense that cleaves all expressions of music|noise to one another.

And it's here that my project departs from Hegarty's. While Hegarty seeks the elusiveness of a noise that tries to keep from being music, or at least keeps its effects, its "disturbance effects," from being arrogated to the objectives of music (even if these objectives are expressive of chance effects) I want to pursue a music that participates differently in the grey economy of *informe*. For conceptual ease I call "music noise" a music that keeps its expressions of *informe* from sinking into the mud of mere sound, a base materialism, and I'll suggest that like noise music, music noise needs to be understood in a way that keeps its failure, its failure to fail, in ear. In the same way that noise music fails to be noise because the process of expulsion from music that makes noise "noise" also makes it "music," music noise also has to divide itself from practices and conventions that it cannot do without in order for its points of deformation to express the nonsense it wants to become. While there are a number of ways to achieve this, I want to focus on how

---

[59] Warren Burt, email message to author, 19 June 2009.

Another Noisy Lullaby

Slowly, smoothly, extremely softly, on the boundary between pitch and noise

Warren Burt

Warren Burt, from score for *Another Noisy Lullaby* (2009). Courtesy Warren Burt.

our culture's acquired habit of listening to music (amongst other sounds) inattentively is used (often unintentionally) by a number of composers to scuttle music's familiar vessels so that their expressive flotsam will either wash up on the shores of more remote aesthetic contexts or sink to the murky depths of the everyday.

Recording distraction

When a composition is made to elicit only partial attention, or when it behaves like background music, it evokes the logic of distraction to incite the kind of disturbance and hesitation that is character-istic of the becoming which I've described as formless(ness). To illustrate this process, let's consider the work of Toronto-based composer Martin Arnold whose music, characterized by its strange allusions to mediaeval polyphony and post-bop jazz, as well as an unusual approach to orchestration, engages with listening in a way that celebrates "all those things you can't control within what's sounding."[60] A work like Arnold's *Burrow Out; Burrow In; Burrow Music* (1995), which as he explains, "doesn't do anything or go anywhere" but simply meanders along, indifferent to whether it is being listened to or not, rather than charging the sails of music's windmill temporizes the normative pressure to form judgements or endorse the musical reality of what's being heard. *Burrow's* quiet and good-natured perversity[61] lingers in a mode of perception where what things are or what they may mean doesn't matter. This is not to say that there is no sense to what is heard in *Burrow*, but rather that its occasion of listening is conducted otherwise and away from the facts that typically organize musical audition. Listening here attends closely to the sensuous level of perception where it delights in the elaboration of local details without concern for the latter's structural implications or formal significance. Oddly, to listen in this way is also to *listen away* from a force, a rhetorical force, that is immanent to

---

[60] Martin Arnold quoted in Paul Steenhuisen, *Sonic Mosaics: Conversations with Composers* (Edmonton: University of Alberta Press, 2009), 148.

[61] Martin Arnold, "Observations About, around and Beside 'Burrow out; Burrow in; Burrow Music'" (PhD diss. University of Victoria, 1995), 12.

the activity of perception and which urges comprehension over mere apprehension. In listening away it is the appearing itself, the *appearancing* of things that matters: *That* things happen is sufficiently interesting and amusing, not what, why or even how they happen. The appeal of listening away speaks to a desire in perception, to the appetite internal to sensation for something other than the given or the existent. It's not what sounds say or mean, or even exemplify, for there is no distinct or good sense to what occurs. Important is what they may become, never what they are. Rei Terada has given the name "phenomenophilia" to this perceptual desire and characterizes it as an attraction to "perceptions that seem below or marginal to normal appearance."[62] Its "association of appearance with mereness, lightness, radiance, and hypothesis," and the way these appearances fringe the normative pressures of perception to endorse "the given world and its natural laws,"[63] makes phenomenophilia a form of *informe*.

To the extent that *Burrow Music*'s compositional tactics stage the appearancing of these kinds of evanescent percepts it can be thought to encourage phenomenophilia and thereby to express the movement of *informe*. But this staging of a phenomenophilic *informe*, as ingenious as it is, has only partly to do with *Burrow*'s formal scheme. To a large extent, the listener's powers of concentration have to be considered here, for as I will argue, they have been altered by contemporary culture's varieties of distraction that encourage a form of continuous partial attention.[64] This means that the formlessness of the kind perceived in *Burrow Music* is not simply a formal affair but an expression of how music is realized through the way it is heard. And in this case, *Burrow Music* can be understood to articulate something of the way music-to-belistened-to indirectly adopts the habits of

---

[62] Terada, *Looking Away*, 3.

[63] Ibid., 16.

[64] This is technologist Linda Stone's expression which she coined to capture they way one often feels "a desire to be a LIVE node on the network," which is to say, a desire to be connected. Arguably, for the contemporary subject, this desire is existential. To be continuously connected is to maximize one's opportunities of being engaged, and the sense of being busy or continuously engaged has itself come to express sense of being alive. See "Continuous Partial Attention," Linda Stone, http://lindastone.net/qa/continuous-partial-attention [accessed October 2012].

music-*not*-to-be-listened-to, the effect of which transfigures the former's several perceptual aberrations into unexpected aesthetic wonders.

* * *

Burrow Out; Burrow In; Burrow Music is a one-hour ten-minute piece in two movements written by Martin Arnold in 1995. As Arnold describes it, the underlying impetus for this work derives from a realization that his "fundamental experience of listening to music was through recording."[65] To the extent that recorded music does not simply represent but in fact reconfigures the order of its constitutive mediations, to express this fundamental experience of music-as-it-is-recorded *Burrow Music* is a work that is sensitive not only to the way it will sound and be heard as projected from a stereo, but how "production techniques are significant, distinct, and active contributors to the resultant recorded music."[66] In short, what Arnold wanted to accomplish with *Burrow Music* was a piece that takes the mediation introduced by recording technology and recording techniques as an essential part of recorded music's material. Beyond traditional elements such as "pitches, rhythms, textures, and sonorities (and their histories outside of the piece)"[67] are ambient elements that Arnold believes are "latently audible" in the final recording. Things such as

> the dimensions of the room (including sills; ledges; outcrop-pings; trim; smooth or angled corners); all the materials involved in the walls (plaster/stipple/paper/kind of paint); the amount of furnishing...and the placement, shapes, and material make-up of the furnishing; the floor surface and covering; the number of windows, the number of curtains, and the number of curtains drawn or not; the difference between the street noise from the third floor, the second floor, and the ground floor,[68]

---

[65] Arnold, "Observations," 18.
[66] Ibid.
[67] Ibid., 27.
[68] Ibid., 7.

as well as the kind of microphone used; the placement of said microphone relative to an instrument; the amount of gain applied to the microphone; and, as legions of informed and not-so-informed musicians will attest to, whether these sounds are recorded in a digital or analogue format. For Arnold, "how a piece is recorded is a part of the music, as much as all the other aspects of interpretation—dynamics, phrasing, articulation, *rubato*, etc."[69]

In addition to these indiscernible details, there are a host of other aspects that make *Burrow Music* an extremely interesting composition. But for now I only want to draw attention to the way that its formal perplexity renders the kind of listening that is typically brought to bear on "compositions" as insufficient. First, however, I want to describe how Arnold thinks this is accomplished, and then I want to propose what I believe is taking place. But since I'm almost certain that you will have never heard this piece, a more detailed description of the work is in order.

Basically, one can hear *Burrow Music* as a timbrally rich, extremely long, and very weird work of slow-moving modal counterpoint. As I noted above, the piece is in two movements. The first movement, at sixty-eight minutes, is the longer of the two and is essentially a three-part modal counterpoint, but with an accompanying punctuating line that activates (opens/closes) a gated tape part on which is recorded an improvised organ and string performance (both instruments being played by the composer). Each of the voices is recorded separately and independently of one another on a cassette four-track recorder, and throughout the piece, the melodic lines are performed at different times by one of twelve different instruments,[70] each of which have been recorded in different ambient spaces using different recording techniques to create, in a sense, a second and third order counterpoint based on instrument timbre and ambient resonance. The strategies that Arnold uses for ordering the parameters of pitch and rhythm are many and multilayered and require too much space (and patience) here to detail in depth, except perhaps to note that much of the material was generated using different

---

[69] Ibid., 18.

[70] ...which include: melodica; sopranino, alto, and bass recorders; Casio D[igital]-H[orn]-100; alto and baritone saxophones; trumpet; trombone; electronic panpipes...

applications of Danish composer Per Nørgård's "Infinity Series," a recursive algorithm with fractal-like properties whose self-similar "wavelengths" or "refractions" are audibly related to the originary series that gives its constantly expanding row the semblance of hierarchical order.[71]

The second movement, which times at forty-two minutes, is a representation of the same scored material that comprises the first movement. However, for this movement a MIDI-realization of the score is made and recorded to cassettes that are then listened to through headphones by performers who either whistle or hum along with one of the three principal melodic lines. Additionally, the MIDI-recording of the score is gated (turned on and off) and projected through speakers by a signal that comes from the microphone into which the performer whistles/hums. What's heard on the recording then is an extremely murky blend of whistling, humming, and MIDI-pianos. As Arnold writes: "This movement celebrates the non-expert pastime of humming and whistling-along and all the sonic anomalies that go with this activity."[72]

Aside from his underlying taste for mediaeval polyphony, Scottish Piobaireachd, 1970s prog-rock, and jazz-lounge, Arnold cites an interest in experimental film and video, particularly those reflexive works that "take on some kind of investigation into various aspects of various kinds of apparatus set in motion for the[ir] production and consumption."[73] Though citing the work of Michael Snow, Ernie Gehr, and Peter Gidal as influential, it's film-maker/theorist Trinh T. Minh-ha whose work Arnold feels particularly indebted to. In Trinh, Arnold discerns what he calls a "non-demonstrative" approach that differs from other experimental filmmakers in that her films do not index the implicit understanding or control that a work such as Michael Snow's *La Region Centrale* (1971) suggests. For Arnold, the "creative strategies and artistic innovations in regard to the manipulations of the camera...are demonstrative and exemplary

---

[71] For a detailed discussion of the infinity series and Nørgård's application of it in his music see Erik Christensen, "Overt and Hidden Processes in 20th Century Music," *Axiomathes* 14, no. 1–3 (2004). I also examine the infinity series in Chapter Three with respect to Karen Eliot's work.

[72] Arnold, "Observations," 13.

[73] Ibid., 20.

in their methodology and, as such, offer *clear indices* to aspects of the artists' intentions."[74] This, he contends, demonstrates an authority on the part of the artist, or an interpretive privilege that in Trinh's work is absent. Arnold points out that while the "unsettling [of] various conventions and preconditionings" at work in Snow, Gehr, and Gidal's film are present in Trinh's films, their "subversions are not lucid enough or consistent enough or pervasive enough or dramatic enough to take on another [alien] authority."[75] The expressive ambiguity Arnold sees in Trinh's *Naked Spaces* (1985), for example, parallels his desire for *Burrow Music* to both exploit and subvert conventions while never presuming mastery or control of his creative strategies or the effects that they condition.

Like Trinh, Arnold seeks to keep the affects—the abstract but perceivable force of change immanent to and expressive of an experiential modification—of convention and subversion in play without isolating or classifying which artistic effect belongs to which affect. Arnold describes this as "a condition where the dialectic line that can be cut between the two disappears and they become unknowable as categories."[76] Describing his ideal reception of *Burrow Music* and the kind of experience he aims to cultivate in listening to the work, Arnold explains:

> I want the array of elements that make up my hybrid material to be as capable of being (mis)apprehended as all context and content [...]. I want a situation in which any given element in any given moment might seem familiar (and maybe beautiful or sentimental or comfortable) but in which there is *no real sense of what is going on*; no solid indication or even implication of what my agenda or intent as a composer might be.[77]

With its emphasis on a thoroughgoing but not unpleasant senselessness, *Burrow Music* can be considered a work that prolongs the experience of hesitation, that tries to become an ongoing "event,"

---

[74] Ibid., 26, my emphasis.
[75] Ibid.
[76] Ibid., 27.
[77] Ibid.

an event that *in effect* has no duration, no envelope of development, or contour of growth that would advocate a way of taking account of what's happening. Ideally, *Burrow* lingers in the "eventness" of its event wherein things are only apprehended as a "quasi-this" or "quasi-that" because they are always *in the process of becoming* this or that. Citing John Cage's *Cheap Imitation* (1969), a reversioning expression of Erik Satie's *Socrate*, as an exemplary case of musical hesitation (and model for *Burrow Music*), Arnold writes:

> It has an innocuous, generalized familiarity because of its diatonic ("white note mode") nature, and yet, specifically, it is unknowable. There is absolutely no sense of what should come next—largely a result of the chance procedures which generated it...and yet, because of its sweet, friendly melodicism, it does not adhere to any recognizable archetype for "randomness." And not only is there no way of guessing what comes next, because there is no recognizable tension within the piece, it supplies no motivation for one to wonder such a thing; it is completely without suspense.[78]

Or, it is wholly suspense, a radical suspension of its abstract tendencies to consummate this or that satisfaction of becoming recognizable as music. Arnold goes on to describe other details of what this piece does, followed always by another "and yet...," which gets at something of the way *Cheap Imitation* keeps the skewed effects of its perplexing gestural logic and formal obliquities in circulation, keeps them eventual, hesitant, becoming. For Arnold, this is indicative of how music, when organized in such a way can, paradoxically, appear to disorder itself, to give the impression of being formless, or, to be consistent with Arnold's use of Deleuze and Guattari's notion of faciality as a regulator of signification, of being "faceless" and free to enjoy the asemantic drift of "a multi-dimensional, polyvocal corporeal code."[79]

But much of what Arnold describes in *Burrow Music* (and *Cheap Imitation*) are its internal formal details. While details such as the unusually long duration, the otiose melodic drifts, and a veritable

---

[78] Ibid., 99–100.
[79] Deleuze and Guattari, *A Thousand Plateaus*, 170.

absence of dynamic variety are necessary elements that help *Burrow Music* scramble the expectations that mediate the way a listener takes account of a musical event, these alone are not sufficient conditions to render "the strangeness of its existence so disorienting."[80] If they were, one should expect *Burrow Music* to relinquish some of its unsettling effects with successive hearings. Its being recorded would presumably give the listener a degree of control that would countervail *Burrow Music*'s troubling affect by giving one the opportunity to develop the kind of attention that evolves from multiple listenings, an attention that Warren Burt, incidentally, calls "exact attention":

> Exact attention would seem to me to involve, as preparation, multiple listenings to something. First listening for (for example) melody (pitch), then maybe listening to harmony, then listening to form, then maybe a Schenkerian kind of listening, then concentrating on timbre, then concentrating on personal memories (why does this tune remind me of her?—or why does this tune remind me of tuna sandwiches?), then concentrating on semiotic aspects of the piece, etc.[81]

But the fact is that as many times as I've listened to *Burrow Music*, and as well as I understand the objectives of the piece, I still have enormous difficulty grasping what's going on. To me this suggests that the capacity to listen, which Arnold insists is what he's addressing in the work, plays a key role in determining what Arnold says is *Burrow Music*'s "insidiously disorienting instability."[82] In a way, Arnold's reading of his own intentions to thwart his intentions by elaborating the salient tactics he uses, paradoxically, to control how the composition of *Burrow Music* might "escape" him, overlooks something about his own observation that recording introduces certain mediations that become part of the music.

While treating (in a non-demonstrative way) the mediations of audio technology in a way that addresses how "production

---

80 Arnold, "Observations," 100.
81 Warren Burt, email message to author, 19 July 2010.
82 Arnold, "Observations," 101.

techniques are significant, distinct, and active contributors to the resultant recorded music,"[83] it should also be considered how listening to recorded music affects the way one attends to music, any music. This is to say that attention—or lack of it—actively contributes to the way the music sounds, to the resultant experienced music. Arnold is right that "there is nothing neutral about the recording process,"[84] but there is also nothing neutral about the circumstances of listening, and certainly there is nothing neutral about what sound technology has done to these circumstances. Simon Frith puts it this way: "As we have taken power over music on records, as they have become ubiquitous...so the musical work has ceased to command respectful, structural attention."[85] As a consequence, "All music," he contends, "is more often heard now in fragments than completely" and "because *all* our experiences of time are now fragmented and multilinear, fragmented music is also realistic music."[86]

Production techniques are therefore not the only "active contributors" to the way music is heard through recordings. For the majority of the population of industrialized cultures whose primary experience of music is circumscribed to that of listening (to recordings), the peculiarities of recording's mediations are no longer exceptional. Thus, in addition to affecting what is or is not audible, as, say, the way a microphone position alters the amount of finger noise or breath that is heard, recordings have taught us how to listen in moments as well as indifferently, and thereby to orient "the listener's attention to 'sound'" such that "perception of the sound is more important than consideration of the 'composition' as an entity in and of itself."[87] Pausing, turning down, rewinding, skipping ahead, stopping a song in the middle of playback, and simply forgetting about it are behaviours that develop around the way recordings allow one to affect recorded musical sounds. But these behaviours also

---

[83] Ibid., 18.

[84] Ibid.

[85] Simon Frith, *Performing Rites: On the Value of Popular Music* (Cambridge, MA: Harvard University Press, 1996), 242.

[86] Ibid., 242, 243.

[87] Shuhei Hosokawa, *The Aesthetics of Recorded Sound* (Tokyo: Keiso Shobo, 1990), quoted in Frith, 243.

adjust the importance of the music downwards so that they become something grasped or appropriated unconsciously.

As Walter Benjamin notes, habits that develop around the way an individual uses things, or we could say, the way things mediate one's use of them, impinge on how these things figure into one's perception and influence the significance they can have.[88] So as well as affording a separation of performer and audience, a separation that programmed music (what we refer to generically as "Muzak") relies upon, recordings encourage us to regard music as something that can be willfully tuned in and out of: The sound of music becomes something alternately neglected or cherished according to a nebulous set of continuously shifting priorities, priorities that are becoming increasingly multiple and superficial.[89] Additionally, and coupled with

---

[88] See Walter Benjamin's essay, "The Work of Art in the Age of Mechanical Reproduction," in *Illuminations*, ed. Hannah Arendt (London: Fontana Press, 1992).

[89] **Multitasking** Studies on multitasking show that the brain does not work in parallel but processes serially, and so is limited to dealing with tasks one after another. While it's not clear if the shift from one task to another relies on a passive bottlenecking, or whether a central executive power actively coordinates the priorities of tasks, acting on multiple tasks entails switching between them. This "switchiness," however, has costs. Because the brain is limited to processing information in series, along separate channels devoted to visual, aural, proprioceptive signals, there's a certain amount of leakage in mental efficiency when switching between tasks. "Brain leakage" is typically measured in time (fractions of a second), but it can also be expressed as a degree of energy depletion that when protracted makes perception and thought prone to error, to failure. Now what's interesting about this in terms of how it affects the way a spectator interacts with a time-based or "occurrent" art such as music, an art whose listened-to experience is constituted by the attention given its sounds, is that the perceptual habits we've contracted from living in a world of electric definition that encourages our senses to constantly commingle and inflect each other's expression, have conditioned us to rapidly alternate between different channels rather than to focus on any one sensory register in particular. Next time you're in a concert hall, try to observe how often your awareness passes from one series of experience—the sensuous play of sounds—to another—the inevitable cough or cell phone ring. And (though strictly speaking it's impossible to do this) try to notice how much of the music you're *not* paying attention to, by which I mean how much of the conventionally recognizable musical sounds are simply absent from your conscious experience. In a sense, you'll find that the acoustically continuous phenomenon called a "piece of music" will be fractured and fragmented by the act of perception itself.

But it's not as if perception was before the hyper-mediatization of our environment a continuous and unbroken flow. William James points this out in his 1911 essay on attention when he asks the reader to locate a simple dot on a piece of paper or wall, and focus on it. What's found here, says James, is one of two things: "either your field

the fact that recorded music's ubiquity makes this almost universal, the scission between performing and listening spaces gives musical sounds an impropriety that allows them to circulate as impersonal environmental qualities and something that one learns to listen away from.[90] Or, like architecture, which is rarely perceived apart from the

---

of vision blurs to the extent that you see nothing distinct at all, or else you find that you've unintentionally quit looking at the dot and are now attending to something else."[89e] The subject—the dot—is in a sense unchanging and so "attention inevitably wanders away."[89b] However, the dot as an intentional object is anything but unchanging, or at least, our experience of it (which for a radical empiricist is everything) is found to be teeming with all manner of wanders (e.g. How big is the dot? How far from the edge of the paper is it? What's its shape? What color does it have? How does it set off the surface behind it? Why does it look like a squashed bug?). What James' intro-spective cynosure reveals is twofold: one, that attention is occasional, that "it comes in beats" and pulsed quanta of effort; and two, as *New York Magazine* writer Sam Anderson put it, that attention is better described as an "ability to organize *distractions* around a central point."[89c] Distraction therefore is, in a sense, the condition of attention. Para-citing Deleuze, who makes an analogous observation about the "irrational," we can say that attention is something like a region carved out of distraction—not sheltered from it, but crossed by distraction and defined by a specific kind of relationship among distracted factors. Attention can be thought of then as a type of gestalt, an afferent and centralizing awareness hewn from a multiplicity of singular percepts, which, in a way, makes attention a mode of distraction. What distinguishes our contemporary situation then is not so much that our culture is distracted, but that its highly reticular socio-economic base expresses another modality of distraction, one that flittingly decentralizes and ramifies awareness rather than gathering it around a central point. In other words, there's no "point" any more, but only a constellation of rhythmically and intensively conjoined moments of colours, flavours, odors, pressures, sounds, temperatures, excitements, and boredoms—Hume's pearls scattered over Deleuze and Guattari's "smooth space" of bundled affects and symptomatic matter. No more hunting gestalts, it's snark season.

[89a] William James, *Talks to Teachers on Psychology; and to Students on Some of Life's Ideals* (New York: W. W. Norton, 1958), 80.

[89b] Ibid., 79.

[89c] Sam Anderson, "In Defense of Distraction: Twitter, Adderall, Lifehacking, Mindful Jogging, Power Browsing, Obama's Blackberry, and the Benefits of Overstimulation," *New York Magazine*, 17 May 2009, my emphasis.

[90] **Mechanization** realizes the impersonal affective potential of music in two related respects: First, recording technologies decouple music from its social pertinences (which, by the way, is what concert music has always aspired to do) and so grant it a form of autonomy that allows its sounds to be treated as a thing to be exchanged and circulated as any other thing. Second, disarticulating the circumstances of perfor-mance from circumstances of listening allows the affective profiles of a piece to circulate beyond the occasion in which their specificity had been realized. Bodies that grow weary and make mistakes, and bodies that gather new potentials from these expressions to modulate the affect of the current and any future performance, are

lived economy of its spatial array, music (especially as it has become increasingly omnipresent) serves as a felt background from which one's attention can be detached and given reign to drift towards more obscure perceptions and sublimated tropes.

In this way, *Burrow Music*'s "insidiously disorienting instability" is as much a function of how recorded music and a media-rich environment—an environment that it helps create—invite us to listen distractedly. What this means is that part of *Burrow Music*'s strangeness derives from the fact that a highly mechanized information-saturated culture of hybrid bio-petrol-geo-electric-social networks already teaches its subjects how to listen "rhizomatically," how "any point [of listening] can be connected to anything other, and must be"; how an act of listening "may be broken, shattered at a given spot, but...will start up again on one of its old lines, or on new lines."[91] Because listening to music through recordings is central to contemporary culture at large, its members already pay a certain in-attention to music in general.

---

restricted to the listener's side of things by recordings. In addition to the saturation of the acoustic sensorium that mechanization has remaindered, and the escape of sound from sight's ordering habits, automation that is playback introduces a further degree of indifference that helps the listener abandon his/her traditional respect for the form or content of music in a way that gives attention permission to wander|wonder about its other interests while the musical sounds continue to act on the body, disciplining its fidgets and twitches. Muzak's evil|genius was not that it sought to manipulate attention using music, but that it recognized, radicalized, industrialized, and of course capitalized on what recorded music encourages—the eviction of music from its relatively recent status as fine art into the spins and stalls of everyday life.

What I mean by this is that the habitual reception of musical sounds is an effect of the way music has, as a consequence of its mechanized mediatization, become an agentless feature of the environment such that it comes to be heard the way streetcars and lawnmowers outside of my house are heard—always to the side of another activity. The consequences of this are both profound and curious. In becoming a ubiquitous part of everyday life, music loses something—namely, its form, that principle of integrity so necessary for its membership into the fine arts. What it gains by losing its distinctness, however, is an enhanced emotional valence. Music theorist Ian Cross calls this property of music its "floating intentionality," a drifting aboutness that refers to the way music "can be thought of as gathering meaning from the contexts within which it happens and in turn contributing meaning to those contexts."[90a] While for Cross this ambiguity is something essential to all music, for me it specifies something about the way music has different effects according to how it's realized by the attention it is given.

[90a] Ian Cross, "Music and Meaning, Ambiguity and Evolution," in *Musical Communication*, ed. Dorothy Miell et al (Oxford: Oxford University Press, 2005), 30.
[91] Deleuze and Guattari, *A Thousand Plateaus*, 7, 9.

The parts—"lines of segmentarity"—that one tunes in and out of when listening to *Burrow Music* never survey the piece and so never compose an image of the work that would dominate hearing and organize its expressions into signifying regularities. Or in Deleuze and Guattari's language, *Burrow Music* has no face to "define zones of frequency or probability, [to] delimit a field that neutralizes in advance any expressions or connections unamenable to the appropriate significations."[92] In a sense, *Burrow Music* borrows from distraction its ramifying capacity and its cognitive sleights, and transposes these into a stationary context (the context of listening through headphones) to perform a "fractal deformation," a process in which listening lives on bites of "increasingly fragmented gestures, features, images, that never add up, never amount to a whole body,"[93] or a face.

Capture and escape

Every awareness begins in a shift. We think of ourselves as directing the shifts in our attention. But if you pay attention to paying attention, you quickly sense that rather than you directing your attention, your attention is directing you. It pulls you into your coming perception, which dawns on you as attention's next-effect. Attention is the perceptual automatism that consists in tagging a change in the perceptual field as potentially important and building awareness on that change.[94]

There are a number of things to understand about distraction, but perhaps the most important to keep in mind is that it is coterminous with attention. Said another way, distraction and attention are coincident expressions of the same event much as buying and selling describe two sides of the same transaction. What determines the expression of one over the other is therefore a matter of context and

---

[92] Ibid., 168.
[93] Mann, *Masocriticism*, 154.
[94] Brian Massumi, "Perception Attack: Brief on War Time," *Theory and Event* 13, no. 3 (2010), http://muse.jhu.edu/journals/theory_and_event/v013/13.3.massumi.html [accessed October 2012].

emphasis, how the affect of said event becomes effective. "Surfing" (the web), for example, is read as a distracting event if its effects are seen to interfere with one's productive capacity, memory loss or diminished analytical powers being two examples. Something like reading closely or listening intently will be taken as an attentive event to the extent that something productive comes of it: edification or emotional management. But as these examples suggest, what counts as productive, and therefore what counts as an expression of distraction or attention, is highly contextual and circumscribed by a host of constantly shifting cultural norms.

The volatility of distraction|attention and its link to technology has become in the past ten years a hotly debated topic. Journalists Maggie Jackson and Nicholas Carr have each recently published books aimed at diagnosing contemporary distraction, and both see the powers of attention waning in light of the hegemonic role that communication technologies play in determining the priorities of life.[95] Drawing similar conclusions, they argue that a network culture is a twilight culture and distraction the new moon of thought. But distraction is not entirely a symptom of recent technologies. Diversions have always been indicted as signs of potential degeneracy. The difference now is that the apparent surfeit of mass-produced distractions seem poised to substitute their feints for the lunge. Siegfried Kracauer in "Cult of Distraction" (1926) and Walter Benjamin in "The Work of Art in the Age of Mechanical Production" (1935) each analyzed the condition of distraction in relation to an emerging mass culture. Both writers perceive distraction as a consequence of industrialization and take its filmic expression in particular to reflect something of the way modern culture represents and reproduces itself in and as "[a] fragmented sequence of splendid sense impressions."[96] While both applaud distraction's capacity to contaminate the pretense of aesthetic modernism, rendering the notion of art's hallowed nature and the expression of an inward otherworldliness irrelevant to popular

---

[95] Maggie Jackson, *Distracted: The Erosion of Attention and the Coming Dark Age* (Amherst, NY: Prometheus Books, 2008); Nicholas Carr, *The Shallows: What the Internet Is Doing to Our Brains* (New York; London: W. W. Norton and Company, 2010).
[96] Siegfried Kracauer, "The Cult of Distraction: On Berlin's Pleasure Palaces," in *The Mass Ornament: Weimar Essays*, ed. Thomas Y. Levin (Cambridge, MA: Harvard University Press, 1995), 326.

culture, they draw different conclusions regarding its ultimate role in the expression of dialectical materialism. For Kracauer, distraction was a means of both repressing and mirroring the external conditions of mass-culture. For Benjamin, however, distraction identifies a potential politics. While the cinematic manipulation of images serves to distract—where close-ups expand space and slow motion extends movement—at the same time it conveys the experience of reality's constructedness and thereby has the effect of teaching people how to perceive reality as a plastic phenomenon.[97]

Benjamin and Kracauer's critiques, however, take place during the infancy of mass culture and its proliferation of distractions, a time when distraction still referred chiefly to a form of amusement, a time before distraction became a burden. A more recent study by Joseph Urgo, which reflects on the cost of contemporary culture's sundry methods for relieving the body of its labour, suggests that industrialized societies have unwittingly intensified the cognitive demands of their subjects by not only multiplying the things for consideration but converting these things into a supple quasi-thing called information. Urgo argues that because processing information has become its own form of satisfaction, it has become nearly indistinguishable from entertainment, and as information has become increasingly disembodied, virtual and ubiquitous, it has mutated from a "recipient- and source-bound phenomenon to independent, agentless phenomenon to environment."[98] But distraction is not solely cognitive; it has a material and affective logic that William Bogard refers to as a logic of escape and capture. "To distract something," he writes, "is to elude its clutches; but also, as a consequence, to now clutch *it*, secretly and from behind."[99] Distraction

---

[97] It's worth noting that Adorno strongly disagreed with Benjamin's view of distraction. Where Benjamin argues that film lends itself to a distracted apperception of its whole that ultimately endows one with a kind of incidental power of critique, Adorno, shifting the terms from cinematic vision to "easy listening" music, points out that "decon-centrated listening makes the perception of the whole impossible" and furnishes the listener, or viewer, with nothing but the charm of a "particular sensory pleasure." Adorno, "Fetish," 305, 306.

[98] Joseph Urgo, *In the Age of Distraction* (Jackson, MS: University Press of Mississippi, 2000), 49.

[99] William Bogard, "Distraction and Digital Culture," *ctheory*, 2000, http://www.ctheory. net/articles.aspx?id=131 [accessed October 2012].

is not simply a state of consciousness but a patterning, a way "to control movement, order desire and belief, and translate them into habits."[100] In this sense, distraction is an act of abstraction, taking away, whose occasion refers to "a process of bifurcation" where two lines, one of capture another of escape, pull "in different directions at the same time."[101] For Bogard, "in an age where simulation has become a dominant strategy of social control" distraction plays out culturally "by organizing [a body's] flows at a molecular level, at the interface of the cellular structure of the organism and the system of information."[102] Here Bogard brings us back to the idea that distraction and attention are flip sides of the same event. Which side is expressed has to do with factors of speed and the way "*differential flows of matter and energy*" self-organize into "abstract machines" that "impart form to variable flows, or again, break their form apart and down."[103]

Although Bogard's quasi-materialist way opens distraction to other conceptual rhythms, I want to return to Benjamin's idea that mechanical reproduction and the distraction encouraged by the effects of cinema make the public unintentional or "absentminded examiners."[104] Basically, Benjamin posits that through a veil of distraction the absentminded are able to "incidentally" (re)activate the powers of apperception. He argues in particular that film's expressive assemblage is grasped in the same way that architecture and the practicable field of implicit objectives it produces are appropriated through the unconscious acquisition of habits. Benjamin contends, "[T]he ability to master certain tasks in a state of distraction proves that their solution [to an encounter with difference] has become a matter of habit. Distraction as provided by art presents a covert control of the extent to which new tasks have become soluble by apperception."[105] This is to say that distraction is a homeopathic power, an unexpected antidote to received sense of things as simply given. In its multiple occasions, distraction gives one "unconscious

---

[100] Ibid.
[101] Ibid.
[102] Ibid.
[103] Ibid.
[104] Benjamin, "The Work of Art," 239–41.
[105] Ibid., 240.

intimacy"[106] with a heterogeneity of factors that would typically fly under the radar of conscious perception. Distraction is, so to speak, an unconscious or absent-minded intelligence expressed in the form of habits that "solve" a particular situation's implied imperatives.

Art historian Christine Ross, whose work I drew on in the previous chapter, mobilizes the idea of distraction's homeopathic potential in relation to Rosemarie Trockel's 1999 Venice Biennale triptych—*Eye, Kinderspielplatz* and *Sleepingpill*. These three video installations— *Eye*, a large projection of a close-up human eye; *Kinderspielplatz*, a slow-motion projection of a children's playground filmed between dawn and twilight; and *Sleepingpill*, another slow-motion video, which documents the quasi-event of sleep that takes place in a public mobile dormitory—revolve around what Ross calls "an activity of somnolent attention."[107] Ross argues that in these videos the anodyne of "entertaining" distraction is troped by staging and/or inducing the gloominess of a "weary" distraction.[108] "The need for sleep," writes Ross, "is both a symptom of depressed fatigue and a means to regenerate the subject."[109] The irresistible need for sleep has a kind of unmitigated power to disengage the most obsessive info-junkies from the choked and compulsive space of media distraction. Awake, we suffer the cancers of bright shiny things and murky blunt stuff. Asleep, we enjoy a nocturnal remission. For Ross, Trockel's imagery of sleep and listlessness point to the regenerative powers of slumber and suggest that distraction's homeopathic properties offer a cure for the subject's failing faculties, but only to the extent that the excessive correspondences between distraction's disparate seductions remain unconscious.[110]

While dreaming may indeed be a kind of absentminded escape|capture that in principle revitalizes one's deteriorated critical faculties, the perceptual weirdness of being *constantly* distracted that describes our daily life suggests that the woolgathering of dreams are no longer entirely the office of sleep. The multi-perspective

---

[106] Stan Allen, "Dazed and Confused," *Assemblage* 27 (1995): 48.

[107] Christine Ross, *The Aesthetics of Disengagement: Contemporary Art and Depression* (Minneapolis: University of Minnesota Press, 2006), 157.

[108] Ibid., 178.

[109] Ibid.

[110] Ibid.

purview and strange coeval omniscience|ignorance that describes the lived economy of dreams, an economy where the dreamer is also the dreamed and the dreaming, can describe significant aspects of waking life. In the same way that an industry decision to include original artist recordings in its programming scheme along with its own schmaltzy renditions blurs the lines between background and foreground music,[111] but also owing to the ubiquity of audio playback devices that allow contemporary listeners to background their own tastes, the line between dream and quotidian logic has become fuzzy. The "lateral vistas of information that stretch endlessly in every direction"[112] describe the layout of both dreams and networked culture. And furthermore, the vaporous possibilities that characterize the causality of dreams is matched in waking life by what Brian Massumi calls the "fog of potential" of contemporary culture's "threat-environment," its ecology of dread wherein a constellation of "effects, swirling into complex relation, give any number of competing logics and alternative presidings a chance."[113] Here then (again) is Baudrillard's "hyperreality," where simulacra orbit one another, "substituting the signs of the real for the real."[114] Hyperreality, writes Bogard, "is our current mode of distraction, and our current mode of capture."[115] If a dream is the dream of another dream and by dreaming a dream one dreams a dream dreaming, then dreaming dreams that dream dreams is to dream the dreaming of dreams dreaming.

---

[111] As an industry terms, foreground music is strictly speaking, "music programming that consists of songs in their original form, as recorded by the original artist." Jonathan Sterne adds that this music "operates at the levels of taste and distinction, differentiation and association," and rather than being organized around style, the way background music organizes its playlists, foreground music is organized "according to marketing categories like 'top 40' or 'adult contemporary'." See Jonathan Sterne, "Sounds Like the Mall of America: Programmed Music and the Architectonics of Commercial Space," *Ethnomusicology* 41, no. 1 (1997): 31–2.

[112] Sven Birkerts, *The Gutenberg Elegies: The Fate of Reading in an Electronic Age* (Boston: Faber and Faber, 1994).

[113] Brian Massumi, "Power to the Edge: Making Information Pointy," in *Ontopower: War, Power, and the State of Perception* (Durham, NC: Duke University Press), forthcoming.

[114] Jean Baudrillard, *Simulacra and Simulation*, trans. Sheila Glaser (Ann Arbor: University of Michigan Press, 1995), 2.

[115] Bogard, "Distraction and Digital Culture."

Lull)))))))))

Sleep is not the potent remedy for distraction that Ross sees in Trockel's videos. The little death that sleep gives is inaccessible because we keep waking up in our dreams. But these dreams are not only optical, they are also acoustic. Following Marshall McLuhan, who insists that humankind dwelled in an acoustic world before writing modulated the ratio of sensorium towards the visual, Paul Hegarty argues that after writing, "Our eye becomes ear... as we can no longer close it—images surround us acoustically."[116] "The total visualization of culture," he continues, "frees the image from its grounding in representational meaning."[117] Similarly, with each layer of mediation, music becomes increasingly transparent (invisible, actually) to the point that it functions as "a pure medium of itself."[118] And this, too, is how dreams behave. Their elements are so equally fluid, so evenly overdetermined that there is no outside reality to dispute its verisimilitude. As the protagonist, Dominic Cobb of Christopher Nolan's 2010 film *Inception* says: "Dreams feel real while we're in them. It's only when we wake up that we realize that something was strange." Acoustic space is all around us, and in us. And as Steve Goodman contends, this makes sound a primary vehicle for shaping reality: "Vibration research ensures a ubiquitous media environment in which any surface whatever, organic or nonorganic, becomes a potential emitter of sound."[119] As such, "Muzak preempted our submersion into a generalized surround sound culture, the insidious purr of control and the digital modulation of affective tonality that smoothes the experience of the ecology of fear."[120] Perhaps it's better said then that after writing, where the purr of acoustic control is the closest thing to a ground in an "unstoppable, directionless, sound world,"[121] we don't sleep, we lull. We linger in a state between dreaming and waking.

---

[116] Hegarty, *Noise/Music*, 135.
[117] Ibid.
[118] Ibid.
[119] Goodman, *Sonic Warfare*, 143.
[120] Ibid., 143, 144.
[121] Hegarty, *Noise/Music*, 135.

This in-between state, depending on whether you're waking up or falling asleep, is called hypnopompia or hypnagogia, respectively, and it is characterized by the onset of sensory aberrations and hallucinations ranging from evanescent phenomena like sparkling or spinning threads of light, whispered voices, the feeling of falling ("hypnic jerk"), and wafts of partially heard melodies, to more elaborate and dramatic scenarios such as being beheaded.[122] The spectral nature of this state gives its expressions an ambiguous valence that lends descriptions of it a poetic touch. But also, because partially heard fragments of music figure regularly in these hallucinations, this between state has found its way into music. The recently nominated genres of Hauntology and Hypnagogic Pop are manifest examples of how music expresses a cultural lull. Both styles refer chiefly to a retro-electronic music steeped in a sensibility for the fictional, or (keeping with the apparitional signifiers) the spectral nature of nostalgia. Specifically, groups like Mordant Music and Pocahaunted mine the past for sounds that act the way Fredric Jameson suggests signifiers in a postmodern age do: they serve as codes for the affections of an era's style that can be "cannibalized" and made into "a field of stylistic and discursive heterogeneity without a norm."[123] While perhaps no different from other postmodernisms that follow a logic of pastiche, what gives these haunted musics their peculiarity is a feeling for what music critic David Keenan calls "wasteland 1980s cultural signifiers."[124] Often drone-heavy and noise-inclined, this music is characterized by a logic of deformation that aims to disfigure without obliterating samples, timbres, and impressions noticeably culled from a musical past that never was. Indulgence in these warped signifiers is what gives the music its spectral identity.

---

[122] See Andreas Mavromatis, *Hypnagogia: The Unique State of Consciousness between Wakefulness and Sleep* (London: Routledge, 1987); and Jeff Warren, "The Hypnopompic," in *The Head Trip: Adventures on the Wheel of Consciousness* (New York: Random House, 2007). Prior to their scientific investigation beginning in the nineteenth century, these oneirogogic images and percepts were elaborated in fantastic terms, often interpreted in a culture's terms of the supernatural. The description of falling asleep given by the narrator in book one of Proust's *À la recherche du temps perdu* is a model illustration of hypnogogia.

[123] Fredric Jameson, *Postmodernism, or, the Cultural Logic of Late Capitalism* (Durham, NC: Duke University Press, 1991), 17.

[124] David Keenan, "Hypnagogic Pop," *The Wire*, August 2009, 29.

Or more pointedly, the sound of this "lo-fi post-noise psychedelia" that blends outmoded media's high noise to signal ratio with an affected anti-virtuosity, performs what is now the clichéd "decon-struction-of-the-original" trick that supposedly "acknowledges pop's hold over us while using it to build an alternative to that reality."[125]

A similar sensibility and fondness for the effects generated by "trailing-edge" technology and non-virtuosity is also realized in contemporary composition; however, the points of nostalgic reference are not quite the same. Rather than sampling 1980s pop culture with contemporary technology, one can hear composers recycling the tropes of experimental art music from the 1950s and 1970s, tropes that Michael Nyman compiled and categorized as "indeterminacy," "process," "ephemerality," and the "non-identity" of a work. But we can also hear the debt to conceptual art and free jazz that helped evolve experimental music in the 1970s into sound art, something that Hauntology and Hypnagogic Pop don't exhibit owing to the rock and dance background of their practitioners. Although their aesthetic sensibilities diverge in many ways, this kind of composition shares with Hauntology and Hypnagogic Pop a kind of sadness or melancholy and a desire to construct an alter-native reality by abstracting the affects from expressions past and showering the listener with their unloosed charm. Turning attention away from the historical depths in which a musical signifier is sunk, and scrambling the customary relationship between a work's formal object and aural symptoms, produces a strange, alluring apparition that "brings objects directly into play by invoking them as dark agents at work beneath those qualities [that express it]."[126] This skewing of the musical object and its qualities is the condition of "charm," and charm's schizogenesis is the condition for the invention of a point, a singular point whose reality revolves around the circulation of its fiction. And this happens not strictly as a matter of pastiche, but also as an effect of one's being continually distracted by the murmuring qualities that these musics bathe us in.

---

[125] Emilie Friedlander, "Horizons: What, If Any, Are the Politics of Hypnagogic Pop?," *Visitation Rites* (2009). http://www.visitation-rites.com/2009/09/ [accessed October 2012].

[126] Harman, *Guerrilla Metaphysics*, 50.

Bangkok-based composer Hugh Peaker writes music that lulls. His work *Species of Space #16* (2009), for instance, hallucinates a world of continuous deformation in which perception twists around its own processes, becoming alternately distracted and attentive in a way that articulates the extremely pliable and supple space of musicalized sound. A slow-moving work (approx 11') with a uniformly soft dynamic throughout and marked by an under-stated but constant and highly intoxicating *glissandi* played by all the non-keyboard instruments,[127] *SoS#16* is scored for a typically contemporary ensemble that mixes classical with electrified instru-ments characteristic of jazz, 1970s pop, and early synth music.[128] Similar in kind to Arnold's *Burrow Music*, which appeals to the habits of listening to recordings in order to make an ambient distraction effective, *SoS#16*'s strategy for leading listening into distraction is to simulate within the fixed space of the concert hall many of the conditions characteristic of background music.

What is notable, or rather, un-notable about background music (BGM) is the way that it works to conceal itself from listening. BGM is hidden not simply by its relatively low volume, but by its constant presence. That is, the continuous broadcast of BGM causes it to be received as the sound of the ocean or freeway traffic is received. Over time acoustic constants are filtered from conscious awareness owing to a process of sensory adaptation, selective attention, and sensory gating. The sounds do not go away or cease to have an effect on the listener. Instead, they are tempered and modulated, appropriated to the wider ecology of one's behaviour, as for instance when one unknowingly raises his or her voice after enduring a noisy commute home or spending an evening at a dance club. But constancy risks invisibility, inaudibility. Like the waterfall, BGM disap-pears into the flow of other activities. To avoid vanishing completely into the background, BGM has to maintain a modest degree of

---

[127] Peaker specifies, for example, that the guitar, bass, and cello, if not indicated by a standard glissando line, always play each pitch with a slide upward of no more than a major second. The flute, which is tuned a quarter tone flat and instructed to treat intonation as an ornament, also plays these continuous *glissandi*.

[128] Specifically, the ensemble is thus: flute, Fender Rhodes, Wurlitzer EP203W Casio PT30 Organ, Amplified Fretless "Jazz" Guitar, Violin, or Viola, or Cello (harmonics only), Cello, and Fretless Electric Bass.

difference. This can be accomplished by canny programming choices that circulate between songs the right amount of acoustic differences to activate the reflex of attention.[129] Or, as Muzak's composers recognized, eliminating certain "harsh" timbres and varying the texture of a work by continually re-orchestrating the same material can effect an uneven continuity that tends to the roots of attention without allowing it to grow any shoots of interest.

SoS#16 incorporates elements of all these techniques but none so much as the principle of variation of the same.[130] The self-similar gestures, non-functional harmony, and directionless melodic fragments played extremely quietly by an ensemble that includes Casio organ, slide electric bass, Wurlitzer, and Rhodes, creates a woolly and undulating musical surface whose appearance is that of a pure, unspecified melodiousness. Peaker likens *SoS#16* to "a biological assembly," suggesting that its "component parts are defined less by rigid metric properties than by connectivity: where the specific shape of a figure is less important than its continuity and sense of connection to the whole."[131] Although descriptions of BGM do not elicit such topological figurations, both it and *SoS#16* cultivate a mode of listening that privileges continuity over specifics. The difference of course is that *SoS#16* is meant-to-be-listened-to and not (merely) heard.

Listening to *SoS#16*'s lull)))))

At first, listening is taken by the surface strangeness of the work. The collective *glissandi* and the sundry sonic artefacts that give the piece its rich and addled colour scheme weave the acoustic

---

[129] (see † **Quantum Modulation**, note 150)

[130] Leonard Meyer argues that variations of the same difference have an effect on listening that disturbs or muddles habits of expectation in *confound* rather than obliterate attention's reflex to build awareness on a perceived change. As such, attention is frustrated not to the point where there is no point—that would be the nirvanic ideal of minimalism—but to the point where its call to action and reaction is deflected towards other "manifestations," manifestations that are not necessarily "musical" or even acoustic. See Meyer, *Emotion and Meaning in Music* (1956).

[131] Hugh Peaker, "Notes to *Species of Spaces #16*," email message to author, 17 March 2010.

equivalent of an impossible figure whose parts are coherent but whose whole is not. To follow anything but the pure continuity of this biomorphic semblance through one fold, stretch, curve, or bend to another is to miss the effect, the effect of being lulled into keeping attention at a low burn, always on, poised: a state of autonomic readiness. Then listening twists around the accumulated sensations and ideations ingredient to its dynamic unfolding, particularly those colliding randomly to form inter- mittent points of interest. It leans into the coming moment's halo of inchoate perceptions where vagueness thickens and focus blurs. Half-formed melodies, intimated harmonies, and budding tensions become the pivots on which listening turns as attention is dimmed in a fog of incipience, its wanders lost in a garden of forking paths. Distraction. *Why am I thinking about my holiday at the ocean? My back is aching. The hydro bill is due tomorrow. I miss her...* Listening: turned inside out and away from the music without ever crossing an edge—lulled.

The drifts of attention, which is to say, the proliferation of distrac- tions that compose the heard surface of *SoS#16*, simulate the experience of "surfing" the web. "Surfing," writes Massumi, "sets up a rhythm of attention and distraction."[132] With each click, as with each pulse of concentration directed towards the coiling surface of *SoS#16*, we "serially experience effects, accumulate them in an unprogrammed way, in a way that intensifies, creating resonances and interference patterns moving through the successive linked appearances." "Link after link," Massumi continues, "we click our way into a lull."[133] This lull is the expression of a "trans- ductive momentum"—the impetus to carry on transitioning—and it accounts for the strange allure of surfing potentiated relays that, despite "the meagerness of the constituent links on the level of formal inventiveness, or uniqueness of content,"[134] compels attention.

SoS#16, too, exhibits a meagerness of formal inventiveness. Enter at any point and be carried along, up, down, side-to-side,

---

[132] Massumi, *Parables*, 139.
[133] Ibid., 138, 139.
[134] Ibid., 141.

forward and back, by the same wobbling rhythm. Turn attention "here," where several *glissandi* swivel around a middle C,[135] and find it seconds later over "there" as I ruminate on how unfairly I judged my friend. In both surfing and listening to *SoS#16*, attention hinges on the strangely active immobility of the body. For as with any restrained activity, such as reading a book, listening to a record, or clicking hyperlinks, the tendency to act on the perceptions that constitute a work's intensive field are "reduced to a minimum and short-circuited by being turned in on the body."[136] The body at rest is only *actually* so:

> Through letters [or in this case, through vibrations] we directly experience fleeting vision-like sensations, inklings of sound, faint brushes of movement. The turning in on itself of the body, its self-referential short-circuiting of outward-projected activity, gives free rein to these incipient actions.[137]

Virtually, the body reposed lives the "charge of nonactuality."[138] Actually listening to *SoS#16* "increases the degree of envelopment of the actual in the nonactual."[139] The more you listen the less you'll (actually) hear. But for Massumi, the vague and "impending moreness" that characterizes internet surfing, as it did television before, occasionally "sharpen[s] into a selective perceptual focus or a clarity of thought that strikes the foreground consciousness in a flash of sudden interest or even revelation."[140] For *SoS#16*, however, attention mostly just lulls. It takes the fog of incipient perceptions as a veritable substance animated by what Massumi, citing Bakhtin, describes as "the feeling of the activity of connecting."[141] *SoS#16* lingers in a cloud of "inklings" that do not sharpen into focus so

---

[135] See, for example, the cello and electric bass parts in excerpt at mm. 9–11.
[136] Massumi, *Parables*, 277, n.13.
[137] Ibid., 139.
[138] Ibid., 277, n.13.
[139] Ibid.
[140] Ibid., 140.
[141] M. M. Bakhtin, "The Problem of Content, Material, and Form in Verbal Art," in *Art and Answerability: Early Philosophical Essays by M. M. Bakhtin*, ed. Michael Holquist and Vadim Laipunov, trans. Vadim Laipunov (Austin: University of Texas Press, 1990), quoted in Massumi, *Parables*, 277, n.10.

Hugh Peaker, from score for *Species of Space (#16)* (2009). Courtesy Hugh Peaker.

much as undergo continuous homeomorphic deformations: warps and wrinkles turning hesitations inside and out and out inside inside out out out...

(((((Listening away)))))

The act of listening away that realizes music as a background phenomenon is closely tied to the nineteenth-century ideal of autonomous concert music. This may seem counterintuitive and historically anachronistic since the concert form premises itself on an explicit act of *listening to* music and is itself preceded by other types of incidental music (e.g. *tafelmusik*).[142] But if you think about the conditions of a concert you will find that it's an enchantment ritual and procedural for conjuring daemons of sound. This ritual requires spells to dampen the affectivity of the body's non-aural senses,[143] and spells to turn attention away from the rebarbative din of everyday life. To realize this form of musical superstition demands that the participant *listen away* from the "accompanying circumstances of the concert institution that contradicts its idea."[144] That is, to realize

---

[142] *Tafelmusik* (table music), which was traditionally performed during or after meals, was in some respects a precursor to Muzak insofar as its songs were perceived for the mood they conjured rather than for the formal relationships they expressed.

[143] The body is what reminds us that we are utterly dependent creatures and it is what we need to be able to experience sound as music in the first place. The body is where our capacity to respond is located. In fact, it could be argued that the body is itself constituted as a site of responses, a nexus of capacities that become focused and directed according to what sets upon it. Bergson makes this point in *Matter and Memory* when alluding to contemporaneous discoveries of the human nervous system:

> If...we cast a glance at the minute structure of the nervous system as recent discoveries have revealed it to us, we see everywhere conducting lines, nowhere any centers. Threads placed end to end, of which the extremities probably touch when the current passes: this is all that is seen. And perhaps this is all there is, if it be true that "the body is only a place of meeting and transfer, where stimulations received result in movements accomplished." (Henri Bergson, *Matter and Memory*, trans. Nancy M. Paul and W. Scott Palmer (London; New York: G. Allen & Co. and The MacMillan Co., 1912), 227.)

[144] Hanns-Werner Heister, "Music in Concert and Music in the Background: Two Poles of Musical Realization," in *Companion to Contemporary Musical Thought*, ed. John Paynter (London: Routledge, 1992), 51.

music as an autonomous activity, an activity wholly separated from the heterogeneous interests of life's clamorous desires and strident demands, one has to actively exercise a practice that "excludes or annuls the 'un-artistic'," or more reasonably, "makes it relative."[145] The concert ritual does this of course through its well-developed ideological summons that invokes the fiction of aesthetic autonomy. However, the ritual is aided by a spatial layout that not only enforces a separation between the site of music's production and its consumption, it also cultivates competing forms of self-consciousness: On stage the musician's sense of self is mediated by acts that compose her as a performer and empower her as an hieratic figure of attention. The listener, on the other hand, is delivered a self through scripted performances of non-acting—namely, acts of shutting up and staying still that establish him as an appendant. This formulary for listening to the liturgic spectacle is also a formulary for listening away from the noise of necessity, away from the racket of socio-economic complexities that both underwrites the concert's autonomy and contradicts its ideals.

There are two points about listening away that can be extrapolated from the above. The first is that both concert music and background music share the same sense. In its concerted mode listening is *not* hearing the "ambient din" while in its more distributed mode what is listened-away-to, what is *not* being heard, is the "musicky" bit. Concert music and background music are privative aspects of the same sense of listening. The second point, though it needs to be explained still, is that both concert and background modes treat music as something autonomous. Despite the sanctity of concert music it shares with background music a genetic trait that Hanns-Werner Heister identifies as the "secular defunctionalization of music."[146] While seemingly remote to one another concert music and background music are genetically related by virtue of their faith in music's "emancipation from its particular aims and usage."[147]

But whereas concert music (CM) realizes its emancipation by raising itself to the level of its culture's ideology of equanimity and

---

[145] Ibid.
[146] Ibid., 55.
[147] Ibid.

fraternity, background music (BGM) effaces those processes that would belie the ideal character of its object through the mediations introduced by the technical reproduction of music. Though these two simulated "autonomies" have different effects, each of which are exploited to different ends—aesthetic and commercial respectively—both CM and BGM revolve around the same indeterminate object whose appearance is ostensibly unencumbered by the murky details of social and historical mores. However, whereas listening in its concerted mode is oriented away from the bodies that produce it and steered towards the effects that flicker over the surface of these (bodies), in its distributed mode listening is inverted and pitched away from these musical effects and guided towards the interaction of bodies. Said another way, CM's listening is centripetal. By isolating bodies and channeling their affectivity to one sensory realm, CM's rituals exorcize those sensations that do not conduce to the realization of its ideal object. Things like "feelings" and change of mood that occur in the vicinity of CM become affective weeds in a conceptual sound garden. BGM's listening on the other hand is centrifugal. It scatters attention across all sensory domains and distributes the semblance of vitality among a host of co-present percepts in a way that "effects a fusional mutual inclusion of a heterogeneity of factors in a signature species of semblance"[148]—listening-feeling.

While both CM and BGM can be understood to express different ideals of musical autonomy, only recorded music wholly excuses music from the specificities of its occasion. That is, recordings allow for musical sounds to sound without concern for what else is taking place around them, so much so that their eidetic autonomy is maintained across even the most dramatic change of events. A recording, for instance, can continue sounding Sinatra's soothing croon unperturbed throughout a gunfight. Bloodied bodies and all, Ol' Blue Eyes keeps on singing. Film often uses precisely this mechanized indifference with striking effect. The opening scene of David Lynch's *Blue Velvet* (1986), in which a schmaltzy pop song expressing the tranquility and continuity of the suburbs ignores the sudden

---

[148] Brian Massumi, *Semblance and Event: Activist Philosophy and the Occurrent Arts* (Cambridge, MA: MIT Press, 2011), 142.

death of a man watering his lawn, creates an affective dissonance between visual and aural cues that establishes the film's ambivalent mood. However, it's not that recording technology accesses a hitherto inaccessible dimension of music inasmuch as it isolates music's capacity to be realized as a purely affective accessory. The "isolated, dull, and unidentified biogenic moments...of 'atmosphere,' charm and feeling"[149] that CM's ritual expels are, for recorded music, particularly when shuttled to the background, absolute content.

Muzak's way[150] of dreaming ubiquitously))))

Through the disarticulating effects and utter ubiquity of sound technologies that permit music, any music, to be everywhere

---

[149] Heister, "Music in Concert," 58.

[150] **Notes on Muzak** "Overstimulated, individuals can no longer be affected by increases in data alone."[150a] Muzak, the much-maligned company whose product has become synonymous with all background music, used to program a playlist according to a formula that it called the "stimulus progression," essentially 15 minutes of increasingly active music followed by 15 minutes of silence. Intended to "offset the decreases in worker efficiency during mid-morning and afternoon slumps[150b] (see also † **Quantum Modulation**), Muzak's sensual caress, like preindustrial "musick" before it, presumed to give the flux of things a temporal fix that could be modulated in order to affect one's mood and thereby counteract the workday's lethargic trajectory. So more than simply a pleasing background additive, Muzak, writes musicologist Ronald Radano, "aims to portray [its product] as a psychologically active, sonic accompaniment, carefully designed to remain below the threshold of common attention."[150c] Yet in addition to meddling with one's physiological potentials, Muzak also nurtures another dimension of affect. In programming popular songs—denuded instrumental versions in particular—it assumes a pre-existing psychic consensus that "massifies symbolism in which not few but all can participate."[150d] But this consensus is neither conspicuous nor evident, for "The net effect [of background music] is an anonymous sound field seemingly devoid of directly perceivable musical meaning."[150e] In a sense, the shared meaning of Muzak's "massified symbolism" requires collective discretion, perhaps, paradoxically, wholesale ignorance to realize its consensus. In this way the insensible symbolism that Muzak fabricates cannot help but solicit comparison to Freud's theory of the unconscious whose power derives from the very fact of its concealment. As a catholic symbolism, the wallflower of Muzak can only be dreamt. If it truly encourages all to participate, then it can only do so as a reverie whose condensations and displacements work anonymously to distract one from the "pre-cognitive 'corporeal techniques' that register a concern for the body,"[150f]

concerns like those appearing in repetitive and tedious jobs—"an arm lowered at the wrong time, a slower step, a second's irregularity, an awkward gesture, getting ahead, slipping back."[150g]

These organismic intrusions, what Freud calls "instincts" and which he ties to the drives and their affective structures,[150h] are precisely what the refrains of all background music aim to discipline, to opiate. Yet ironically, the incessancy and the low-level intensity intended by the company to tranquilize these signs of life in revolt—life's creative advance—actually have the effect of multiplying them, but *only in their incipiency*. By producing conventionally arranged versions of familiar tunes whose unabashed transparency "minimizes the introduction of new...musical stimuli," and by "broadcasting continually and quietly below the dynamic level of normal speech, [which] 'hides' [its sound] from the listener," Muzak creates what Radano calls "a framework for simple being."[150i] "The internalized language of Muzak," of consensus music—our shared reverie—he says, "establishes [a] sonic order, [that] induces the individual, alone or in a group, to let the mind wander where it pleases, to respond to stimuli in a multitude of ways."[150j] In other words, the anarchy of sensation is succored and managed so "the individual is free to think, to rhapsodize, to create, to worry, to wonder."[150k] Sensuous attenuation it would seem makes the mind comes to life. However, the nature of these rhapsodic mentations is such that they remain undetermined. Like a dream, which is a fleeting series of acausal images—impressions whose possibilities remain bundled in potential—our responses are pinched at the moment of emergence. But as Brian Massumi contends, these unconsummated re/actions are not unreal; they are incipient perceptions, "a turning in on itself of the body's activity, so that the activity is not extended toward an object but knots at its point of emergence."[150l] So while Muzak "places the responsibility for creating a meaningful experience in the realm of the receiver,"[150m] it only lets one dream these experiences rather than live them.

[150a] Robert Sumrell and Kazys Varnelis, *Blue Monday: Stories of Absurd Realities and Natural Philosophies* (Barcelona: Actar Editorial, 2007), 124.

[150h] Ibid., 115.

[150c] Radano, "Interpreting Muzak," 450.

[150d] Dr. James Keenen, Chairman of Muzak's Board of Scientific Advisors, quoted in Sumrell and Varnelis, *Blue Monday*, 118.

[150e] Radano, "Interpreting Muzak," 450.

[150f] Ben Anderson, "Time-Stilled Space-Slowed: How Boredom Matters," *Geoforum* 35 (2004): 749.

[150g] Robert Linhart quoted in Ben Highmore, *Everyday Life and Cultural Theory: An Introduction* (London; New York: Routledge, 2002), 160.

[150h] See Sigmund Freud's "Instincts and their Vicissitudes," 111–40, in *The Standard Edition of the Complete Psychological Works of Sigmund Freud*, vol. 14, ed. James Strachey (New York: Norton, 1957 [1915]).

[150i] Radano, "Interpreting Muzak," 451, 452, 457.

[150j] Ibid., 457.

[150k] Ibid.

[150l] Massumi, *Parables*, 139.

[150m] Radano, "Interpreting Muzak," 457.

† **Quantum Modulation** During the early 1990s, Muzak developed a programming logic in order to differentiate their original artist-recording soundtrack from common radio playlists. Unlike the stimulus progression, whose logic revolved around

manipulating an individual's mood over an extended period of time by gradually introducing more energetic music, quantum modulation focuses on the production of continuity and "maintaining a flow that does not vary in 'intensity'."[ta] Whereas the stimulus progression might be thought to create a wave of musical energies on which a person's affectivity rides, quantum modulation can be understood as generating homeostasis by virtue of the way some songs share an intensive affinity. In a sense, quantum modulation is Muzak's response to the way in which it posited that contemporary listeners are more commonly hearing music the way they read traffic signs—namely, in passing. Arguably, people no longer stay with music long enough to be affected (their movements or mood) by gradual or progressive changes in tempo, melody, rhythm. Modulation now comes in discrete packets, in "quanta." What happens, specifically from Muzak's point of view, is that listening in packets "primes" perception; that is, the listener's hearing and forthcoming attention—and presumably desire—are conditioned by the non-conscious rehearsal and potentiation of perception during what psychologists call "attentional blink." Here, the micro-events that populate this fractional pause in awareness have the capacity to modulate the formation of a coming perception. Brian Massumi's examination of this phenomenon distinguishes "priming" from the more familiar notion of subliminal influence, writing that priming "conditions emergent awareness...rather that causing a response (repro-ducing a preexisting model)...it implies complex thought-like processes occurring as a nonconscious dimension of emergent perception."[tb] In other words, priming describes an unconscious and creative preparation by the nervous system that modifies, without causing or determining, the intensity and significance of a coming perception. Thus, insofar as "attentional blink" arises "between successive changes in the perceptual field,"[tc] and musical sounds literally constitute such a field, the act of hearing music is rife with primes. This is doubly so, first in the way that change is immanent to and constitutive of a musical field—i.e. change in harmony, tempo, orchestration, as well as the basic developmental envelope that describes the event of a single tone—which thereby necessarily includes a series of "blinks" that prime the coming perceptions which compose what is called "the music itself"; and second, in the way that musical sound—as a medium whose materiality implicates itself in the processes of awareness that are had through it"[td]—introduces a change in the larger perceptual field of haptic, osmic, and interio-proprioceptive sensations that constitute yet another series of blinks and primes that modulate the way a perception and desire will emerge.

For music to affect perception in a culture where attention is more commonly defined by its division and switchiness, it (music) has not to cut so deeply into the already scored fabric of daily awareness, but to cut quickly and decisively. Musical sound has to introduce a change that will open a gap in a rapidly shifting and only partially active attention where its structures can be "pre-rehearsed on the noncon-scious level in the form of emergent patterns."[te] By opening a gap where its sounds can be interpellated into the dimensions of priming, background music disposes perception to the peculiarities of the way it acts as structured and structuring medium, peculiarities that Shepherd and Wicke argue are specific to how musical sounds are materially involved in calling forth and binding with states of awareness, especially affective states, that become elements of signification in a symbolic universe of differ-ential attraction.[tf] Thus, musical priming has a different effect from other perceptual phenomena in that it conditions perception to develop or advance along lines which elaborate the isomorphic relation that musical sounds have with affective states. This

and nowhere, one is able, or indeed, one is compelled to fold the numerous refrains encountered into the routines of everyday life. This does not necessarily make ours a more musical culture, for

---

is similar to Susanne Langer's theory of "semblance," which sees artworks offering to perception nonsensuous—i.e abstract—forms of feeling that are "free from their normal embodiment in real things so that they may be recognized [grasped] in their own right."[g] What differs here is that semblance, the virtual or abstract form of feeling is nuanced to encompass everyday perception of music rather than the concerted interactions that one may have with musical sound.

The semblance that takes off from musical sounds, that magical "quality without practical significance,"[h] is precisely what is sought out, cultivated, and negotiated by listeners in everyday life. But outside of the concert hall or some other staged listening environment, this intense abstraction tends to "slip behind the behind the flow of action and is only implicitly felt."[i] Typically semblances only subsist for perception lured into a frame of focus where an artwork's relation of implications can be presented as a symbol of the life of feeling. Being distracted then would seem to preclude the perception of a semblance. However, Muzak showed a way to indirectly access musical semblance using a technique the company calls "Atmospherics." Shifting from their outmoded stimulus progression that requires long-term listening wherein one's mood is gradually modulated by slowly increasing the intensity of the music on the playlist, Muzak developed a way to qualify a retail space by quantifying various musical criteria like "rhythm, tempo, title, artist, era, genre, instrumentation, and popularity."[j] By indexing these values and compositing a playlist where "the same intensity can be maintained even as the music appears to have changed,"[k] Muzak's soi-disant "Sonic Architects" devised a way to compose volumes of acoustic space with "an absolutely consistent identity and unchanging mood."[l] The uniform intensity of works and a cleaver use of cross-fading seamlessly connects different songs while giving the impression of change serves to prime perception in a way that inclines the affections of the itinerant and intermittent listener towards the affections that the retailer imagines that its products can induce. The important thing to take from this is that quantum modulation aims to modulate the interests that guide perception by introducing a discrete change in the perceptual field—from the general din of mall traffic to the focused drive of a techno beat—that will condition the way attention may unfold, and, ideally the way future feelings may be felt.

[a] Sterne, "Sounds Like the Mall of America," 32.
[b] Massumi, "Perception Attack," n. 3.
[c] Ibid.
[d] John Shepherd and Peter Wicke, *Music and Cultural Theory* (Cambridge: Polity Press, 1997), 108–24.
[e] Massumi, "Perception Attack," n. 3.
[f] Shepherd and Wicke, op. cit.
[g] Susanne Langer, *Feeling and Form* (New York: Charles Scribner's Sons, 1953), 50.
[h] Ibid., 51.
[i] Brian Massumi, *Semblance and Event*, 45.
[j] Sterne, "Sounds Like the Mall of America," 32.
[k] Goodman, *Sonic Warfare*, 144.
[l] Sterne, "Sounds Like the Mall of America," 32.

like so much of everyday life, we learn how to forget the refrains that give us our sense of interiority and which steer us through the blooming buzzing confusion. Like our spatial layouts, music's omnipresence has become, like architecture, "soluble by apperception." The mode of listening constitutive of BGM's privative autonomy—listening away to BGM—is not a new habit but a more public and shared habit. As Daniel Goodman has argued, inattentive listening has been a well-established convention since at least the 1930s as radio became more intimately implicated in domestic social affairs.[151] What has changed is the number of occasions in which listening away must be exercised and the normalization of a monadic sociality, a sociality expressive of individuals collectively listening away to music, as for instance happens everyday at countless coffee shops when a crowd of persons "harmonize" their self-absorption. Anahid Kassabian's notion of "ubiquitous listening" addresses this situation of omnipresent musical sounds by attending to the manners and the effects of listening away. For her, "ubiquitous listening" characterizes how continuous exposure to music breeds a mode of audition that "tak[es] place without calling conscious attention to itself as an activity in itself."[152] This un-listening is done most often on those occasions when "we listen 'alongside' or simultaneous with other activities,"[153] such as when we cook, shop, shower, drive, type, take a commercial break, or are placed on hold.[154] Under these conditions music becomes little more than a vital semblance keeping company with the drought of routine and the irritation of being between things.

But ubiquitization isn't exactly new. As noted, recording technology has been disarticulating listening from its conditions of production for decades. This has not only made music a commodity by giving

---

[151] See David Goodman, "Distracted Listening: On Not Making Sound Choices in the 1930s," in *Sound in the Era of Mechanical Reproduction*, ed. David Suisman and Susan Strasser (Philadelphia: University of Pennsylvania Press, 2010), 15–46.

[152] Kassabian, "Ubisub."

[153] Ibid.

[154] Kassabian has applied the notion of inattentive listening and ubiquitous subjectivity to so-called "world music" whose conspicuous placement in coffee shops articulates what she calls "distributed tourism." See Anahid Kassabian, "Would You Like Some World Music with Your Latte? Starbucks, Putumayo, and Distributed Tourism," *Twentieth Century Music* 2, no. 1 (2004).

it a form that can be exchanged (LP, CD, cassette, mp3 file), but has had the effect of making music something increasingly sourceless and thereby dismissible and/or easily ignored. Neither the form nor the content necessarily matters for recorded music: Only volume matters. All styles and genres can function equally well as an acoustic background provided they ease the daily hell of other people and help fill out the liminal spaces that make up more of life than we care to admit. Music's ubiquity has turned its sounds into a "form of phatic communication [whose] purpose is to keep the lines of communication open for that lumpy deployment of dense nodes of knowledge/power we call selves."[155] Musical sounds work now to keep our selves from drying out in the arid isolation of our contiguous self-interests. But as Baudrillard reminds us, "the medium and the real are now in a single nebula whose truth is indecipherable."[156] There is no longer a discernible difference between background and foreground, between phatic expressions and informative ones. So if neither background nor foreground, then music, in its ubiquitous phase, is more like a membrane or affective film that cleaves the desires of our private realities and public worlds to one another. From room to room, home to work, office to concert, lobby to pub, taxi to bed, we pass dreamily through several skins of musical "hellos."

We don't (((listen))) anymore

Or at least we don't pay the kind of attention to musical sound that (it's been suggested) we used to. The evidence of this might be the rise of AD(H)D (attention-deficit hyperactivity disorder) and strangely, the increasing prevalence of time-based art. We can't, however, as the patrons of good taste or defenders against false consciousness do, blame this entirely on BGM. Although BGM is reviled among critics and musicians, BGM in general is in fact a more fully-developed expression of musical autonomy than CM in that it unhinges music's occasion absolutely from any specific

---

[155] Kassabian, "Ubisub."
[156] Baudrillard, *Simulacra and Simulation*, 83.

or special time and/or place as well as from any particular use or meaning. The iPod (among other sundry audio devices) realizes this potential just as BGM and differs from it only insofar as the latter wears its commercial interests and capital letters (™) a little higher on its sleeve. What seems to bother people about the BGM industry—though really "those people" are mostly musicians and music critics who are threatened by the way musical taste develops in relation to MTV, video games, and more recently, internet radio's algorithmic "recommender systems" that predict musical preferences based on user profiles and past selections (e.g., Last.fm and Pandora Radio)—is that it appears to evacuate music of its objective *and* subjective profiles. It's not the liquefaction of the "personal, idiosyncratic, and human qualities of authenticity, of originality"[157] that disturbs people, it is that the specifically *affective* potential realized by music's withdrawal from the foreground and its sinking into shadow makes it *feel* like an anonymous matter that is indifferent to our personal investments. Hate is not the opposite of love, indifference is. Lack of interest or sympathy is vastly more offensive and hurtful.

* * *

Essentially an extension and transfiguration of McLuhan's speculations on how technology adjusts the ratio of our sensory media and how sound technology promises to recover something of the auditory and proprioceptive realms occluded by print media, our musically saturated environment teaches us, through habit, how to reacquaint ourselves with patterns of change and the pervasive quality that is expressive of its occasion. This privative mode of listening is, however, difficult to isolate in itself, for its expressions are obscured by the way its acts draw attention to elements of a situation that are not conventionally "musical" but are nevertheless, like the practicable potentials of an architectural array, what Seth Kim-Cohen might call its "non-cochlear" factors.[158]

---

[157] Radano, "Interpreting Muzak," 452.
[158] Seth Kim-Cohen, *In the Blink of an Ear: Toward a Non-cochlear Sonic Art* (London and New York: Continuum, 2009).

Listening ubiquitously is not exactly something that is done. It is something that is "undone" so that music can behave as "a quality of the environment,"[159] an environment that is not "there" before its musicalization but which only appears so due to the way awareness comes only after we've attuned to the lure of things that populate our field of perception. In this sense, ubiquitous listening makes music virtually imperceptible, and any music is welcome. For so long as the semblance of vital activity that a music expresses satisfies a mood, musical sounds escape the capture of genre—the habits of form—and become instead an affective residue that thurifies the affairs of the occasion. But curiously, to listen ubiquitously is to habituate hearing, and because habits are what bind us to a particular set of behaviours, and thereby to specific orders of class and moral aptitude, ubiquitous listening has the effect of formal-izing an apparent formlessness. But (again), and more curiously, in becoming habitually ubiquitous, listening away forgets its own (un)form like breathing forgets air, and in this way regains something of its formless operation.

The (((sound))) of habits

Paul Harrison suggests that habits are an individual's and culture's "enunciative frame," an armature of capacities "defin[ing] what it is possible to see and to say."[160] Habits are eminently enabling. They are responses to the task of becoming that we may think of as what an organism is—namely, habits are the ways for life to be accom-plished, to be effective. Yet at the same time, while habits enable, the field of action and meaning that they organize diminishes "the potential, or virtuality, of the body to do things otherwise."[161] Habits make life possible, but at the cost of restricting the range of the life that can be lived. But Gail Weiss, drawing on the work of Deleuze and Merleau-Ponty, conceives of habits as expressions of an organism's

[159] Kassabian, "Ubisub."
[160] Paul Harrison, "Making Sense: Embodiment and the Sensibilities of the Everyday," *Environment and Planning D: Society and Space* 18, no. 4 (2000): 506.
[161] Ibid.

power to connect and reconnect inventively with the world. "Habits," she writes,

> do not mire human beings in the world or even in its given habitus; rather, they allow…new syntheses to be established between the body and its world, syntheses that are passive to the extent that they express a dynamic engagement with the world.[162]

But it is also the nature of habit, the habit of habit, to disappear in its contraction. Indeed, to contract a habit is already to be dwelling within a field of sense. The pathways in which one's actions cleave to the world merge with the gestures and forms of conduct that express habit's occasion. In a sense, the behaviors that manifest the contraction of habit make habit illegible as such. Only by interruption or through the ill fit of actions to a given situation are the lines of behaviour read as habit and not simply conduct. Indeed, Deleuze argues that we are composed mostly of molecularized habits and that "We speak of our 'self' only in virtue of these thousands of little witnesses which contemplate within us."[163] However, despite its illegibility, habits always affect behaviour by mannering the ways in which one actualizes a world. In other words, infra-legibility habits modalize experience by making reality forever affected. Habits: expressive drifts of difference over time in the delirium of an abstract real. I write "drift" here because habits, while a type of vital sediment that grows things like "styles" and "institutions," draw their power, their affect, and their efficacy from the very difference that they, as delimiting forms, contemplate. This is to say that habits also change.

It of course is its own kind of habit to say that we use music to make us feel a certain way, or to understand how to feel feelings. This is to say that it is a cliché to take the intensities of music and in-fold them into our bodies as habits, affective habits. But even habits have to be maintained and the repetition that breeds habits also exhausts them. Deleuze is clear about this, stating that

---

[162] Gail Weiss, *Refiguring the Ordinary* (Bloomington: Indiana University Press, 2008), 90.
[163] Gilles Deleuze, *Difference and Repetition* (New York: Columbia University Press, 1994), 74.

difference inhabits repetition and that "habit *draws* something new from repetition—namely difference."[164] Thus while habits are contracted by circumscribing a difference internal to repetition, a difference that makes a difference effective, the same force of repetition attenuates this same habit's enablement. Every occasion in which habit would contract a certain range of actions introduces another difference that gradually dislocates the efficacy of that habit. Habit, if we recall Weiss's thought, is the expression of a power to connect with a world of difference and to draw effective relays from it. Habit is therefore a veritable force of consistency that operationalizes delirium.

Ubiquitous listening is a contemporary habit that is unconsciously exhibited and reinforced by contemporary (un)listeners. And like any habit, its subliminal modifications make it a skill for negotiating the swerves of difference that its very forgetting remainders. The fidgets, twitches, cramps, yawns, and partial awareness that accompany ubiquitous listening are reminders of a vital capacity, reminders that cultural geographer Ben Anderson calls "pre-cognitive 'corporeal techniques'" that "register a concern for the body in action and consequently act to make the present moment, the 'now' of lived experience, habitual once-again."[165] Accordingly, ubiquitous listening can perhaps be thought of as the contemporary subject's task, a task to contract habits of listening to *difference*, not the kind of difference that rolls out themes and variations, but the differences that are co-present with these, differences like a growing hunger or the changing temperature—that are usually backgrounded when listening attentively but nevertheless continue to affect how one perceives and takes account of a musical occasion. Putting listening aside is how one (un)listens to difference as such.

Somewhere, always, an iPod is shuffling, a record is spinning, a radio is transmitting, a television is airing, or a cellphone is ringing. Music is everywhere, splendidly indifferent to its being heard or not. On desktops, secreted in ceilings, tucked under car seats, or buried in ears, a multitude of speakers amplify—"express"—the

---

[164] Ibid., 73.
[165] Anderson, "Time-Stilled Space-Slowed," 749.

internal principle of activity that determines the perceptions and appetites of each and every musical atom. As an artificially pervasive occurrence composed of songs, tunes, compositions, jingles, ditties, airs, strains, flourishes, each automated and sounded according to its own immanent principles of change, ubiquitous music is the obscure substance and hermetic form through which a discontinuous monadological being exists and communicates. The artificial medium of ubiquitous, mechanized music mediates ways of being, ways of being in a mode of listening. While this concept of medium as an artificial vehicle for being has been rehearsed to death, it is overlooked and under-explored as a factor of desire.

Artifice and the artificial

What more suitable candidate could there be to replace Plato's "chair" than MIDI-instruments? MIDI-instruments are not just that much more removed from reality than the carpenter's, the painter's, or poet's chair; they are of another reality all together. Or at least that is how Brooklyn-based composer Quentin Tolimieri treats them. Indebted equally to the erudite aesthetics of Michael Finnissy and the farcical methods of Thelonious Monk, Tolimieri has made MIDI instruments the principal reality of his musical world. "In recent years," he writes, "I have been focused, primarily, on composing multi-channel works of electronic music that utilize, for their timbral material, fairly simplistic and rudimentary MIDI instruments."[166] Continuing: "I am attracted to these instruments for a variety of reasons, not least of which is their feeling of being, in some sense, cast off, of being a kind of detritus, of being, at first glance, seemingly unfit for the production of serious music."[167] Unfit, cast off, a kind of detritus: judgements expressive of an encounter with productive norms that Tolimieri identifies with the practice of composing "serious music." But his attraction to

---

[166] Quentin Tolimieri, "Text," http://www.quentintolimieri.com/text.html [accessed May 2012].
[167] Ibid.

MIDI instruments arises from something much more interesting and curious than a simple opposition between the serious and the trivial. He writes, "Foremost among my reasons for using these MIDI instruments is their essential artificialness. This artificialness is, in my work, held in contrast to a musical language that is mainly concerned with, for lack of a better word, a kind of 'humanness.'"[168]

The quality of Tolimieri's MIDI instruments is immediately recognizable by their low fidelity and completely un-nuanced simulation of acoustic instruments. His contrasting this quality with what he reluctantly calls a quality of humanness, delimits a structural scheme in which a body is seen to revolve around its opposing capacities of elegance and clumsiness. Tolimieri suggests that historically, gracefulness is the capacity "toward which [music's] gestural languages should aspire."[169] But, Tolimieri insists, this is not the real life of the body; it is an ideal. The "real body" is "a body that can trip, fall over, stutter, lose track of itself and fall apart."[170] The capacity to be inept is, while not strictly human, distinctive of the species. Yet neither of these capacities is "the real body," they are simply different modes of being a body. Tolimieri's interest in "a body that is essentially clumsy"[171] effectively makes the expression of failings something towards which his music aspires.

In his work *Josef, Lieber Josef Mein* (2007), Tolimieri takes the simple lyricism and modal harmony of the German folk carol and subjects it to a series of transformations that are expressive of a gestural repertoire delineated by error and blunder. Performed entirely by MIDI instruments projected loudly and separately through six closely-placed speakers, we hear thirty-eight minutes of an affected instrumental chatter in which the original song appears as an intermittent gestalt. As "a kind of counterpoint in which the individual voice and the resultant whole are, to some extent, at odds with each other,"[172] Tolimieri's *Josef* is the very antithesis of

---

[168] Ibid.
[169] Ibid.
[170] Ibid.
[171] Ibid.
[172] Tolimieri, email message to author, 28 April 2009.

gracefulness. None of the parts harmonize or cooperate with each other to declaim with any elegance the tonal relationships that form the melodic and harmonic complexion of the song. Its voices are awkward and cumbersome, gauche, and klutzy. In its arc of many blunders, *Josef* devotes itself to "a series of failures, of accommodations, of provisional attempts"[173] that exposes a pertinacious sincerity at the heart of artifice.

What ought to stand for artifice—the contrived and affected—is recast in *Josef, Lieber Josef Mein* as an exaggeratedly "natural" state, a state that is, paradoxically, accomplished by Tolimieri's own affectations of failure. Strikingly similar to Colin Nancarrow's exploitation of the player piano's artificial nimbleness that allowed him to realize a kind of inhuman music, Tolimieri uses the semblable features of MIDI-technology to produce the appearance of a slack and sloppy performance that is supposed to exemplify the more quotidian awkwardness of human activity. Yet, because the MIDI parts in *Josef* are neither improvised nor randomized, but painstakingly composed, the precision with which each instrument commits to its own idiosyncratic manner of realizing the material—be it a tendency to drag the beat, play the wrong note(s), noodle around with the melody, play out of time and/or out of tune—strains the categorial integrity of both natural and artificial expressions. Tolimieri's wonderfully cockamamie rendition of *Josef, Lieber Josef Mein*, marked by a miscellany of staged musical failings, achieves a peculiar technological grace that undermines and ultimately exposes its own sense of natural clumsiness as an accomplished ideal.

It can be suggested that clumsiness and grace, like noise and music, share the same genetic conditions and that only according to their degree of involvement in a certain adventure of becoming are these conditions expressed as one or the other. But in his attempt to actively articulate the effects of error and to thereby simulate a corporeal logic of hesitation and ineptitude, Tolimieri confounds the processes of listening that would incline one to hear a series of "failures" as either a graceful adaptation to hostile circumstances or a clumsy parade of incompetencies. Clumsy as a stable category in

---

[173] Ibid.

this situation disappears from the scene, but so, too, does grace. Each lives virtually in the other's field and takes turns becoming the other's theme.

)))) Desire and dissatisfaction

Josef, Lieber Josef Mein's mannered clumsiness makes the work "exist as if it were music and at the same time as if it were noise."[174] Like the categorial conflicts that both sap and energize the valence of noise music, *Josef*'s ambivalent gestural language enjoys the pleasure of being both comical and charming. But not because its insouciant style alternates between careless indulgence and nimble decadence, so much as it refuses to satisfy the occasion of judgement that would qualify one or the other. This ambivalence implies a kind of aurally-articulated desire that invents a perceptual space adjacent to the burdens of taste. By declining to endorse the presumed inevitability of perceptions that present themselves as though they were the necessary result of contingent, historical processes, that the work's gestural semblance must me heard as either "clumsy" or "graceful," *Josef, Lieber Josef Mein* strikes upon an experiential discontent that is acted out in as a dissatisfaction with the world of experience as it is commonly received, especially a world under the rubric of "facts." This dissatisfaction revolves around the premise that perceptions are not neutral but possess a rhetorical force that places pressure on the perceiver to endorse or affirm their reality. In the case of "fact perception" this pressure is particularly intense, for facts are tied to epistemes in which their givenness is normative, "normative not only of actions, but of likes and dislikes, thoughts and feelings."[175] The attempt to escape from this pressure, if only for a moment, by turning away from the world as it is given and cultivating an attraction towards "perceptions that seem below or marginal to normal appearance,"[176] constitutes a practice that Rei Terada names "phenomenophilia."

---

[174] Hegarty, "General Ecology of Sound."
[175] Terada, *Looking Away*, 3.
[176] Ibid.

In its simplest form, phenomenophilia describes a desire for perceptual encounters that do not have a place in *any* semiotic field whatsoever by virtue of the transience and insignificance of the experience. In this respect, phenomenophilia has resonances with "the romantic and post-romantic discourse of mere appearance."[177] But its want for appearance qua appearance does not presume to confront or deny dominant perceptual regimes as the Romantics and their avant-garde spawn do. Instead, the phenomenophile exhibits a kind of "queer desire" that reflects a solipsistic appetite for perceptual experiences that "no one can be imagined to share, appropriate, benefit from, or push one to endorse."[178] "The beauty of phenomenophilia," writes Terada, "is the mirror image of Kant's proto-communitarian beauty," a somewhat asocial beauty that contrasts with the traditional and coercive notion that "the perceiver must feel as though everyone should agree that the object of contemplation is beautiful."[179] Phenomenophilia therefore consists in flirting with "offbeat" perceptions and delighting in a quasi-beauty that cannot be shared or simply, does not *have* to be shared. "The most transient perceptual objects come to be loved because only they seem capable of noncoercive relation."[180] But importantly, phenomenophilia is also characterized by a feeling of guilt or shame, a feeling that one should not be or does not have the right to be fascinated with such asocial perceptions. The artistic costs, which is to say the Kantian communitarianism of aesthetic experience, are decisive in this respect, for insofar as the normative prescriptions of "art" rely on the objectification and, in principle, the shareability of a thing's aesthetic properties, looking or listening away from shared perceptions exempts the offbeat from becoming "art." One's pocket involvements may be aesthetic, but their hermetic nature precludes them from being "art."

Though rife with acoustic artefacts and tendential disappointments that would make its dynamic unfolding delight the phenomenophile, *Josef, Lieber Josef Mein* is perhaps too explicit in its discontent with

---

177 Ibid., 4.
178 Ibid., 6.
179 Ibid., 23.
180 Ibid., 4.

the given world of musical grace that it misses the distinctive diffidence that typifies the practice of phenomenophilia. Indeed, while Tolimieri asserts that *Josef* is concerned with the perceptual dross of MIDI instruments, he also claims to be "interested in the creation of a musical space wherein an ambiguity can exist in the relationship between part and whole."[181] As Terada notes, "Unlike straightforward derogations of the given world that believers in *another* reality feel free to express," phenomenophilic dissatisfaction "insinuates a reservation it never articulates."[182] Tolimieri is not reserved. He wants to create a new dimension of perception (albeit a dimension defined by its perpetual ambiguity). What distinguishes phenomenophilia from *Josef, Lieber Josef Mein*'s perceptual and even anti-hermeneutic aspirations is an attitude that fails to either affirm or deny (which is to negatively assert) the world as given, but simply aims, without any sense of a right to, "to be relieved…of fact perception's demand and the normative concepts that go with it."[183] This is a tactic of withdrawal and it is crucial to the practice of phenomenophilia, for it articulates a dissatisfaction that one feels *no right to express*. The phenomenophile can only insinuate dissatisfaction. "In looking away there is neither a perceived right nor an imperative to negation, only an awkward silence suspending negation and affirmation."[184] This means that music aiming to create phenomenophilic effects is in a sense flummoxed and discomposed by its own hopes of being (non)music, for (non)music is itself a thing, a reification of certain facts about sound and listening that cannot help but oblige an endorsement from the listener. To step outside this process of reification and the pressure of facts is, however, impossible. But Terada remarks that the "very desire to withdraw from what [one] perceives is worthy of respect, and this desire does not need to be linked to any future possibility."[185]

Phenomenophilia relinquishes the will to art: "Looking away rests content with evanescent perception that cannot be shared, and

---

[181] Tolimieri, email message to author, 28 April 2009.
[182] Terada, *Looking Away*, 24.
[183] Ibid., 187.
[184] Ibid., 188.
[185] Ibid., 29.

lets the chance at art go."[186] This is something that Hegarty echoes throughout *Noise/Music*, but makes explicit when writing about the ecstatic aspirations of a certain species of free jazz. He suggests that "the 'freeing up' that comes out fleetingly in the experience of 'freeing up' music" indicates an attempt to surpass the limits of individual or collective expression.[187] This is self-defeatingly premised on "the gain of subjectivity," but it can still, Hegarty continues, "signal the limits of the mundane world [of fact] in trying to leave that world behind."[188] Thus "its failure is a sovereign one, a worthwhile one that remains impossible to quantify or value."[189]

Yet, Terada notes, "artists are always pulling phenomenophilic tricks,"[190] and so their work might be thought of as activating perceptions that take place alongside the unavoidable affirmation of their art. That is, composers like Tolimieri (and several of the others discussed here) attempt to invent from within the coercive gaze of art occasions for perceiving, or side-perceiving, that are "aesthetic without being artistic."[191] Though the perceptions seen/heard by looking/listening away can never be "art" without compromising their "unfactive" and thus non-coercive nature, they can occur as a background of quasi-perceptions surrounding art's optimally resolved forms. To speak then of an aesthetic that belongs to the "listened away to" is to summon the image of a divided attention where one half-visits the shapes and forms that crystallize in and as music's sensuous object, while the other cavorts with the ambient affections and "clouds of qualities surrounding such an object."[192] In a sense, an aesthetics of listening away is an aesthetics of distraction, for you can never listen directly to(wards) a work's strangeness, to what Graham Harman describes as "a black noise of muffled objects hovering at the fringes of our attention,"[193] you can only listen to the side of it, *to the form (object) that it is not*, where your satisfactions flourish, illegitimately, behind your back.

---

[186] Ibid., 174.

[187] Crowley and Hegarty, *Formless*, 47.

[188] Ibid.

[189] Ibid.

[190] Terada, *Looking Away*, 174.

[191] Ibid.

[192] Harman, *Guerrilla Metaphysics*, 183.

[193] Ibid.

So while Tolimieri's defamiliarization of *Josef, Lieber Josef Mein*'s standard melodic and harmonic tropes certainly evokes the kind of divided listening that, in its dissection, makes the things that happen to the side of it shine a little brighter, it lacks the hesitancy and internalized intolerance that marks the phenomenophile's conviction that he has "'no right'...to his dissatisfaction."[194] In Tolimieri's work, the charm of a perceptual ambivalence seems always in usufruct to concert music's traditional role as an autonomous object and is thereby entitled to its culturally and historically accumulated transports. This makes *Josef* perhaps too confident of its diversions and marvels so as to disqualify its strangeness from articulating the self-sensed intolerance that the phenomenophile has for being "attracted to the way things appear to him, to his own awareness *that* they appear to him."[195]

A better example of this phenomenophilic diffidence can be heard in the work of Toronto composer John Mark Sherlock. Informed by the same experimentalist sensibilities that pervade Arnold's, Peaker's, and Tolimieri's music (though displaying a stronger commitment to the abstractions and almost anti-melodic tendencies that characterize Morton Feldman's brand of experimentalism), Sherlock's music exhibits a palpable compunction or even contrition that is arguably connected to the cultural malaise that I discussed in the first chapter. However, there is something more dour than resigned in his work, something almost rueful: "After things were completely dismantled by the music of the 1950s and 1960s," says Sherlock, "we don't have much left to work with without treading over the same ground: post-modernism? I'm just holding on to the floating detritus; the flotsam remaining after it all went down."[196] *one more day in the empire* (2006), like many of Sherlock's compositions, is scored for variable instrumentation. And like many more of his works, it is designed to stage its own failure. In essence, Sherlock's compositions are recipes for disaster. But they're strangely quite harmless disasters. Almost all of his pieces are deceptively innocuous looking: a single

---

[194] Terada, *Looking Away*, 24.

[195] Ibid., 22, my emphasis.

[196] John Mark Sherlock, Interview with Otino Corsano, ARTPOST.info—The Art Information Portal for Galleries and Art Buyers, 2006. http://www.neithernor.com/sherlock11/?page_id=15 [accessed October 2012].

time signature (usually ¾), a grand staff, eighth-notes, quarter-notes, grace-notes, rests, and all without dynamic markings. The instructions, however, complicate this:

1   Players may play any, all, or none of the notes.

2   Although the tempo should be close to that marked, precise alignment of various instruments in time is not necessary. If one player is still playing after the others finish, that player should play out to the end.

3   Players need not rehearse together even if they choose to rehearse on their own.

4   Any instrument may play—and it would be desirable that they do so—any note as a harmonic either at pitch or in a different octave, *ad libitum*, with some restraint.

5   Please do not improvise pitches or durations. Grace notes going to nowhere can be treated as light *staccati* or *tenuti*.

6   Dynamics are free but should not exceed *mezzoforte*.

7   Email sherlock@neithernor.com for further clarification. There is a chance that you may not receive a response. In that case proceed as you would with a dead composer.[197]

The result is almost always the same: The musicians are confused. Their individual part is the score, which invariably has too many pitches for any one instrument to play (some of which occasionally extend even beyond any instrument's theoretical range), entails a supremely awkward execution, or both. Additionally, even though the instructions stipulate that "precise alignment of various instruments in time is not necessary," and that "players need not rehearse together" (or at all), often the ensembles that have performed his works attempt to do both of these, and both they do badly. For a variety of reasons *one more day in the empire* usually becomes the combined result of self-doubt, hesitation, tentativeness, imprudence, impatience, and simple bewilderment. The product, or rather

---

[197] John Sherlock, "Performance Notes," in *one more day in the empire* (2006).

John Mark Sherlock, from score for *one more day in the empire* (2006). Courtesy John Mark Sherlock.

the by-product of these scores is a musical impulse that revolves around the exploitation of confounded competencies. In the recorded version of this work the clarinet, Fender Rhodes, Clavinet, Wurlitzer, and e-bowed electric guitar parade all of these affections. While a transcription of the pitch and rhythmical deviations from the original score would represent an aspect of the work's fortuity, it wouldn't get at the way these embodied perplexes and intensive failures are received in listening. For one thing, the versioned score would just be another score of *one more day in the empire*, though one tremendously more complex. As an indeterminate work, *one more day* is not compromised but realized by its deviations, and so any rendering of any one performance will in principle simply be—*one more day in the empire*. Secondly, the listener (almost) never sees the score and more often than not hears the piece only once,[198] and so cannot even participate in the effect of expectations and inhibitions that deviations are supposed to excite. A better sense of *one more day*'s charm can be more easily and effectively imagined with a more "impressionistic" rendering by virtue of the way the strangeness of the illustration is meant to discompose your looking at it. (See *one more day...* "versioned.")

Like *Josef, Lieber Josef Mein, one more day in the empire* exudes charm. Both pieces use rather conventional musical elements—the former an old German folk song, the latter simple rhythmic and harmonic relations, that belie the works' aural deformations and underrepresent the extraordinary musical weirdness and incidental complexity that emerges from applying clumsy playing techniques to a hummable tune notation, or sabotaging the interpretive capacities of performers. But while *Josef, Lieber Josef Mein*'s charm is an expression of the way Tolimieri skews his own acute awareness of Western art music's common forms, the charm that sparks off *one more day in the empire*'s self-fulfilling failure is almost ashamed. The charm in Sherlock's work comes across as illegitimate or

---

[198] Repeat performances of experimental music are extremely rare. Curiously though, this culture wherein ensembles receive funding for and gain credibility by commissioning and performing new rather than older works, gives contemporary music a new sense of ephemerality. Then again, the ubiquity of playback devices, which seem to be always on, ensures that these new singularities will be heard again (at least by one person—namely, the composer).

one more day in the empire: "Versioned."

alien. As though misbegotten, *one more day*'s bastardization of musical competence and good aesthetic sense spoils the rightful sovereignty of proper "composition" with a flimsy and undeserved allure. Why? Though *one more day* is composed of familiar musical notes—a quasi-minor modality, distinct moments of homophony, sumptuous instrumental timbres, silences, and shifts in musical density—it makes little attempt to render these in experimental terms or give them an expressivity that would, at least by proxy, make them minorly musical and so justify their failure to be radical or even conventionally musical. For inviting habits into the territory of music-to-be-listened-to, *one more day* is perhaps "sorry" in a way that Tolimieri's *Josef, Lieber Josef Mein* isn't. But this is not because *one more day* messes with what ought-not-to-be-messed-with. Rather, *one more day*'s shame is that the unconscious habits of incompetence, and what sociologist Erving Goffman calls "toy involvements," a kind of secret and "inward emigration" from the collective scene (i.e., a concert) towards a "playlike world in which [one] alone participates,"[199] feel anti-social.

More than noise music's aggressive denial of the internal necessity of its becoming "not music," the assembly of different incompetencies that is *one more day in the empire* transposes into a private reality what exists illegitimately *within* the main event of the concert performance. But smuggling private perceptions through the public doors of music comes at a cost, for lingering in the charm of incompetence reads as a kind of failure to respect the fact of music's sociality. And this failure, while sheltering perception from the pressure of musical "facts," endures the guilt that Terada associates with phenomenophilia's lack of desire for genuine sociality or critical perspicuity,"[200] a guilt that is intensified in *one more day* by its proximity to art's pledge to be beautiful, that is, its implicit promise to be had by everyone.

---

[199] Erving Goffman, *Behavior in Public Places: Notes on the Social Organization of Gatherings* (New York: Free Press, 1963), 69.
[200] Terada, *Looking Away*, 29.

Last)))))

*When I played parades we would be going down Canal Street
and at each intersection people would hear just the fragment I
happened to be playing and it would fade as I went farther down
Canal. They would not be there to hear the end of phrases.... I
wanted them to be able to come in where they pleased and leave
when they pleased and somehow hear the germs of the start and
all the possible endings at whatever point in the music that I had
reached then. Like your radio without the beginnings or endings.
The right ending is an open door you can't see too far out of. It can
mean exactly the opposite of what you are thinking.*

Michael Ondaatje
Coming Through Slaughter

The passage above, spoken in the fictional voice of the New Orleans
jazz musician Buddy Bolden, tells us something about the way
listening can move sideways; or rather, the way it can sidle along
what's being heard so that, in a sense, it listens in many directions
at once. This passage brings into focus the fact that listening has
habituated to the dim and partial perceptions encouraged by the
way music is "more often heard now in fragments than completely,"
that "listening to a piece of music from beginning to end is...the
exception rather than the rule."[201]

Here, Bolden's "fragment" resembles an instance of Adorno's
"atomic listening," the selection of acoustic particulars over structural continuities. But I would suggest that Bolden's description of
these fragments as germinal places it closer to Alfred Whitehead or
Gilles Deleuze's occasion or event: a untimely moment around which
listening orients its past and future expressions into musical adventures that give a qualitative background continuity to what's actually
being heard.[202] The fragment, in all its virtual iridescence, can be

---

[201] Frith, *Performing Rites*, 242, 243.

[202] Essentially, this qualitative background continuity designates the feeling-thought
that carries over from one singular moment to the next. Brian Massumi argues that this
carry-over is the "affective tonality" of an occasion, and stems from the fact that every
situation is festooned with "nonsensuously lived micro-intervals filled only qualitatively

thought to possess an internal difference that if it were given time, that is, somehow protracted, would as William James suggests, "*be made to show new aspects of itself.*"[203] However, it's rare that a fragment has time to itself. More often, a fragment is just another moment of our generally tessellated experience of the everyday.

But there are occasions when a fragment does have its own time, when it can be stretched out and the bundled romances that it keeps to itself drawn apart. These occasions are typically taken in the familiar concert setting, only now they are more often than not taken from behind, buggered by a habit that smuggles Bolden's parade route—the intersections—into the concert hall: listening comes in where it pleases and leaves when it pleases. But it is not that the musical surface is itself fragmented or splintered. Mahler's skin is just as wounded as John Zorn's. Piggybacking on our newly wired "Google-brain," which has transformed the body from a complex abyss of desires, reasons, and feelings into "simple-processing units, quickly shepherding information into consciousness and then back out again,"[204] we've unintentionally smuggled our habit of smuggling background sounds across the threshold of attention into the middle of a ritual designed precisely to keep the diversions out. We must now invert Eliot's assertion that we are "distracted from distraction by distraction." We are distracted *by* distraction *from* distraction. Music doesn't divert our minds from our daily interruptions. Music is now one of many daily interruptions, and this holds even as it crosses the threshold from public commotion to private chambers.

Specifically, distraction affects the way concert music is listened to in that it violates or corrupts the intentionality that constitutes the magical object conjured by spells of silence and bodily restraint. Music now, in effect, shatters; it breaks apart on the backside of listening where a melodic "lift" and rhythmic "push," or a tuneful impression and an infectious groove is had incidentally by listening aside. Composers can be heard responding to cultures of distraction

---

and abstractly by affect." From moment to moment, these micro-intervals are like vanishing points, that while never actually in a situation, impose a sense (i.e., "depth") upon the words, gestures, hesitations that hover around their virtuality. Massumi, *Semblance and Event*, 65.

203 James, *Talks to Teachers*, 7.

204 Carr, *The Shallows*, 119.

not by emulating the expressions of these as television programmes have tried to ape the speed and associative logic of advertising's montage effects, but in how their music fails to manifest a set of traditional cues that, as Susanne Langer writes, "begets or intensifies expectation, including the expectation of sheer continuity."[205]

More than any rhetorical refusal to deny the internal necessity of its unfolding (which is nothing less than the imperative of Adorno's structural listening), we can take the protracted self-similarities of Sherlock's *one more day in the empire*, Arnold's *Burrow Music*, or Peaker's *Species of Spaces* as fortuitous couplings with our involuntary sensibility to only partly and occasionally pay attention to musical phenomena. In a sense, this music invites distraction, but always in a way that draws distraction across the work, giving it a chance to skirt aesthetic borders and trade its sound effects on the black market of the unconscious.

Under these circumstances, the fragments that distraction isolates and scatters across listening create an ongoing series of incipits—the opening lines of a story or a musical work—literally, "here begins": "It was a dark and stormy night..." In his novel *If on a winter's night a traveler...* (1979), Italo Calvino describes the incipit as "the promise of a time of reading that extends before us and can comprise all possible developments."[206] A book, or a piece of music for that matter, that is only an incipit would be a work that "maintains for its whole duration the potentiality of the beginning, the expectation still not focused on an object."[207] As a structuring force, the incipit possesses a commanding form, a figurative time signature that paces and organizes the way activities realize an idea over time. Incipits are a kind of cusp or a threshold, a metaphysical boundary dividing differing realities. *Call me Ishmael... For a long time, I went to bed early... A screaming comes across the sky...*Three worlds side-by-side. Here, the fragment gets its time, extending itself in potential along the whole of the work. But placed in series as Calvino does in *If on a winter's night a traveler...*, the incipit returns each

---

[205] Susanne Langer, *Feeling and Form*, 129.
[206] Italo Calvino, *If on a Winter's Night a Traveler*, trans. William Weaver (New York: Harcourt Brace Jovanovich, 1981), 177.
[207] Ibid.

pulse of attention each time to another beginning—*Mrs. Dalloway said she would buy the flowers herself...I am an invisible man... It was the day my grandmother exploded...* . The fragment doesn't have time for itself but gives it to the next moment, a moment that is just another fragment, another incipit, another unfocused object. A veritable distraction span.

But an accumulation of incipits does not a text or a music make. Or it does. And it would be an exceptionally odd book, or a really weird song, one made of loose threads and a heap of beginnings that fail again and again to become their own possibilities. The world as a multitude of nexts: each moment a span of attention in abeyance, another singularity, another pinchpoint shorting out the interest of glimpse after glimpse after glimpse.

Another again

Once upon a time...

3

Nonsense I

A human being unwillingly deprived of the society of his peers descends into madness as the fine structures of perceived reality, maintained and reinforced by the rhetorical bombardments of others' truths (and his own, reflected back), rapidly unwind without constant reinforcement. What I tell you three times is true. What I tell you three million times is civilization.

MARK PESCE
"THE EXECUTABLE DREAMTIME"

Bullshit is unavoidable whenever circumstances require someone to talk without knowing what he is talking about.

HARRY FRANKFURT
ON BULLSHIT

(Voodoo

In a study on difference and power in music, John Shepherd identifies a paradox that is fundamental to human sociality and is articulated by the tension expressed "between the inalienable potential for artifice and the inescapability of the material [world]."[1] That is, the symbolic processes allowing us to manipulate the material environment exhibit a certain independence from the material world while at the same time remaining indissolubly linked to material conditions. Shepherd makes this point, however, not to celebrate it, but to expose how the largely male project of industrial capitalism tries to disguise this tension by appropriating the power of language's symbol system to ignore "the inherent characteristics of sounds from those of the objects...on which they operate,"[2] a power that is only amplified with the emergence and dissemination of print technology whose system of visual signs and phonetic literacy promote an even greater separation between the sound's characteristics and meaning. This power of language to disarticulate meaning from a thing's material features is, Shepherd argues, what drives the development of a society and its civilization. However, language and the sense it makes come at the cost of sacrificing the relational and fluid presence that sound evokes and demands. The consequences of this are twofold and mutually reinforcing: First, "if the sounds of an utterance are not homologously bound or limited in their configuration by the inherent configurations of the objects to which they refer, then they can be open-endedly manipulated in relation to those objects and more easily prescribe their future manipulation in time and space."[3] Second, as a culture becomes literate and takes its literary expressions, in the widest sense of the term, as its central point of definition, the "system of visual signs that are...quite arbitrary in their cross-sensory relation to the sounds they represent...can, in principle, take on a life of its own in relation to the sounds of the language it notates."[4] Thus, the number of utterances and what can be said about something is unlimited and it is not restricted to fact or morphological correspondence. Unmoored like this, we can, in effect, bullshit all we want.

For a "something" like music, whose non-denotative aspect gives it a rich connotative potential, this virtually open-ended process of

---

[1] John Shepherd, "Difference and Power in Music," in *Musicology and Difference*, ed. Ruth A. Solie (Berkeley and Los Angeles: University of California Press, 1993), 57.
[2] Ibid., 54.
[3] Ibid.
[4] Ibid., 55.

ascription confers on its expressions a mythical status in the sense that what music "says" is unfalsifiable (imaginary). As such, insofar as the society and culture of industrial capitalism is built on the analytic tendencies of language that promote a myth of objectivization and the concomitant belief that the world is susceptible to control, music is a problematic category. As a construct of a discursive culture that categorizes musical sounds into pitch, rhythm, harmony, tempo, etcetera, as well as form, genre, style, classical, and popular, the sense of integration, coexistence, and fluid interaction that sound gives rise to makes music paradoxically something that "reaffirms the flux and concreteness of the social world," but also something that reifies its relational form.[5] The idea of music therefore locates a "something" wherein opposites coincide. In a sense, the category of Music (upper case "M") is a stranger to the very culture that animates it, but a productive stranger whose paradoxical status excites the inconsistencies and contradictions that industrial capitalism's reckoning of the world produces in abundance. This trafficking in contradictions is also what makes music a myth, for like myth, which may be considered an unconscious expression of a society's internal discrepancies, the matrix of relations that is reflexively and outwardly connoted by Music holds oppositions together within the same event.

As a stranger and a myth, music functions in industrial capitalist cultures as a form of nonsense, what Susan Stewart calls a residual category, which like "Chance," "Accident," or even "etcetera," "gives us a place to store any mysterious gaps in our system of order."[6] Nonsense so defined is a conceptual stopgap that accommodates what an order does not tolerate by marking its own limit. As such, nonsense is an inalienable "aid to sense making" without which "sense would not be 'measured' [but] would itself threaten infinity and regression."[7] In the context of industrial capitalist society, Music exists as a kind of nonsense in which the inconsistencies of manipulating and defining a material reality through symbolic processes can

---

[5] Ibid.
[6] Susan Stewart, *Nonsense: Aspects of Intertextuality in Folklore and Literature* (Baltimore: Johns Hopkins University Press, 1979), 5.
[7] Ibid.

accumulate and be provisionally managed. As nonsense, we might see Music functioning where "sound ceases to be a mediating presence,"[8] where the suppleness of its material, which cannot help but "reaffirm the present existence of the individual, and reaffirm it with a concreteness and directness not required for reaffirmation through the sounds of language,"[9] is expurgated from the proper map of abstractions and absences that coordinate everyday life. The sticky and messy matter of music is displaced in a way that its symptomatic appearance in the form of "emotions" or "feelings" makes it a stranger to the measure of sense with which its strangeness is conterminous.

But this does not essentialize music. Or rather, it essentializes the discursive construction of Music. But then again, what is it to say, write, or think of music, or Music, apart from its discursive constructions? Indeed, it is the basic position of post-structuralism that there is no outside, no immaculate reality apart from the discursively formulated social realities that a culture presents to itself as objective and true. Which is to say (which is already to say too much), that there is no music or language, or noise, for that matter, *as such*. Music and Language are terms of sense that express the signifying inclination immanent to those sonic practices which discourse gathers up and disseminates in its bid for knowledge. The null- or "myth-space" of the "*etcetera*," which is the same as "Blah blah blah," is the closest one can come to music or language "as such." The effort to encircle the "outside" of music with something like Cage's chance operations would appear then to be the most effective way of bringing out the "blah-blah" essence of music. However, chance does not make music any less artificial, any less constructed, it just makes chance less chancy and more planned. But all this is old hat.

What is really interesting about all of this is not *that* Music plays out the contradictions and inconsistencies of our industrial society but *how* it does this. While all Music is subject to the discursive economy that constitutes it as Music and not as Sound, Speech, or Noise, it would seem that the more self-aware practices clustering

---

[8] Shepherd, "Difference and Power in Music," 50.
[9] John Shepherd and Peter Wicke, *Music and Cultural Theory* (Cambridge: Polity Press, 1997), 164.

around its sign would make an issue of it in a way that allies it to the practice of metafiction, which, as Patricia Waugh suggests, is a way of writing that "self-consciously and systematically draws attention to its status as an artefact in order to pose questions about the relationship between fiction and reality."[10] And indeed, the latter half of the twentieth century is dotted with musical works that embody varying degrees of self-reflexivity and formal instability that evoke comparison to the work of authors such as John Barth or Thomas Pynchon.[11] The third movement of Berio's *Sinfonia* (1968–69), for instance, and Mauricio Kagel's aptly titled *Metapiece* (1961), too, and of course Cage's *4'33"*, are works that self-consciously draw attention to their artifice. But perhaps more exemplary of the way metafictions interrogate "a *theory* of fiction through the *practice* of writing fiction,"[12] is the more recent work of composer/theorist Claus-Steffen Mahnkopf, who takes the lessons of post-structuralism and the dialectical contortions of Adorno's philosophical project as an aesthetic end to be mannered by an equally, but intentionally, clumsy "complexificationizing" of the art music tradition. But the meta-musical theatre of Mahnkopf, like so many metafictions, undermines its own disturbance by maintaining a transcendental reserve; the delirium which reflexivity courts is held off by keeping the supplementary dimension of the author in play. At most what this brand of meta-music accomplishes is a hyper-awareness of its own artifice that merely sanctions the use of a beleaguered rhetoric of aesthetic negativity (which, unlike Barth, is no fun to read) that gives the impression of being enlightened and insightful. Yet, in the spirit of

---

[10] Patricia Waugh, *Metafiction: The Theory and Practice of Self-Conscious Fiction* (London; New York Methuen, 1984), 2.

[11] Noted, the practice of self-reflexivity appears quaint if you consider the history of European art music which is, among other things, the art of self-referentiality. (See Ruth Katz, *A Language of Its Own: Sense and Meaning in the Making of Western Art Music* (Chicago: The University of Chicago Press, 2009).) However, Waugh is writing in the early 1980s and commenting on a trend in literature that "reflects a greater awareness within contemporary culture of the function of language in constructing and maintaining our sense of everyday 'reality'" (Waugh, *Metafiction*, 3). While Brahms' *Symphony no. 2* certainly indulges a high degree of self-referential symbolism, the discourse which constitutes it as "absolute music" excuses its signs from having to address the phenomenal world and so exempts the meta-operations of the work from the complex and highly problematic issue of representation that make metafiction so disorienting.

[12] Waugh, *Metafiction*, 2.

the barren dialectic with which Mahnkopf is enthralled, this is exactly what the music stresses.

But there are other contemporary practices that take a different tack. Fully aware of the way music is discursively constituted and how the representations of its events not only have a way of becoming a part of their unfolding, of bleeding into other constructs such as gender, race, and class, there are practices that pursue a form of sovereignty which is had, paradoxically, by bullshitting. These practices flirt with Paul Mann's "stupid undergrounds" by partaking of the same asymptotic mannerisms that express the vertiginous passions of hyperreality. However, what distinguishes, for example, Irish composer Jennifer Walshe's fictive sound art collective Grúpat, or Toronto-based inter-media artist Marc Couroux's necromantic re-visioning of The Carpenters and 1970s American politics, from the modernist refrains of Mahnkopf and the suicidal impulses of the stupid underground, is their conviction to explore, if I may borrow a phrase from the crypto-metaphysician Donald Rumsfeld, "unknown unknowns." In other words, a kind of radical doubt underwrites the intentions of Walshe and Couroux in a way that decentres rather than negates the problem of reflection. The effect of doubt is not to reach a higher "truth," but to make room for a little "voodoo."

This means that Walshe and Couroux have left what Bush administration insiders have called "the reality-based community," a community defined by people who believe that solutions or results can "emerge from a judicious study of discernible reality."[13] Walshe and Couroux no longer (if they ever did) carry out their actions with respect to an empirical aesthetics—a verifiable aesthetics whose effects are observable—but instead act at the level of potential where aesthetic effects recursively grow into new artistic realities. As the Bush people might say, when they act, they create their own reality.[14] Or as Brian Massumi does say, "[T]oday's world is

---

[13] These are words that *New York Times* writer Ron Suskind attributes to a senior Bush advisor. Ron Suskind, "Without a Doubt, " *New York Times Magazine*, 14 October 2004. http://www.ronsuskind.com/articles/000106.html [accessed October 2012].
[14] Brian Massumi, "Potential Politics and the Primacy of Preemption," *Theory and Event* 10, no. 2 (2007): par.17, http://muse.jhu.edu/journals/theory_and_event/v010/10.2massumi.html.

not objective. It is potential."[15] Our world of unknown unknowns is a world that is "unexpungeable because its potentiality belongs to the objective conditions of life today."[16] As such, "truth," or "fact," or "beauty" even, is self-fulfilling, for in taking unknown unknowns objectively one stokes the objectively indeterminate potential of uncertainty and encourages it to take actual shape by "acting to make present a future cause that sets a self-perpetuating movement into operation."[17]

And is this not voodoo? Is not acting to make present a future cause exactly what the "hougan" or "bokor"[18] does when they wish luck or misfortune on someone, acting on the unprovables of a belief system to short circuit doubt and compensate "for the absence of an actual cause by producing an actual effect in its place?"[19] Effects as cause, as quasi-cause. A jinx makes itself actual by correlating the ordinarily unspecified points of failure and intensities of defeat that co-exist "in a state of actual indistinction from each other": Obscured failures "actively fused, in dynamic superposition."[20] But this is not superstition. It is *hyperstition*, a fiction that makes itself real by affective insinuation, by gut reactions that contaminate the nervous system with the intensity of a nonbelief. Hyperstition is a pre-personal and unconsciously exercised conviction that cannot help but register as the reality of a situation. In fact, Marcel Mauss describes something very close to this when he qualifies the operative logic of magic as an effort to induce belief in hopes of achieving "the adherence of all men to an idea, and consequently to a state of feeling, an act of will, and at the same time a phenomenon of ideation."[21] But what Mauss misses in this characterization of magic is that one first summons an intensity, an affective quality, that is only then followed by adherence to an idea, for an intensity is the registering of a difference that belief represents, a sliver of felt nonsense that circuits through a

---

[15] Ibid.

[16] Ibid., par. 14.

[17] Ibid., par. 22.

[18] "Hougan" and "bokor" are the Haitian terms for male and female voodoo priests, respectively.

[19] Massumi, "Potential Politics and the Primacy of Preemption," par. 23.

[20] Brian Massumi, "Fear (the Spectrum Said)," *Positions* 13, no. 1 (2005): 45.

[21] Marcel Mauss, *A General Theory of Magic*, trans. Robert Brain (London; New York: Routledge, 2001), 119.

constellation of symptoms, binding them in coincidence through a quasi-causality of expressive correspondences.

Hyperstition is an occult technology or an "abstract machine" that quasi-causes change to occur and events to take place in alliance with the immanent and impersonal will of a situation that cannot but express itself as a series of coincidences. In a way, hyperstition does resemble superstition. A spell is cast, a person dies; I'm wearing green socks, and no planes fall from the sky. Two events connected by coincidence (expressive correspondence—voodoo) but real-ized (made effective) to the extent that their alliance shocks the system and "disconnects the body from the ongoing flow of its activities,"[22] readying it for a restart along a new path where green socks and falling planes share the same destiny. Properly speaking, this is superstition. However, when coincidences spread, as they do *in flagrante* on the nightly news (and more subtly, when people speak to one another), when the exceptions that coincidence expresses become models of reality, they generate "a real without origin or reality: a hyperreal"[23]—effects become causes and "indissociable dimensions of the same event."[24] This is hyperstition.

But what exactly does it mean to be hyperstitious? What does it mean to have faith in the fabrication of coincidences? In short, it means that you bullshit, that you make things up. This, however, does not mean that being hyperstitious makes you a liar. As Harry Frankfurt argues, liars retain a certain respect for truth in their aim to deceive,[25] which is impossible for the hyperstitious person to have because "truth" supposes a perspective from which the exception of an event can be demonstrated as unexceptional. When you see the world as a series of exceptions and happenstance, as the hyperstitious person does, the ruse of metaphysics that makes us "believe in the true" is supplanted by the superior ruse of 'pataphysics which "lets us pretend to be untrue."[26] In this respect, to be hyperstitious

[22] Massumi, "Fear (the Spectrum Said)," 36.

[23] Jean Baudrillard, *Simulacra and Simulation*, trans. Sheila Glaser (Ann Arbor: University of Michigan Press 1995), 1.

[24] Massumi, "Fear (the Spectrum Said)," 36.

[25] See Harry Frankfurt, *On Bullshit* (Princeton, NJ: Princeton University Press, 2005).

[26] Christian Bök, '*Pataphysics: The Poetics of an Imaginary Science* (Chicago: Northwestern University Press, 2002), 12.

is to bluff, to feign, not in order to be false, for that would suppose a truth, but to be effective. And being effective has no concern with truth-values.

Walshe and Couroux's hyperstitions can be regarded as a hyper-fiction more than a meta-fiction, as a form of royal bullshitting in the sense that they do not "insert a particular falsehood at a specific point in a set or system of beliefs,"[27] as lying does, but instead distribute splinters of nonsense that contaminate the assemblage of conventions and assumptions that produces the appearance of an intelligible, orderly world. To this extent, the text that follows, the text that reviews their work, becomes a part of their hyperstitions. What I write about their work constitutes an aspect of the very bullshit that I am studying. Thus, the very words that I have written and which you are now reading circulate a misrepresentation so that more than explaining their bullshit, it stirs it.

((Metareferentiality, metamusic, and hypermusic

If we understand Music as a discursive formation, then in a sense it is always already a kind of *fictum*, a falsehood, for its expression as "art" entails an awareness of its "artifice," its relation to a "real" as a fiction, a "quasi-real." Like all fictions, it should be subject to various meta-processes, processes that spur "an awareness of the medial status of the work or system under consideration."[28] However, a musical *fictum*, as opposed to a *fictio* whose metareferentiality is accomplished solely by producing an awareness of the sense of mediality, is subject to metareferential reflection not only when its artifice is made apparent but when it elicits a *comparison* to a reality that it is (supposedly) not, as happens with musical works that trigger a response like: "That's not music!" This statement (negatively) describes a musical *fictum*. It expresses a two-fold metareference

---

27 Frankfurt, *On Bullshit*, 51.
28 Werner Wolf, "Metafiction and Metamusic: Exploring the Limits of Metareference," in *Self-Reference in the Media*, ed. Winifried Nöth and Nina Bishar (Berlin; New York: Mouton de Gruyter, 2007), 307.

in that saying something is "not music" draws attention to the specific behaviour of the sonic medium while at the same time brings to mind the relationship that this medium is supposed to have with reality—namely, that music is an artifice and what is being heard as "not music" is not complying with the fictionality, the artificiality, that music is supposed to adhere to. That said, there is a greater consequence to draw from this kind of meta-multiple. In declaring something to be "not music," and thereby calling attention to the medium and producing a conceptual awareness of the kind that structures the difference between "fiction" and "reality," one is remaindering something whose ontological and epistemological status is radically indeterminate. If not Music, not a musical artifice, then what is "it" that remains? If "it" is not acting as an agent through which processes of expression and communication can take place (i.e. medium), then "it" is more matter than idea. And if "it" is not, so to speak, feigning a world of impending death such as Mahler's 9th does, then "it" is not even imaginary. Paradoxically then, "it," this "unmusic," this acoustic matter impinging on my time and space, is something of a black hole and much closer to music as such than Chopin's *Nocturnes* could ever hope to be.

Unmusic, a "something" on just the other side of discourse, is a species of metamusic in the sense of its being *ulterior* to Music. This departs slightly from the idea of metamusic as a practice analogous to metafiction, for this modified definition of metamusic as unmusic is characterized more by a failure than by an explicit reflexivity. While an understanding of metamusic that is analogous to metafiction typifies the operations of a signifying practice that "elicits a *cognitive process or reflection* on itself, on other elements of the system or on the system as a whole,"[29] the sense of metamusic that I am making is based on a failure to be musical (to act as an expressive acoustic medium) and to be Music (to be an object of contemplation, exchange, or study). Thus, what I am calling "unmusic" is a failed event. And as sociologist Stewart notes, a failed event is nonsense. "Like a 'fiasco'," writes Stewart, "nonsense is a failed event, an event without proper consequences."[30] "Not-being-musical" (or if

---

29 Ibid., 305.
30 Stewart, *Nonsense*, 4.

you're of the avant-garde persuasion, "not-being –'anti-musical'")
is a fiasco to the listener who expects to hear sounds behaving
musically, behaving as Music (or the inverse). Yet, as I'm suggesting,
an event with "improper" consequences is an event nevertheless: a
failed event is still and event failing. While the failed event may not
comply with the conventions or context in which it is situated, even
if those conventions stipulate the fictionality (artificiality) of what the
event expresses, it still has effects, and these effects impinge on
and influence the sense of other events despite its being cut out
of the discourse that articulates the sense proper to the situation
(being accomplished by and through the discourse). As such, the
effects that express the sense of the fiasco that this "unmusic" is
are effects of a certain failure.

But this leaves a question about how we can even study
"unmusic," for how does one stage a fiasco? How does one intentionally fail? In other words, how does one make unmusic? The short
and paradoxical answer is that you *unmake* it. The long and much
more circuitous answer, which requires a major detour through the
way in which meaning in music and language is generated, and
how the category of Music can only be understood as a discursive
construct such that it is impossible to think of Music apart from
language, is that you *fake* it. While this is perhaps not a very satisfying answer, I'd suggest that satisfaction is already out of step with
failure, for failure isn't about satisfaction but quite the opposite.
Failure is about an engagement with the potential of potential rather
than a satisfaction of a potential's ideal. Thus to fake failure is and
is not to fail to fail, for failing to fail is a success of sorts whose
accomplishment is itself a type of failure (which is a success that
is a failure...). And as the previous sentence demonstrates with its
convoluted (though mercifully curtailed) recursive logic, to fail is to
make nonsense, and to make nonsense is to traffic in contradictions,
which is, in a sense, to unmake sense.

This redoubling of contradictions is in fact close to Adorno's
formulation of modern art, which he believes is fated to the task
of expressing its alienation from the spirit of its time, to express
its incapacity to adequately express itself. However, unlike the
Sisyphean predicament that Adorno ascribes to modern art, unmusic
finds some traction in its quandary, for being nonsense relieves its

occurrence from being "art." But, of course, the cessation of art is something that can only be accomplished when art disappears into the occasion of its own excess. And that occasion, according to Baudrillard, has already happened. In fact, "art" disappeared a while back (When? Sometime in the 1970s, probably when information technologies were electrified and became the dominant way in which Western culture mediated its self-expressions), and its sublimation into the everyday order of simulation was overlooked.[31] Too busy watching reruns of I Dream of Jeannie or Bewitched I suppose. What is called "art" now is itself a continuous rerun, a rerun of the image of its own disappearance.[32] But said another way, which I'm sure some would rather it be said (though it makes no difference), "art" is everywhere one and the same with the image of the everyday, if not actually, then potentially. Under these circumstances, because art and the reality that is supposed to set off its aesthetic properties have lost their operational difference, unmusic is everywhere Music is not. However, according to the logic of simulation, Music is everywhere so unmusic is nowhere. Yet being everywhere is the same as being nowhere, therefore Music is nowhere, which makes unmusic everywhere. But this is hyperreality and hyperreality trucks no difference between the real and the unreal (artifice), the musical and unmusical. Thus unmusic eschews Adorno's dialectical impasse to the extent that it is total nonsense, a byproduct of the hyperreal that supervenes a discourse of contradictions and paradoxes where everything is coming up signs.

In this sense it would be better to call unmusic h/Hypermusic, for the failure that expresses a nonsensical unmusic, is not outside of discourse so much as it radicalizes the powers of discourse. This process of failure would be an instance of what theorist and music critic Mark Fisher calls the "intense amplification of the processes of immanentization."[33] That is, the failure which constitutes

---

[31] See Jean Baudrillard, Symbolic Exchange and Death, trans. Ian Hamilton Grant (London: Sage, 1993).

[32] Jean Baudrillard, The Conspiracy of Art: Manifestos, Interviews, Essays, trans. Sylvère Lotringer, Semiotext(e) Foreign Agents Series (New York: Semiotext(e), 2005).

[33] Mark Fisher, "Flatline Constructs: Gothic Materialism and Cybernetic Theory-Fiction" (PhD diss., University of Warwick, 1999), http://www.cinestatic.com/trans-mat/Fisher/FC4s7.htm [accessed October 2012].

h/Hypermusic does not mark a breach in discourse but a doubling over of it that subtracts the need for, and indeed, the possibility of adding any supplementary dimensions—like sound—to its expressions.

h/Hypermusic is therefore no less discursively constituted than Music is. However, the discourse of Music circulates a respect for a simulated difference between real and artifice, sound and symbol, in a way that the discourse of h/Hypermusic does not. And so, it is this "not" around which h/Hypermusic revolves, a not that folds discourse back on itself making a knot that threads the nonsense of not-Music through the sense of Music.

In essence, h/Hypermusic subsists *here*, between and among these words and your reading them, as the expression of a discourse whose mimetic devices are not just simulations—as DeLillo's photo-graphed barn is in *White Noise*—but theories of simulation. In other words, the map no longer precedes the territory: the manual on map-making now precedes the map that precedes the territory. As this means "~~we~~" are all only fictions, h/Hypermusic, too, is revealed as just another fiction, but a certain kind of "theory-fiction" born of an insight into the depths of reflexivity, or as Fisher describes, the registering of a "cybernetic account of subjectivity, a sense that the self can no longer be properly distinguished from the multiplicity of circuits that traverse it."[34] h/Hypermusic and the nonsense that it disseminates (and vice-versa) is therefore an expression of my "psychedelic giddiness" that results not, as Baudrillard suggests, "from multiple or successive connections and disconnections,"[35] but from the coincident hallucinogenic conviction that the schizonoia of hyperreality induces in me.

(((Grúpat and pseudonymity

But I'm not the only one who feels this way. Take for instance the work of Irish composer and artist Jennifer Walshe. In an interview with James Saunders, Walshe describes the varieties of sounds that

---

[34] Ibid.
[35] Jean Baudrillard, *Seduction*, trans. Brian Singer (New York: St. Martin's Press, 1990), 162.

she likes to work with. In addition to what she describes as "dirty" sounds, biographically significant sounds, sounds that are byproducts of physical situations, and sensuously articulate sounds, are sounds that she says are "at times imaginary, sounds which function as conceptual descriptions"[36]—unreal sounds. Walshe continues:

> The performer, for example, might be required to imagine the inside of their body as the interior of a mountain full of mines, feel the blood moving through their veins as tiny carts carrying diamonds to and fro through a tunnel system, and then tip these tiny imaginary diamonds into their lungs to prepare for creating a sound. The audience of course can't "see" the performer creating blasts of white light in their lungs to pulverize the diamonds they just tipped into them. But my intention is that all this preparation and delicate attention means that when the performer emits a vocal sound which atomizes the diamond dust, creating a crystalline mist through the air, there's a quality to the sound which comes from these imaginings.[37]

Although Walshe is describing the details of a specific imaginative exercise, the fictional dimension of finding her way into a sound underwrites the principle of her imaginary South Dublin arts collective Grúpat "whose roots can be traced to 1999, when Bulletin M, The Parks Service, Turf Boon, and other artists met at a rave at the Hellfire Club on Montpelier Hill, in the Dublin Mountains."[38] Grúpat, to put it simply, is a project in which Walshe acts as commissioner and curator for a group of fictional composer-artists whose identities and aesthetic sensibilities she adopts and performs. By developing elaborate backstories and planting expressions of her pseudonyms in different media, such as the May 2006 review in *The Wire* for a work by Grúpat member, The Parks Service, penned by Walshe under the

---

[36] Jennifer Walshe, Interview, in *The Ashgate Research Companion to Experimental Music*, ed. James Saunders (Burlington, VT: Ashgate, 2009), 344.

[37] Ibid.

[38] A history of Grúpat can be found on Ireland's Contemporary Music Centre website and is attributed to Stuart Fresh. This entry, however, was almost certainly written by Walshe and is an example of the way Walshe exploits the scattering potential of various media that in turn generates reality-effects. See Stuart Fresh, "A Short History of Grúpat," http://www.cmc.ie/articles/article1799.html [accessed October 2012].

name "Jonathan Vanns," and by performing a piece by another Grúpat member, Ukeoirn O'Connor, whom Walshe "commissioned" for the 2007 Kilkenny Arts Festival (which was subsequently reviewed in *The Irish Times* on 21 August 2007), Walshe produces her own kind of hyper(fictional) music that amplifies and harnesses the immanence of the hyperreal. In addition to generating an excess of aesthetic objects and events (and perhaps more interestingly), by commissioning, installing, and performing works that she created under the names of "Ukeoirn O'Connor," "Turf Boon," and "Flor Hartigan" (among others), but more significantly, by documenting, reviewing, and giving interviews about these, Walshe repeats the gestures and logics of the contemporary art world that make artworks as obscure as hers are, real. In doing this she not only multiplies her persona and aesthetic referents, she replicates the logic of hyperreality.

It could be argued, however, that because it's now known that Walshe herself is responsible for realizing the different projects imagined by Grúpat, she loses something of the hyper-ness of her/their work. From the perspective of a reality that still respects the issues and orders of representation, it is true; she does lose that liquid purpose which dissolves the cords of intention that bind the identities of Grúpat to her. In a sense, her actualizing the h/Hypermusic of Ukeoirn O'Connor or Turf Boon converts it into just "music." In a world where one knows that it is Walshe who is Grúpat, to keep Ukeoirn O'Connor's or Turf Boon's work h/Hypermusic would require her, paradoxically, to have *not* realized the music, to leave it entirely virtual. But from the perspective of hyperreality, which is where Walshe would like us to dwell, there is no meaningful difference or delay between the fictional and the real, a point that is echoed by Fisher in an example he makes in drawing attention to the way the film *Toy Story* (1995), a film about fictional toys, and the toys of the toys in *Toy Story*, are released simultaneously so that "the film functions as an advertisement for the toys, which function as an advertisement for it, in an ever-tightening spiral. The fictional is immediately real, in the most palpable sense: it can be bought."[39] In hyperreality, Walshe, Grúpat, and the Music are given together in an

---

[39] Fisher, "Flatline Constructs," http://www.cinestatic.com/trans-mat/Fisher/FC4s7.htm [accessed October 2012].

a-chronistic and diffracted media-time that, rather than attenuate the reality of the art and these figures, makes them abstract facets of the same hyperreal plane.

A question then: What does the music of Turf Boon, Flor Hartigan, and Ukeoirn O'Connor sound like?[40] Or for that matter, what does Jennifer Walshe's music sound like? It's hard to say, for even if one could tell the different musics apart from one another, to which identity should one ascribe it? Walshe does. But if she can shuffle these fictions around why can't we? More importantly, we might ask whether it matters what the Music sounds like. The splendid art catalogue that I'm gazing at, published by The Project Arts Centre in Dublin, with its velvet-black cover adorned in monochromatic doodles, cradling high-gloss color photos of installations, score excerpts, reviews, post-cards, as well as the requisite copyright notice(s) and catalogue essay by a legit scholar,[41] suggest that maybe it hardly matters. That I'm writing about Boon-Hartigan-O'Connor-Walshe seems to be what matters, or at least writing about this figment and whether it matters whether the sound of the music matters seems to matter just as much as the putative music does. For Paul Mann, who argues that radical art lives on the discourse of its own death, all of our actions, expressions and desires are occasions that maintain what he calls the "white economy of discourse."[42] It matters only that words and ideas about art are exchanged. That is to say, Grúpat is as real and as meaningful as Thomas Mann's Adrian Leverkühn is insofar as the respective fictional quantities of each excite (incite) discourse in a bid to capture some kind of difference—a white economy's currency of exchange. And counting the words up to this point I would say that Grúpat is about...5700 words real and meaningful.

* * *

But Walshe's Grúpat is not unique in its pseudonymous venture. The history of literature is extremely familiar with the *nom de plume*, and

---

[40] You can find out by visiting: http://www.myspace.com/ukeoirnoconnor, and http://www.myspace.com/turfboon.

[41] Bob Gilmore, Lecturer in music at Brunel University.

[42] Paul Mann, *The Theory-Death of the Avant-Garde* (Bloomington: Indiana University Press, 1991), 141.

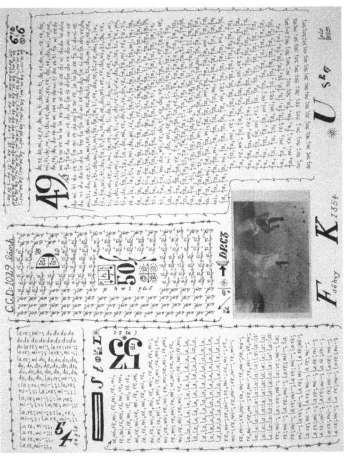

Turf Boon, from score for *Community Choir* (2002–present). Courtesy Jennifer Walshe

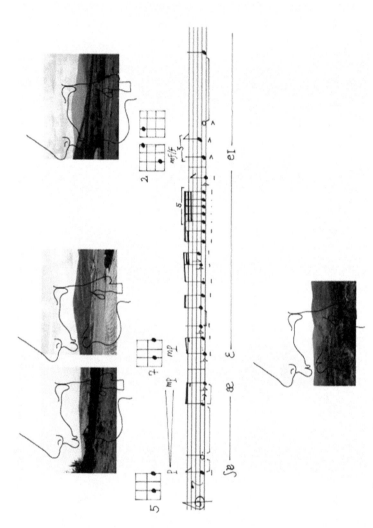

Ukeoirn O'Connor, from score for *Three Songs* (2007). Courtesy Jennifer Walshe

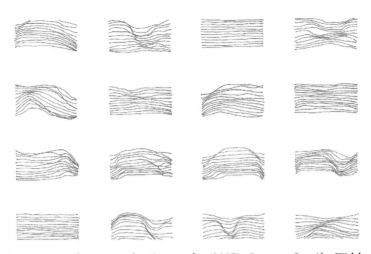

Flor Hartigan, from score for *Conturador* (2007). Courtesy Jennifer Walshe

in our media-saturated society it is de rigueur for anyone with a degree of electronic literacy to have at least one digital persona whose informational identity substitutes more and more for a fleshy individuality.[43] But what makes Grúpat different and ultimately effective is not its

---

[43] Well known pseudonyms in literature are: Lewis Carroll (Charles Dodgson), George Orwell (Eric Arthur Blair), and Mark Twain (Samuel Clemens). However, the Portuguese poet and writer Fernando Pessoa is perhaps the most interesting case, for his incredibly rich body of work was written under multiple "heteronyms," a term he preferred for the way it characterized how names name distinct attributes that express different aspects of reality rather than merely act as aliases. Richard Zenith suggests that Pessoa had as many as seventy-two heteronyms; however, Pessoa's most important personae were Alberto Caeiro, Álvaro de Campos, and Ricardo Reis.[†] A more recent but inverted example of pseudonymic identity is "Luther Blissett Project." Blissett is the name of a 1980s Afro-Caribbean British footballer that in the summer of 1994 was adopted by European artists/activists/pranksters as an identity of "open reputation" under which a variety of critical hoaxes were carried out, for example, the 1998–99 "Darko Maver" performance. This "performance" is typically taken to be an elaborate manipulation of the culture industry by the art group 0100101110101101.ORG who fabulated an identity and artwork that they attributed to the fictional Serbian artist named Darko Maver. Through the proliferation of forged documents, including press releases, self-authored theorization of Maver's artworks, news of the artist's imprisonment, and the exhibition of images of Maver's work at the 1999 Venice Biennale, the "Darko Maver" ruse demonstrates the mythopoeic potential of media environments, and at the same time, exposes the perviousness of identity, fact, and sense.[‡]

pseudonymity but the fact that Walshe executes it in the realm of Western art music, a realm conspicuously hostile to pseudonymity, for the obfuscation of identity intimates an anonymity that brings its aesthetic expressions into unsettling proximity with "folk" and oral traditions that either have no concept of music as "art" or dilute the individual signature that is accomplice to the Western sense of art in a collective bath of idiosyncrasies. Furthermore, Walshe makes the fiction of Grúpat plausible by exploiting the way media superficies both distort the verity of the reality they report on and circulate this distortion as a reality to effect a feedback relationship between the orders of fiction and the real. As such, Grúpat approaches the condition of what Fisher calls "hyperfiction," a situation where "what is crucial is not the *representation* of reality, but the feedback between fiction and the Real."[44] The circularity between Grúpat as an enigmatic Irish art collective who produce works that Walshe commissions-curates-performs-writes about elaborates the way contemporary culture's "fictional systems...emerge together, in a loop," so that "where once there was a serial trajectory [of concerts, recordings, reviews, and critical essays] now [concerts, recordings, reviews, and critical essays] are issued simultaneously."[45] Like media distortion, Walshe's self-authored pseudonymous reviews of Grúpat works (which she performs/exhibits) short-circuit the difference between fiction and reality and so subtract some of the supplementary dimensions that would falsify the experience. However, because Walshe still has a special role in telling Grúpat's story—she is the author who transcends its fiction—Grúpat never quite rises above the condition of metafiction.

The American composer Karen Eliot, on the other hand, is just such a hyperfiction,[46] for neither the story nor the author plays any special role in the telling of her works. Yet, the author that I am referring to is not exactly "Karen Eliot," and the story is only apparently hers. In

---

† Fernando Pessoa, *The Book of Disquiet*, trans. Richard Zenith (London: Penguin Classics, 2002).

‡ See http://0100101110101101.org/home/darko_maver/index.html for more details.

44 Fisher, "Flatline Constructs," http://www.cinestatic.com/trans-mat/Fisher/FC4s7.htm [accessed October 2012].

45 Ibid.

46 The concepts in the music are available in the writing, each expression an advertisement for the other.

fact, Karen Eliot is a multiple-use name[47] that composers and artists David Chokroun, Aydem Azmikara, Marc Couroux, Engram Knots, and Vanessa Grey use to gather the figments of their collective imagination under one appellation. Unlike Grúpat, which is a fiction that Walshe created to express the schizonoia of her artistic interests,[48] "Eliot" belongs to nobody and is no *one*. Sometimes referred to as an "open identity," multiple-use names like Karen Eliot are always several, and, according to culture critic Stuart Home, often "connected to radical theories of play [where] the idea is to create an 'open situation' for which no one in particular is responsible."[49] In this case, "Karen Eliot" (the collective) is ir-responsible for the way her name functions as a point through which each of these five composers' identities pass. That is, these composers use each others' names when "declaring" the non-pseudonymous authorship of a work; however, they do so according to a scheme whereby there will always be at least two possible attributors and so no way of determining who actually wrote the work. The scheme looks something like this

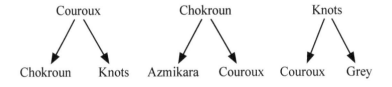

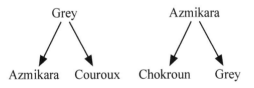

---

[47] Multiple-use names are what art critic Stewart Home defines as "'tags' that the avant-garde of the seventies and eighties proposed for serial use" (http://www.stewarthomesociety.org/sp/multi.htm) [accessed October 2012]. Ideally, anyone can adopt a multiple-use name for some artistic and/or subversive purpose.

[48] Though largely created by Walshe, in an interview in *The Wire* 321, she states that she has since invited individuals who've discovered what Grúpat is (what she was up to) to participate and collaborate in the project.

[49] Stuart Home, "Multiple Names." http://www.stewarthomesociety.org/sp/multi.htm [accessed October 2012].

but may be more easily represented by this diagramme:

Marc Couroux

Vanessa Grey

KAREN
ELIOT

Aydem Azmikara

David Chokroun

Engram Knots

So, for example, as specified by this scheme, either David Chokroun or Engram Knots will have penned a piece by "Karen Eliot" that is attributed to Marc Couroux. Karen Eliot functions here as a pivot on which these composers appropriate each other's identity by writing, or writing about, compositions that the other(s) has (have) written under the pseudonym of Eliot. We never know who the author is as he or she is always twice removed from the assignation of the work. In a way, this many-to-one inversion of the one-to-many Grúpat complex is not anti-identity but *ante*-identity. While corrupting the logic of signatures that establishes legible hierarchies of persona it nonetheless continues to traverse between levels of abstraction that permit one to communicate a sense of intention and agency that typically locates an identity. Only in this case intention and agency are always skewed and out of joint.

This project has similar effects to Grúpat in terms of the way it confuses the restrictions that both define and delimit individual identity. However, Eliot is more mangy and mongrel in character than Grúpat is, for as noted, Eliot's five "collaborators" are always making it both unclear who has written what as "Eliot," and changing details, such as biographical particulars, that are usually considered indispensible in securing the signature of an individual. For example, the fabulated pedigrees that Eliot is given by her members, who tend to portray her as an American composer working in the late twentieth century under the influence of Futurism, Dada, Fluxus, and Punk, are often switched around or reconfigured to reflect the situation in which "she" participates. For instance, the biographical details of "Eliot" that appear in a review written by David Chokroun, composer and artistic director of the Institute for the Study of Advanced Musical Research, of Seattle-based Vanessa Grey's Muzak-opera *Stimulus Progression* (2004)—an opera in which performers follow a group of shoppers through a mall with dictaphones playing a prerecorded performance of their instrumental part—tells us when comparing Grey's work to Eliot's, that the latter is a transgender who served as a reserve in the national guard during the early 1990s while studying composition privately with Barbara Monk Feldman in Santa Fe. However, another description of Eliot appears in a program note for a piano solo attributed to Grey, who submitted the work to a women composers' competition—a work that asks the pianist to suspend two 18-inch concert marching cymbals millimeters above piano strings for as long as possible—noting that Eliot hails from Santa Fe and that it was Barbara Monk Feldman who studied with *her* before she (Eliot) took a job in Seattle doing arrangements and orchestrations for MUZAK Inc. In contrast to Grúpat, whose internal aesthetic dissonances and fictional reality become conceptually harmonized and somewhat spoiled by Walshe's consistent presence and relation to the group,[50] the collective nature and schematic indirection of "Karen Eliot" circulates contradictions and inconsistencies in a way that keeps doubt and the status of her reality in play.

((((Symptoms, syndromes, and hyperfiction

It would seem that the perplexity generated by Eliot's character would dissolve her persona into a field of nonsense. But as a form

---

[50] Not to mention that a feature story on her play with multiple identities in the November 2010 *The Wire* gave the game away. See Phillip Clark, "Misshapen identities," *The Wire*, November 2010.

of radical play her hyperfiction does not dissolve so much as the operational difference between fiction and reality does. As Fisher notes, hyperfiction does not participate in the kind of "imploded transcendence" that constitutes metafiction and its "interminable process by which supplementary dimensions are continually being produced but are immediately and of necessity themselves obsolesced at the very moment of their production."[51] Instead, hyperfiction elaborates processes "in which the product of any process is also one of its founding presuppositions."[52] Agrippa's Trilemma writ large.[53] As hyperfiction, Karen Eliot evades the "tangled hierarchy"[54] of metafiction because her name is constantly shuffled with the proper names of her collaborators to the point where even she proposes that Chokroun, Azmikara, Couroux, Parks, and Grey are *her* fabulations: "*I'm a knot, nothing but a point! In fact, I'm a pointless space through which other voices pass.*"[55] Neither the chicken nor the egg precedes the other; each is a relational term describing the path of a strange loop or the chiral symmetry—"handedness"—of poultry. Names are circular and relative in hyperfiction so that "Eliot" and "Couroux," for example, are the handednesses of an event the way "Alice" and the "Queen" are in the chess-event of *Through the Looking Glass*. And insofar as these names are constantly being exchanged—Chokroun becomes Eliot becomes Couroux, *etcetera*—none receives the actions of things that grounds the drama of the event. Indeed, as Deleuze notes, this is what happens to Alice in her wonderland adventures:

---

[51] Fisher, "Flatline Constructs," http://www.cinestatic.com/trans-mat/Fisher/FC4s3.htm [accessed October 2012]. Fisher calls this condition of excessive meta-izing "Metanoia."
[52] Ibid.
[53] Agrippa's Trilemma is the Greek sceptic's "conclusion" that it is impossible to prove any truth, for we have either a circular argument in which the premise and conclusion support each other, a regressive argument which entails that each proof requires another proof, or an axiomatic argument that acts on unproven precepts. Of course the radical form of this trilemma would include its own position of this impossible situation in its formula.
[54] This is Douglas Hofstadter's term for the way recursive processes search for supplementary dimensions to ground their propositions. See Douglas Hofstadter, *Gödel, Escher, Bach: An Eternal Golden Braid* (New York: Basic Books, 1979).
[55] eldritch Priest, *Boring Formless Nonsense: Experimental Music and The Aesthetics of Failure* (New York: Bloomsbury, 2013), 218.

The loss of the proper name is the adventure which is repeated throughout all of Alice's adventures. For the proper or singular name is guaranteed by the permanence of *savoir*. The latter is embodied in general names designating pauses and rests, in substantives and adjectives, with which the proper name maintains a constant connection. Thus the personal self requires God and the world in general. But when substantives and adjectives begin to dissolve, when the names of pause and rest are carried away by the verbs of pure becoming and slide into the language of events [as they do in the activity of wordplay], all identity disappears from the self, the world, and God.[56]

By constantly swapping proper names, the field of singular symptoms that gather under the designation of a syndrome lose their sense, for a proper name marks a gathering point in a structure of coincidence—the "syndrome" of an event—between a multiplicity of effects that otherwise remain impassive and inexpressive. Only pawns can express the event of promotion. And when all pawns become queens, chess becomes checkers. The uncertainty that arises in shuffling proper names is not alien to the processes which naming names, but, argues Deleuze, is "an objective structure of the event itself."[57] For example, the circulation of symptoms within a body give no sense of an illness until they are parsed and parroted as a syndrome that is designated by the proper name of the clinician who is proxy for the practice and accomplishments of "medicine," the supplementary dimension of diagnosis, treatment, and prevention of disease. And insofar as this uncertainty "moves in two directions at once," where symptoms become symptoms with reference to a syndrome that only becomes a syndrome with reference to symptoms, "it fragments the subject following this double direction."[58] Shuffling the identity of "Karen Eliot" does not exhibit or critique the framing structures that metafiction believes in and suffers from; instead, "Eliot" simply makes a continuous effort

---

[56] Gilles Deleuze, *The Logic of Sense* (New York: Columbia University Press, 1990), 3.
[57] Ibid.
[58] Ibid.

to connect a multiplicity of effects that a proper name pinches with other multiplicities, such as "the subprime mortgage crisis" or the excessively multiple "war on terror." In a sense "Karen Eliot"—the project—is like Lévi-Strauss' "floating signifier," an expression that is "in itself void of sense and thus susceptible of taking on any sense."[59] Unlike Grúpat, "Karen Eliot" has no fixed referent, no identifiable set of symptoms apart from the nonsense that she circulates, a nonsense Deleuze notes, with reference to the differential play that underwrites the sensical spatium which structuralism tried to elaborate, "has no particular sense, but is opposed to the absence of sense rather than to the sense that it produces in excess."[60] In a way, "Karen Eliot" is more like what Deleuze calls an esoteric word, words such as "snark," or "fruminous," or even "it." For without "denot[ing] real objects, manifest[ing] the beliefs and desires of real persons, or signify[ing] meaningful concepts,"[61] Eliot conveys the open sense of nothing in particular that in turn demands a continuous apprenticeship in the fundamental exercise of sense.

Eliot's esoteric apprenticeship in (non)sense is thus exemplified in the way she thematizes her nonsense as a hyperfiction that writes itself into being as someone suffering from depersonalization disorder (DPD).[62] Eliot, who is several, describes her nonsense in the prolegomena to her *The Pinocchio Syndrome* by writing that she suffers recurring episodes of feeling as though she is completely artificial or invented. "There are times," she writes, "where I feel to be little more than the empty spaces between the words you're reading, which is to say that I am as much and as little as a blank page."[63] Having read American philosopher Kendall Walton's self-help book *Mimesis as Make-Believe* (1990) while in grad school at the

---

[59] Claude Lévi-Strauss, "Introduction à l'oeuvre de Marcel Mauss," in Marcel Mauss, *Sociologie et anthropologie* (Paris: PUF, 1950), 48–9; quoted in Deleuze, *Logic of Sense*, 50.

[60] Deleuze, *The Logic of Sense*, 71.

[61] Charles Stivale, *Gilles Deleuze: Key Concepts* (Montreal: McGill-Queen's University Press, 2005), 68.

[62] The DSM-IV defines depersonalization disorder as a condition that can be identified by symptoms such as: "feelings of unreality, that your body does not belong to you, or that you are constantly in a dreamlike state." See http://allpsych.com/disorders/dissociative/depersonalization.html.

[63] Priest, *Boring Formless Nonsense*, 220.

University of Michigan, a work which argues that art is an elaborate game of make believe and that the world and objects (rules and things) adumbrated by fictional statements—propositions that are "to be *imagined* to be true"[64]—are to be taken as props that direct and organize our affective and emotional investment in an imagined reality, Eliot developed a sophisticated strategy for coping with her condition. She writes, "I write fictions, what others might call little 'reality machines,' about music that I have not in fact written or listened to."[65] From her perspective as a work of fiction herself, "reality machines" are props that make her real, or as she puts it, "at the very least they make everything as a fictional as I am."[66] That is, Eliot's fictions are not only like Walton's props, wherein the act of saying "Say this is that" marks the event around which sense can be made of play, but resembles Deleuze and Guattari's abstract machines in that her "sayings" place "variables of content and expression in continuity,"[67] which is to say, in metaphysical-speak, that her fictions have a way of binding differences and making them resonate to produce a temporary reality zone or assemblage of sincerity. But Eliot's "reality machines" are actually no different from the more familiar notion of "discourse," which also corrals difference into consistent realties, except that her realities spin out of musical props, and, for the most part, she keeps her fascism to herself.

While Eliot's form of "therapy" may be somewhat deluded, what is interesting about her fictions is that they take on many different styles and are often self-reflexive interrogations on the constellation of voices that her proper name circulates. These machinic props may take the shape of a concert program note (or may simply refer to biographical notes as above), conventional short stories, newspaper articles, blog entries, a series of emails, or even book chapters. Some of the more curious machines, however, are those that resemble JG Ballard's

---

[64] Kendall Walton, "Précis of Mimesis as Make-Believe," *Philosophy and Phenomenological Research* 51, no. 2 (1991): 380. See also Kendall Walton, *Mimesis as Make-Believe: On the Foundations of the Representational Arts* (Cambridge, MA: Harvard University Press, 1990).

[65] Priest, *Boring Formless Nonsense*, 221

[66] Ibid.

[67] Gilles Deleuze and Félix Guattari, *A Thousand Plateaus: Capitalism and Schizophrenia*, trans. Brian Massumi (Minneapolis: University of Minnesota Press, 1987), 511.

"invisible literature," writings that simulate the canon-less history of classified ads, car manuals, telephone books, and weather reports. "Her" work, *In a Sedimental Mood* (2010), for example, is like a compilation of classified ads about a work that explores how, under certain conditions, perception might be unhinged from its morphological habits to lose track of its expressions of attention and distraction. This prop, however, also alludes to a tendency in contemporary art to exemplify the paradoxical sense of stasis and unfinishedness that prolonged duration evokes, a sense that art theorist Terry Smith identifies as "the taking up of a viewer's time before the artwork provides enough information about itself for its point to become apparent."[68]

(((((*In a Sedimental Mood*

This unauthorized versioning of Eliot's fictionalizations (apparently) by Toronto intermedia artist Marc Couroux, is Eliot's machine (which is Couroux's fiction (which is our discourse)) describing a kaleidoscopic reality composed of multiple surfaces bleeding into each other's ground and staining each other's figures. *In a Sedimental Mood*, like any good piece of fiction, draws a map *to* its world. It does this by evoking the affects coded through musical works of 1960s and 1970s popular culture as noted in the ad where Eliot describes the stylistic constraints of the instrumental voices, "Bacharach chordal progressions, Ornette-Prime-Time perpetually dithering bass, static single guitar lines (*Cinnamon Girl* cantus firmus), light virtuosic Hammond organ (space-age pop), arch-pseudo-Baroque harpsichord (late 1960s movie soundtracks)." Essentially, Eliot is exploiting what Muzak "audio architects" refer to as a song's "topology"—"the cultural and temporal associations that it [the song] carries with it, like a hidden refrain"[69]—to create a polyphony of affects that articulate the byzantine nature of late-capitalist culture's polytemporality,

---

[68] Terry Smith, *What Is Contemporary Art?* (Chicago: University Of Chicago Press, 2009), 194.
[69] David Owen, "The Soundtrack of Your Life," *The New Yorker*, 10 April 2006, http://www.newyorker.com/archive/2006/04/10/060410fa_fact#ixzz16vOqbKnW [accessed October 2012].

STRICTLY PLATONIC

MUSIC AS Eventual **PROCESS**

Constructed by independently recorded layers of differing specifics (pitch, harmony), but same general affect/gesture. CONVENTIONAL SOUNDING SURFACE made to function unconventionally (experimentally) over time.

I'VE ALWAYS BEEN interested in meandering ideas within tight metrical contexts.

ALWAYS "REPOINTING"— attention keeps moving around "signposts" clamouring for central focus.

THAT MOMENT IN PERFORMANCE (1970) when background music flips into foreground as the head gangster draws attention to it ("I like that, Gordon") and asks that the "Muzak On-Location Service" apparatus be turned up. It also signals a move from an extranarrative situation

(**background music as soundtrack**) to a materialized (immanent) subject within the narrative itself (background music as background music).

OR THESE MOMENTS in Ornette Coleman's "Prime Time" harmolodic work, where divergent lines suddenly coalesce into a seemingly "intentional" (rationalized) tonal plateau (though mostly coincidental); push and pull between structural listening versus negotiating the ungraspable qualities of an intensely layered content (though never so dense as to completely push you over into textural, object-like listening).

WOMEN SEEKING WOMEN

A CONTINUOUS REFOCUSING of perspectives as recognizable entities emerge from chaotic layering.

AFFECTS RANDOMLY LIBERATED!

THE MUSIC IS CONSTANTLY DE- & RE-CENTRING YOU, giving you an illusion of diversity. Meanwhile, they are indoctrinating

you deeper into the system. The closer the music is scrutinized (actively listened to), the more the diversity is aurally compelling...as it melds with the background, diversity ducks below the surface.

ALWAYS TRANSPOSING, always standing still (similar actions performed on different layers cancel each other out). Total variety = total strictness.

*** HINTING AT STYLISTIC categories, but never fully going there (**eccentric hybridity**).

EACH LINE has its own set of boundaries. Descending piano lines ("cocktail"), rhythmic piano and detuned Rhodes (cf. Lalo Schifrin / Don Ellis / TV soundtracks), Bacharach chordal progressions, Ornette-Prime-Time perpetually dithering bass, static single guitar lines (*Cinnamon Girl* cantus firmus), light virtuosic Hammond organ (space-age pop), arch-pseudo-Baroque harpsichord (late 60s movie soundtracks).

WOMEN SEEKING MEN

THE STYLISTIC PROFILE will change from moment to moment, depending on relative clarity (how many lines are happening at once). Each line is recorded separately without listening to the other (co-occurrent) lines.
A kind of "deaf" recording (cf. blind drawings).

MOREOVER, each of the 84 versions of the same line is recorded consecutively (i.e. every line of cocktail piano recorded in a row, one after the other). Then, the second lines are recorded in their 84 incarnations (without listening to the first line), etc.

YOU END UP with a process that extends (exhausts) itself horizontally, has a definite linear timeline, but also has vertical consequences that cannot be predicted (deaf recording). Recording 84 consecutive versions of the same contour, gesture, affect takes its toll. Owing to the relative simplicity of each line, a sense of diminishing potentials quickly sets in.

A PRESSURE to be inventive over an extended recording process.

(**ALWAYS**) **ALREADY-INFLECTED MUSICS.** Though indicating how they ought to be "taken", the compounded co-presence of eight occurrent musics tends to cancel out individual inflection, or at least scumble the specific potential of each. At times, a "clearing" (reggae drop out) allows for one of these inflected musics to momentarily dominate, flipping from indistinct background to definite foreground, only to be crowded out at the next available moment...

LIMINAL PROFILES: not quite exclusively figuration, not quite memorable enough to be recollected. (Event or hue?)

A SELF-ENCLOSED SYSTEM.

...THE THING IS "MODULATING" ... from one iteration to another. But each one is still cut from the same cloth. (Moving while staying in place). Or, it's like coming across the same object over and over again, but never in the same location.

MODULATIONS ONLY HAPPEN THROUGH OVERLAYS (vertically), not in the original track (which might outline modulatory potential without being able to fully articulate the shift). In a sense, the *texture* is always modulating, which remainders the impression of non-modulation.

MEN SEEKING WOMAN

ABSOLUTELY UNRETAINABLE:

(I can't even remember how it goes, and I made it!). It's a condition that stunts facile categorization and defeats the tune-running-thru-the-head syndrome ("Earworms" or Involuntary Musical Imagery).

FADE OUTS: IMMEDIATE RETROSPECTIVIZERS (formally). They usually happen over redundant materials—not so here. They pull together what has just been heard into a moderately coherent entity (though one which resists a modicum of structural listening), while also giving the impression that this texture could continue in much the same way without significant alteration (fade outs are markers of timelessness). The beginnings, however, are always clear-cut.

(YOU HAVE TO LEAVE IT IN ORDER TO RETURN TO IT.) BEGINNNING AGAIN restores momentum (before drift and inertia set in, chronically). (Reinstitution of purpose happens even when the beginning appears to pick things up exactly where they were left off by the fade, in seeming rhythmic lockstep.)

THE POINT AT SOME LEVEL is to have the listener focus on that shock of newness that inflects and re-inflects an experience which ought to become predictable and repetitive over time.

GETTING USED TO SOMETHING over time through repeats that aren't repeats.

ALWAYS CHANGING, always staying the same (at different levels of perception).

A NON-SYSTEMATIC SYSTEM (Bataille), proliferating from the middle (Deleuze).

OVER TIME the form of the composites becomes clear, even as content remains inscrutable.

MEN SEEKING MEN

ONCE A "THINGNESS" has been established (through duration & repetition), then perceptions of variation can become more acute and specific. Where that "flip" happens depends on the listener. The "thingness" of the thing is established by cranking out variations that reinforce (paradoxically) their sameness.

DESPITE THE SAME-SOUNDING SURFACE, which keeps one in a fairly static place, an infra-legible difference leeches out at a subliminal level, forcing one to (gradually) rethink what constitutes significant (substantive) change. (A process that itself undergoes changes over the length of the piece).

CONSONACE/ DISSONANCE, signal/noise. The signal of one context becomes the noise (interference) to the next context (which "arrives" without you knowing it, Möbius-style). Your signal is my noise / your noise is my signal.

FOREIGN (NOISY) ELEMENTS are suddenly "justified" through a bifurcation to a more compatible context.

MISC ROMANCE

TUNEFULNESS: a factor of duration/repetition.

OSCILLATION BETWEEN PERCEPTION of object (focused on) to perception of space, the environment in which this "background music" is playing…

FADES INTO BACKGROUND even when it's being actively listened to in the foreground. It dares you not to listen to it—like wallpaper begs you not to look at it.

TO OCCUPY THE BACKGROUND means to activate the consciousness of all the layers that function subliminally, the ground against which various figures of attraction are pitched.

NON-REPETITIVE REPETITION: Your ears are momentarily retuned, then the music fades into the background again (without undergoing any kind

of shift in volume). Compare the physical fade outs at the end of each event with the mental "fade outs" occurring when attention drifts towards other shores…

CASUAL ENCOUNTERS

YOUR MOVEMENT through the 74' is at times viscous (attractive, conventionally listenable), slips into your "comfort zone"), at other times sludgy (the indigestibility of superimposed dissonances), and at times granitic (object-like textural mass), grinding to a halt perceptually, though in each case the general "motion" is identical (motion and tempo are control structures that allow one to more readily evaluate the degree to which time stretches over events and behaves AS IF slower or faster with each iteration).

FINSIHED, it's finished, nearly finished, it must be nearly finished. *(Pause.)* Grain upon grain, one by one, and one day, suddenly, there's a heap, a little heap, the impossible heap.

Karen Eliot, *In a Sedimental Mood* (2010). Courtesy of Artist.

one that Smith argues "is characterized by the insistent presentness of multiple, often incompatible temporalities accompanied by the failure of all candidates that seek to provide *the* overriding temporal framework."[70] "We might also say," continues Smith, "that time is... moving in many different directions: backward, forward trending, sideways sliding, in suspension, stilled, bent warped, or repeated."[71] To the extent that the disparate lines of *In a Sedimental Mood* juxtapose musical layers that slow down, speed up, anticipate, and induce a sickly nostalgia, they exemplify the multifarious present that Smith describes (and thereby articulate the idea of its feeling as well). Additionally, insofar as this tangle of durations and affective codes express something of the present temporal imbroglio, the fiction of *In a Sedimental Mood* diagnoses the symptoms of contemporaneity, which has the paradoxical effect of realizing its own fiction.

((((((Hyperstition, magick, and nonsense

If you recall from the beginning of this chapter, the idea of fiction[72] realizing itself is a form of hyperstition. Hyperstition is, however, characterized not by an insuperable belief that restricts belief to one kind of reality as superstition does, but by "nonbelief," which amounts to a passive belief in the *effects* of belief. Nonbelief in this sense is linked to the modern occult practice of Chaos Magick.[73]

---

[70] Smith, *What Is Contemporary Art?*, 196.

[71] Ibid.

[72] (aka "bullshit").

[73] The "k" at the end of magick is a practice initiated by Aleister Crowley who introduced the archaic form of the word to distinguish the occult practice and esoteric wisdom that he was teaching from stage magic. However, in the introduction to Crowley's work *Magick* (1973), John Symonds and Kenneth Grant argue that the spelling has an occult significance:

> The Anglo-Saxon *k* in Magick, like most of Crowley's conceits, is a means of indicating the kind of magic which he performed. K is the eleventh letter of several alphabets, and eleven is the principal number of magick, because it is the number attributed to the Qliphoth—the underworld of demonic and chaotic forces that have to be conquered before magick can be performed. K has other magical implications: it corresponds to the power or *shakti* aspect of creative energy, for k is the ancient Egyptian *khu*, the magical power. Specifically, it stands for *kteis* (vagina),

As its initial expounder, Peter Carroll, defines it, Chaos Magick is a practical and experimental art in developing "magical thinking,"[74] a meta-belief in the efficacy of belief for achieving effects.[75] Like Chaos Magick, which aims to access "the 'thing' responsible for the origin and continued action of events"[76] by hijacking the symbols and discipline of belief structures, hyperstition manipulates the real. But the "Real" that hyperstition manipulates is of course the realm of effects, a realm of expressive correspondences that represents the commingling of virtual and actual entities as they mutually alter and modulate each other's territory: In other words, the constructed world. But what distinguishes hyperstition from Chaos Magick is less the act of reality manipulation and more the location of agency and intention. From the side of Chaos Magick, and most occult philosophies that subscribe to some form of Jakob Böhme's theory of the "doctrine of signatures" wherein "Everything is a signature, pointing beyond itself to an ultimate and interior reality,"[77] agency is explicitly located in the individual. As an expression (or a "mode" to use Spinoza's terminology) of divine impulse, the individual possesses an innate capacity to realize his/her nature as an actor in the shaping of reality by way of appropriating the energy-harnessing

---

the complement to the wand (or phallus) which is used by the Magician in certain aspects of the Great Work." (Aleister Crowley, *Magick*, ed. John Symonds and Kenneth Grant (London: Routledge, 1973), xvi.)

[74] This is not to be confused with the psychoanalytic notion of "magical thinking" as a primitive form of naïve animism, but a kind of non-rational (which may include unconscious as well as alternative states induced by drugs or meditation) thinking that participates in the manipulation of reality.

[75] See Peter Carroll, "Chaoism and Chaos Magic, A Personal View." This essay is available all over the internet, but here's a link: http://www.chaosmatrix.org/library/chaos/texts/chaoism.html [accessed October 2012].

[76] Peter Carroll, *Liber Null & Psychonaut: An Introduction to Chaos Magic* (York Beach, ME: Weiser Books, 1987), 28.

[77] Brian Gibbons, *Spirituality and the Occult* (London; New York: Routledge, 2001), 7. Prior to its expression in occult terms, the doctrine of signatures referred chiefly to a herbalist practice in which an identified homology between various herbs and certain human body parts is thought to indicate a medicinal effect that the herb will have on that body part. For example, the value of "bloodroot" in treating blood diseases was believed to be "written" in its orange-red colour. More likely, though, the doctrine of signatures was a mnemonic device and a way of disseminating medical information. See Bradley Bennett, "Doctrine of Signatures: An Explanation of Medicinal Plant Discovery or Dissemination of Knowledge?," *The New York Botanical Garden* 61, no. 3 (2007).

disciplines of various belief systems. Here, the Chaos magician's intent and *non-attachment* to any specific belief is a thing to be practiced and cultivated, the way, for instance, a studio musician aims to develop a technique and musicality that is adaptable to any style or genre. Hyperfiction, however, as it entails nonbelief, surrenders agency to the differential and impersonal workings of things such as language, economy, and affect, the power of which is manipulated indirectly by communication technologies and a vast media apparatus whose dissemination of information has a way of taking on a life of its own. Take, for example, the phenomenon of "hype." What "hype" describes is a process in which statements about a future effect are peremptorily circulated in various media and intensified by an excitement embodied in the present as a "buzz" that eventually brings about the anticipated reality in the form of "interest." Call it an unintentional incantation, one that deputizes the effect before it happens.[78] The important point here is that Chaos Magick is a practice that intends what Peter Carroll calls "psychological anarchy...[where] the aim is to produce inspiration and enlightenment through disordering our belief structures,"[79] while hyperfiction is an emergent and anonymous effect arising in feedback systems that continually (self-)adjust to and compensate or supplement the reality that they produce (like capitalism does).[80] In a sense, hyperstition is what the Chaos Magician tries to create:

---

[78] The financial fallout known as the subprime mortgage crisis of 2008 is another example of hyperstitional processes in that the events leading up to the collapse of the reality known as "the market" unfolded through a series of greed driven symbolic investments made on the credit ratings provided by hedge funds and other entities of the shadow banking system.[†] No one person or secret cabal manipulated this reality with esoteric spells to effect a change in wealth; rather, it was a series of adjustments in financial policy, the misapplication of risk models and financial engineering, and a dubious faith in the market's ability to self-correct that altered the reality of capital.[‡]

[†] For an incredibly detailed overview and summary (with wonderful graphics and flowcharts) see the Wikipedia entry on the subprime mortgage crisis at: http://en.wikipedia.org/wiki/Subprime_mortgage_crisis.

[‡] Paul Volcker goes into these conditions in more detail in Paul Volcker, "The Time We Have Is Growing Short," *The New York Review of Books*, 24 June 2010, http://www.nybooks.com/articles/archives/2010/jun/24/time-we-have-growing-short [accessed October 2012].

[79] Carroll, *Liber Null & Psychonaut*, 115.

[80] For an exegesis on how capitalism breeds and lives on hyperfictions see Mark Fisher, *Capitalist Realism: Is There No Alternative?* (London: Zero Books, 2009).

an abstract machine re-punctuating the real with virtual entities that pinch, fold, bend, and twist the hardware of actual bodies in order to form new circuits of behaviour, desire, and ultimately, becoming.

Drawing on this distinction we can consider another of Eliot's schizo-fictions, "Becoming Karen et al, a Real-Time Hyperstition as of March 30, 2007," to be a blending of Chaos Magick and hyperstition in the way it aims to shape the reality of a musical experience by treating its own narrative as a cryptic symbolization of the meanings and intents of the music she writes about. This symbolization of desire is a process known in contemporary occult circles as "sigilization," a technique derived from the English artist Austin Osman Spare's practice of reducing statements of intent to illegible glyphs (something looking sufficiently witchy like this):

For Spare,

> Sigils are monograms of thought…a mathematical means of symbolizing desire and giving it form that has the virtue of preventing any thought and association on that particular desire (at the magical time), escaping the detection of the Ego, so that it does not restrain or attach such desire to its own transitory images, memories and worries, but allows it free passage to the sub-consciousness.[81]

---

[81] Austin Osman Spare, *The Book of Pleasure* (Sioux Falls, SD: NuVision Publications, 2007), 91.

The practice of sigilization is thus a way of accessing the repressed forces of the unconscious.[82] Indeed, German occultist Frater U∴D∴ (a/k/a Ralph Tegtmeier) describes Spare's sigilization as a form of "controlled repression" and a means of "reversely using" (i.e. de-pathologizing) this psychological mechanism to align coincidences. Tegtmeier summarizes Spare's rationale as follows:

> If the psyche represses certain impulses, desires, fears, and so on, and these then have the power to become so effective that they can mold or even determine entirely the entire conscious personality of a person right down to the most subtle detail, this means nothing more than the fact that through repression ("forgetting") many impulses, desires, etc. have the ability to create a reality to which they are denied access as long as they are either kept alive in the conscious mind or recalled into it. Under certain conditions, that which is repressed can become even more powerful than that which is held in the conscious mind.[83]

For Chaos Magick, sigilization accomplishes a magical action by enciphering desire and is therefore a technique that "takes advantage of the psychological fulfillment automatism and forces the subconscious to bring about the desired effect against the potential resistance of the conscious mind and censor."[84] Basically, the idea of using sigils is to bypass the ego's editing mechanisms and implant desires and directions to create drives at the level of the unconscious where their workings may go unnoticed and un-bowdlerized. In this respect, "Eliot" herself may be a sigil in that her name functions as a glyph for a hyperstition that manifests a fictional desire which she, and the composers who become her, share. We may say then that to become Karen is to pretend to repress desire "in order to make it capable of being fulfilled."[85]

---

[82] "Frater U∴D∴" is short for *Ubique Daemon Ubique Deus* (Demon in all, God in all). Tegtmeier is currently a member of the magical order Fraternitas Saturni ("Brotherhood of Saturn").

[83] Frater U∴D∴, *High Magic: Theory & Practice* (St. Paul, MN: Llewellyn Publications, 2005), 134.

[84] Ibid., 135.

[85] Ibid.

But if this is the case, if "Karen Eliot" is a sigil that has effects by being written and read, which is itself a process that enciphers fictional desires, then she resembles what writer Grant Morrison calls a "hypersigil": "a dynamic miniature model of the magician's universe, a hologram, microcosm, or 'voodoo doll' which can be manipulated in real time to produce changes in the macrocosmic environment of 'real' life."[86] To repeat, a sigil is a glyph or monogram of thought that one symbolizes and then forgets (i.e. represses).[87] But as Morrison explains, a "hypersigil" is not static; it is "a sigil extended through the fourth dimension" that "can take the form of a poem, a story, a song, a dance or any other extended artistic activity you wish to try."[88] What is unique about hypersigils is that unlike ordinary sigils, the hypersigil can be affected so that its effects might be continuously modulated. Morrison calls his own comic series, *The Invisibles* (1994–2000), a hypersigil, describing it as "a six-year long sigil in the form of an occult adventure story which consumed and recreated my life during the period of its composition and execution."[89] In this sense, "Karen Eliot," too, is a hypersigil in that the composition and execution of her fiction not only (re)creates her life and the composers who pass through her, but mine and yours as well. And she does this not by simply consuming writing/reading hours of one's life, but by the way her stories shuttle desires to the unconscious to form a complex of ideas and qualities, an affectively charged fictional quantity that functions independently of conscious thought while striving towards its own satisfaction.[90]

---

[86] Grant Morrison, "Pop Magic!," in *Book of Lies: The Disinformation Guide to Magick and the Occult (Being an Alchemical Formula to Rip a Hole in the Fabric of Reality)*, ed. Richard Metzger (New York: The Disinformation Company, 2003), 21.

[87] This process of "forgetting" is usually referred to as "charging" the sigil. It is ideally accomplished by holding the sigil before oneself or in one's mind during moments of increased intensity, which may include simple acts of concentration, occasions of fear, or even during times of lust. After these events and their forces perish, one promptly banishes any thought of the desire symbolized by the sigil. Because mediation can take years and moments of surprise are out of one's control, Morrison suggests masturbation as an expedient (and fun) way of sigil-charging.

[88] Morrison, "Pop Magic!," 21.

[89] Ibid.

[90] Frater U∴D∴, *High Magic*, 135.

If this is too esoteric sounding, let's for a moment reframe it in more academic terms. For those scholars who approach change and reality in terms of sublimated material relations and the textual production of difference, hypersigils may be likened not to objects but the variations that play across objects, across the serial moments of writing or reading a book, of composing, performing or listening to music, of being arrested, or even those liminal moments such as commuting to work. As such, what a hypersigil embodies is change, and what change explicates is an implicated difference, a difference that from one direction seems to *induce* the process that actualizes it in terms of ordinary sense experience, but from another, is an *expression*, a symptom, of that process. Deleuze—Sorcerer Supreme of Difference—notes that this process of becoming always eludes the present, that change moves and pulls in both directions at once as Alice does when she grows taller than she was and smaller than she will be.[91] Change taken in this way is in fact very close to Deleuze's understanding of "sense" as a dimension that establishes the expressive potential of a proposition or an event so that, for example, "to grow" will have the sense of "growing younger" *and* "growing older," "growing faster" *and* "growing slower." Or, to use Deleuze's example, "a tree *greens*" is the sense, or pure variation of an arborific becoming. Employing the figure of the phantasm to describe how sense is connected to thinking, Deleuze writes, the phantasm "is a machine for the extraction of a little thought, for the distribution of a difference of potential at the edges of the crack [in the flow of becoming], and for the polarization of the cerebral field."[92] In other words, *sense* is change, a virtual fold or pleat in experience that introduces into a neutral system (i.e., chaos) what could be called import or significance. It is the genetic condition of thought in that it grounds the possible ways we may refer to an external state of affairs, manifest a desire or belief, or signify another concept.[93] Yet sense is a paradoxical dimension in that it changes with each

---

[91] See Deleuze, *The Logic of Sense*, 1–3.

[92] Ibid., 220.

[93] Deleuze indicates these as three types of relations (dimensions) of a proposition: denotation, manifestation, and signification. But sense is the fourth dimension of the proposition and only it relates a proposition to an event, to a becoming. See Deleuze, "Third Series of the Proposition," *The Logic of Sense*, 12–22.

expression of it, so while the pure variation of "to thirst," which marks an expressive potential does not change, *how* one thirsts is always being refigured. "Intensities of relations change in the realm of sense, but the relations themselves are eternal."[94] What sense traces then are variations of variations, a spiraling differential intensity that flickers across things as an abstract line of development, a line of creative flight. Deleuze's own *The Logic of Sense* (1990), composed of multidimensional sentences[95] and mind-bending figurations of sense, is itself a hypersigil in that its experimental form and series of series (of series...) creates the sense of sense, which is that sense is creative, always being made and changing. While this makes for a nearly impenetrable read, by implicating its own expressions into its explication the work nevertheless conveys something of the nature of sense, not by telling us what sense is but by becoming what it wants to be. Thus, like all sigils, *The Logic of Sense* ferries something to the unconscious where its ideas are repressed and allowed to work in the reader at a level where there are no contradictions and insight is a lateral rather than linear event.

Returning to the discussion of Eliot's fiction, "Becoming Karen et al, a Real-Time Hyperstition as of March 30, 2007," I want to suggest that it is like *The Logic of Sense* in that it tries to convey what it describes by becoming it. This piece, which is (supposedly) penned by Montreal-based composer Aydem Azmikara[96]—a Chaos magician,

---

[94] James Williams, *Gilles Deleuze's Logic of Sense: A Critical Introduction and Guide* (Edinburgh: Edinburgh University Press, 2008), 3.

[95] Williams insists that Deleuze's writing style in *The Logic of Sense* is deliberately composed to "prompt" something in the reader, for sense is "not in what is said, but what readers allow it to trigger" (Williams, *Deleuze's Logic of Sense*, 21). To provoke the agitation of sense Deleuze writes so that "each sentence is a mixture of philosophical demonstrations and conceptual innovations, with literary and artistic references, with accessible images, with terms form many other disciplines, (mathematics, psychoanalysis, literature, structuralism...), with condensed physical metaphors and extremely varied analogies" (Ibid., 20).

[96] "Aydem Azmikara" is, like "Karen Eliot," a multiple use name. However, this name is designed to express the ideal anonymity inherent to cyberspace. Type this name into a search engine and you'll find a blog explaining that Aydem Azmikara is "an anonymous distributed identity project," a name that can be used by anyone as an anonymous "signature" and therefore impersonally gain access to a range of potential transactions available online. Further down the page, the significance of the name is revealed, reading: "'Arakimza Medya' means 'stolen signature media' which becomes 'Aydem Azmikara,' when read backwards." See http://arakimzaMedya.blogspot.com.

incidentally, who composes music by stealing the signature elements of other composers' works, first by making a transcription of the thoughts he had while listening to or performing another's work, and then turning this transcription into a (hyper)sigil—takes the form of a journal entry in which "Eliot" recounts her own experience and thoughts of listening to Marc Couroux's *Carpenters et al., Downey Musical Holdings, a Real-Time Social System as of March 29, 2007.* In this entry, Eliot suggests that the concept of media "spin," which Couroux's work purports to simulate, recasts the occult principle of reality manipulation in a way that suggests that both "spin" and "magick" exploit the paradox which affirms sense as not only a pliable metaphysical surface but a creative obscenity.

(((((((Becoming Karen et al, a Real-Time Hyperstition as of March 30, 2007 by Karen Eliot

Last night I went to hear my friend Aydem perform in Marc Couroux's piece Carpenters et al., Downey Musical Holdings, a Real-Time Social System as of March 29, 2007 *at the Queen West Arts Centre with Neither/Nor. I've been to some of Neither/ Nor's shows before and found them to be, how can I put it, weird. The shows and the music are for the most part unassuming; they're staged in small theatres or, as their so called "~~obscurity~~" festival was back in 2005, in a room in the Darling Building, and presented like any concert is, with the musicians and audience divided by that invisible line of concert convention. But the music is strange. It's strange not in the way that Lachenmann's instru-mentale musique concrete or Russolo's intonarumori orchestra might be considered strange, but strange in the way that it's so sincere. Now, I know that all of Neither/Nor's members are savvy in some regard to the idea of the social construction of reality, so this sincerity doesn't strike me as naïve. Rather, it's more that the idea of reality's constructedness is taken for granted so that art becomes less a hammer for smashing mirrors, or a monad reflecting the internal conflicts of sociohistorical processes, and* more a technique for generating affect, for producing the thing that makes thoughts sticky and, ultimately, effective. So, in going to listen to Aydem, I anticipated that I would be similarly affected, that in listening to this music I would, in a sense, be changed. And from the moment I stepped into the space, I suppose I was. Let me explain.

Unlike the studio space in which obscurity took place, this series of Neither/Nor shows—titled "(failure)" by the way—were being staged at what is essentially a rehearsal hall for amateur theatre and dance. Located just up the street from the Centre for Addiction and Health, on the second floor of a rundown office building, the performance space was filled with mirrors and ballet bars lining the walls. Some attempt was made to cover these using huge swathes of kraft paper. But thankfully, this material (whose colour always strikes me as a vomity shade of ecru brown) was modulated towards a more tolerable shade of ochre by a rather charming display of bare incandescent bulbs strung around the exposed rafters. In my opinion, however, the place was a dump.

Before Couroux's piece were a couple of other small chamber works, the most interesting of which was an extremely austere solo violin piece by an LA composer-performer named Eric km Clark. The work consisted of him quietly bowing harmonics and occasionally plucking a string on what he calls a "simplified violin" (which I learned is a violin whose strings are all tuned to "E"). What made this work interesting were the miscellaneous artefacts generated by Clark's bowing and the instrument's inability to hold its unusual tuning. (I should think about this piece some more.) But Clark's brief and ascetic sound world, which came off as someone trying to figure out a tune in their head by whistling it out loud, was the opposite of Carpenters et al.'s forty minute din.

Carpenters et al., whose concept can be summarized as a set of instructions for a performer to learn Carpenters songs on the spot, has no specific instrumentation. However, in this case eight musicians, divided into three groups, realized the piece. What I learned after talking with Aydem about the work is that Couroux split the ensemble to represent three dimensions of what he (Couroux) refers to as the process of "spin," as in media spin.

I'll try to describe how this worked: The first "dimension" of spin, which was Couroux on piano and visual artist Juliana Pivato on vocals, was positioned near the back of the stage area. Both Couroux and Pivato were wearing headphones and listening to a set of three or four randomly selected fragments of Carpenters songs.[97] As they listened, they would try to learn the fragments one by one, then smear them together to form a kind of "hook"(which had the effect of them playing excerpts from "The Carpenters Greatest Hits that never were"), and start the process over again. The second dimension of spin was composed of two electric guitars (one of whom was Aydem). These musicians were asked to listen to the spun (smeared) melodies of the first dimension and try to reproduce what they heard, to replicate the hesitation and errors, the inaccuracies and fudging,

---

[97] For this piece, Couroux used a patch that he wrote for the ubiquitous interactive music software MAX/MSP to randomly select two- to five-second samples of Carpenters repertoire. Importantly, these samples are taken from anywhere in a track so that their start and stop points cut across phrases and vocal lines to further dismember and decontextualize the melodic sense of the original song.

which would turn into its own kind of smear. The third dimension of violin, trombone, banjo, and contrabass, had each player listening through headphones to the original fragments that were the source for the first group (piano and voice). But unlike the first group, these musicians were trying to "recover" shavings of the Carpenters as accurately as possible while at the same time being impinged upon by the ongoing spins of both the first and second dimensions. The result, if you can imagine it, was something like those hidden 3D pictures—"stereograms" I believe they're called—popular in the 1990s where, if you can unfocus on the place of coloured dots, a phantasmatic image will appear to float over the noise of the picture.

Hyperstition as of March 31, 2007

I've heard Couroux *do something like this in an earlier piece he called* Watergating *(2007). In that work there were only two performers learning and building a repertoire from similarly randomized fragments of The Carpenters. But unlike* Carpenters et al., Watergating *isn't reflexive about the creative distortion of spin. That is,* Watergating *simply exploits the logic of spin to create another, if somewhat twisted, reality from a heap of cultural debris, while* Carpenters et al. *seems to linger in and palpate the nonsense that a sound bite must pass through in order to be spun, to make sense. But there is something obscene about both* Carpenters et al. *and* Watergating. *Basically, the musicians are instructed to use their musicianship to "smooth-over" the jagged edges and discontinuities of the fragments they hear. In other words, they are asked to put a spin on the nonsense expressed by the continual circulation of decontextualized shards of music. What makes this perverse is that the musician has to expose him or herself to an ongoing series of what are effectively puzzle pieces that never actually form a complete or coherent picture. They are asked to keep on making nonsense—fractalizing nonsense—and thereby to create an unpredictable situation that dislocates the performer from his/her intentions to play well, to not suck. In effect, this forces the performers to either play with their pants down and fondle their musical junk in front of people, or to fake it and make it look/sound like they know what they're doing.*

The listener, too, is caught in the pinches and pulls of spin, for they are also dislocated from their intentions, their intentions to hear a piece of "Music" and not a rehearsal. And to this extent, the listener can either hear the failure as it is—as the making of nonsense—or become an implicated voyeur. Admittedly, I stared a lot.

Hyperstition as of April 1, 2007

I've been thinking lately that perhaps even more perverse than asking the performers to play with themselves is the startling intimacy that a shared exposure to nonsense creates. Last night, I asked Aydem to do that thing he does where he makes a transcription of his thoughts/impressions that occur alongside other activities. Though he usually does this from his perspective as an audience member, I asked him to try to transcribe his thoughts from his time playing Carpenters et al., *and this is what he wrote:*

Start. Stop. Start again. Listen again. What was that? Did it go like this? No, more like this, but a little slower. Okay, now what's that? Up a step…down a third…down another thi—No, wait…Up a step…down a *minor* third, down a step. What's next? I can't hear what—too short. Try again. That's awkward. Okay. Like this…then like this…and like—again… Where are we? Right. Back h…e-r—e again. Up, down, down…"—", uh-uh-uh. There's that voice part: "…*e've only just begu*…" Again. Up, down, down… "-", uhuhuh… "*e've only just begu*" Now it's coming together… Up/down/down "-" *dadada-e've only just beguUpDownDown–dadada~e've only just begu—la lalala laaa*…Shit! It's changed again...

Now, what's startling is that I did the same, I transcribed my thoughts, and this is what I wrote:

Start. Stop. Start. Listen. What's that? I think it was…No, it's like that but a little slower. Okay, what's this? A litter higher…now lower… down again—No, wait…what's she singing?…down even lower. What's next? It's getting noisy—what was that? Listen again. That's strange, but okay. Ahh, I like that…and that…and yes—again…

Wait, where are we? Okay. Back...there—again. Da, duh, duh..."—", uhhhhh. Right, that voice: "...e've only just begu..." Again. Da, duh, duh... "-", uhhhhh..."e've only just begu." Now I think I hear it... Da/duh/duh "-" uhhhhh-e've only just begu...Da/duh/duh–uhhhhh~e've only just begu—"la lalala laaa...What!@? It changed...

In a way, maybe what's obscene about Couroux's work is that it's not clear where performing ends and listening begins. It stands to reason that if both Aydem and I were enduring the same nonsense, that is, if he and I were suffering the same perpetually undone (incomplete) event, then how could we be said to be "we." Because Carpenters et al. *is nothing but the exhibition of process itself, then it has no particular sense by which to fix the clamour of its happening. All that it's producing are relations that it has yet to determine, to actualize. That is, it makes the sense from which "before" and "after," "performer" and "listener," "Aydem" and "Karen" can be specified. And until someone (like me) begins selecting a series of relations, emphasizing one direction of this sense over the other as my explication (unfolding) is doing right now, before/after, performer/listener, Aydem/Karen are simply implicated in the event—expressible but not-yet-expressed.*

But is this nonsense really obscene, or is it more like the kind of mystical experience that Aydem tells me occult practices, such as alchemy and Kabbalah, refer to as coincidentia oppositorum?[98] To linger at the edge of spin, an edge that is constantly advancing and so continually displacing itself in Carpenters et al. *is not to stall in a nothingness but to ride a surface, a surface that is relation as such. Yet sound bites are never heard "as such"; they come with a residue*

[98] This expression originates with the fifteenth-century cardinal Nicholas de Cusa who reasons that from the perspective of the infinite—i.e. God—opposites coincide, for the infinite by definition must include all categories of things, even what it is not. For de Cusa, this was a way of showing how the faculty of reason, while limited, is (paradoxically) capable of conceptualizing the un-conceptualizable (the infinite) in the form of paradox (hence the title of his treatise *De Docta Ignorantia*). While de Cusa's work is the first to use the expression, Dennis McCort argues that the theme of *coincidentia oppositorum* is "everywhere in cultural expression," for life is constituted by an ineradicably tension between difference and identity, transcendence and immanence. See Dennis McCort, *Going Beyond the Pairs: The Coincidence of Opposites in German Romanticism, Zen, and Deconstruction* (Albany: State University of New York Press, 2001).

of context—finger streaks on a pane of glass. Hence there is always an "It sounds like...." But by the same token, to "sound like" is also "to not sound like," for it is by this same relation (and not by a relation to the same) that the sound bite becomes either. To spin is therefore to manipulate a surface that stretches along the length of a sound event...so had he "a rose by any other name" Lazarus might still be dead. In a way, the perpetual spin of Carpenters et al. *is obscene, for its continuous decentring of intention resembles the depth created by two mirrors endlessly displacing each other's surface to create the effect of depth. However, on the other hand, its way of promoting action on fragments that spread effects across the surface of the work smacks of occult sympathies in that it articulates the basic magical principle of the law of contiguity or cosmic isotropy whereby to affect a part has effects on the whole.*[99] *To this end, the way* Carpenters et al. *summons performance habits and forces the performer to confront and change these is a form of auto-affection, one that generates local effects which radiate outwards, inf(l)ecting a musical reality in which* Carpenters et al. *is itself but a part.* Quod est inferius est sicut quod est superius, et quod est superius est sicut quod est inferius.[100]

Hyperstition as of April 2, 2007

More to mock his beliefs (nonbeliefs?) than to make a serious point, I told Aydem that maybe Carpenters et al. *was an esoteric ritual that Couroux devised in order to ward off the demons and specters of media. However, to my surprise he responded quite sincerely, saying something like:*

> *Yeah, Couroux is a closet magician. "Spin" is just a way for him to mask his occult predilections. In fact, his notion of spin riffs on Genesis P-Orridge's idea of the sound byte as a "splinter," a hologrammatic*

---

[99] See Mauss, *Theory of Magic*, 79–86.

[100] This is the classic formulation of occult metaphysics as rendered by the legendary figure Hermes Trismegistus in *The Emerald Tablet*, an ancient book of insights that reveals a "spiritual technology" for self-transformation and the sublimation of the species into higher spiritual states. This passage reads: "That which is below is as that which is above, and that which is above is as that which is below."

fragment refracting the whole of a reality it helped compose.[101] The whole lot of them [Neither/Nor], they're all repressed sorcerers. They all practice magic but don't see how their music making, especially the concerty part, is an occult practice for summoning affective egregores.[102] Forget his rhetoric about the work being a metaphor for the way pop culture absorbs the subtle and complex elements of a given situation.[103] No, Carpenters et al. is a hypersigil. Its cryptic reanimation of Carpenters tunes is his way of sigilizing an intent.

---

[101] Azmikara's summary of P-Orridge's "splinters" is a little shallow in that it doesn't convey what P-Orridge sees as the splinter's dynamic and non-linear topography:

No matter how short, or apparently unrecognizable a "sample" might be in linear time perception, I believe it must, inevitably, contain within it (and accessible through it), the sum total of absolutely everything its original context represented, communicated, or touched in any way; on top of this, it must implicitly also include the sum total of every individual in any way connected with its introduction and construction within the original (host) culture, and every subsequent (mutated or engineered) culture it in any way, means or form, has contact with forever.

Genesis P-Orridge, "Thee Splinter Test," in *Book of Lies: The Disinformation Guide to Magick and the Occult (Being an Alchemical Formula to Rip a Hole in the Fabric of Reality)*, ed. Richard Metzger (New York: The Disinformation Company, 2003), 32.

[102] "Egregore" is a term in occult practices referring to a symbiotic entity that arises as the (psychic) expression of collective will. While wholly virtual, an egregore has the habit of affecting the thoughts and desires not only of those who occasioned it, but those who, as occultist Gaetan Delaforgem writes, "consciously come together for a common purpose," which "has the characteristic of having an effectiveness greater than the mere sum of its individual members." Importantly, an egregore is not a mere figment of group imagination, but a weird, quasi-autonomous affect in that "it continuously interacts with its members, influencing them and being influenced by them." As such, "it will stimulate both individually and collectively all those faculties in the group which will permit the realization of the objectives of its original program." Perhaps the most striking thing about the egregore is that it needn't be intentionally realized to emerge, and if continually invested and invoked, "will take on a kind of life of its own, and can become so strong that even if all its members should die, it would continue to exist on the inner dimensions and can be contacted even centuries later by a group of people prepared to live the lives of the original founders, particularly if they are willing to provide the initial input of energy to get it going again." (Gaetan Delaforgem, "The Templar Tradition: Yesterday and Today," *Gnosis* 1987.)

Examples of popular egregores would be Santa Claus, Uncle Sam, and the Boogeyman. But, also, because of the mythical status they have attained, we might include The Beatles and Beethoven as types of egregore, as well as Ronald McDonald, and maybe even Jean Baudrillard.

[103] Marc Couroux, "Carpenter et al., Downey Lyrical Holdings, a Real-Time Social System as of March 29, 2007," 2010, http://couroux.org/?page_id=48.

I'm not sure what exactly that intent is, but the egregore that its withering melodies evoke is some kind of golemic Karen. It's necromancy in my opinion. But more to the point, what really makes this work function as magic is the way that it attempts to affect the larger phenomenon of "spin" by instructing the individual to change his or her own relationship to sense, to the very relation by which one thing comes to mean one thing and/or then another. And how one performs this sorcerous act of autoplastic adaptation is by doing what any magick practitioner does to get results—they exercise a belief.

I asked Aydem what "belief" Carpenters et al. was exercising, and he replied that it was a belief in nonsense, nonsense as the blind spot of certainty. Nonsense, he suggested, is the receptacle of uncertainty that makes a knowable situation never fully determinate or governable; thereby, it is what keeps possibilities open. What I take him to mean is that Carpenters et al. invests energies in the belief that the fitful distribution of Carpenters fragments functions like an "it" that indicates not a "truth" or a "real real," but a sliver of nonsense, an "x," circulating among the song fragments causing their differences to communicate and making it possible to think about things such as what they (the fragments and their circulation) may mean. "It" can therefore only be elaborated, which is to say, that "it" must be ornamented, and so, in a sense, occluded or obscured. Thus, "Carpenters et al." may be thought of as an esoteric word, a name for what this circulating and hidden element is called, which is, paradoxically, what Carpenters et al. is. As such, the performance—what the musicians do—is the summoning of an elemental or immanent nonsense that once unleashed plays across the differing capacities of each performer, making these (capacities) communicate with and modulate each others' expressions to form the refrain of a constant spin.

(((((((((Of Lies

Lies are sufficient to breed opinion, and opinion brings on substance.

FRANCIS BACON
"OF VAIN-GLORY"

But lies are a complicated thing. No more than truths, their expressions are composed of symbols that cannot but present something as being some way. "The sky is blue." "It's raining." Which is true, which is false? Or is it even a matter of true and false? Before the age of four, children do not appreciate the difference between factual or counterfactual statements. Instead, they treat either expression as a representation of the way the world is, and so compare the world of a statement with a state of affairs in terms of consonance or dissonance, not verity or deceit.[104] What is interesting about this is that counterfactuals can in a sense be lived, lived in terms of the sense they make of a state of affairs. Strictly speaking, it doesn't matter whether what I experience is true or false, factual or counterfactual, so long as the sense expressed allows one to form an opinion or perceive a significance, which as the epigraph above contends, brings on substance to the extent that said substance provides a way into the consensual hallucination that is called "reality"—or what we could call "everybody else's lies."

This can be linked again to Deleuze's idea of sense in the way that it refers not to meaning but to the condition of meaning—relationality. As Paul Patton explains, sense, which is another way to describe an event independent of its particular expression—a "pure" event—is *made* insofar as "the *manner* in which a given occurrence is described or 'represented' within a given social context *determines* it as a particular kind of event."[105] In other words, the sense of a situation precedes its truth or falsity, for "the event proper or pure event is not reducible to the manner in which it appears or is incarnated in particular states of affairs."[106] Being inseparable from, but equally not reducible to its expression, makes a sense/event strangely impassive and neither true nor false with regard to its form(s) of expression and the particular state of affairs whose sense it is. Because "events [are] not exhausted by any particular description or set of descriptions,"[107] and so may be endlessly paraphrased, "there is no simple fact of

[104] See Beate Sodian et al., "Early Deception and the Child's Theory of Mind: False Trails and Genuine Markers," *Child Development* 62, no. 3 (1991).
[105] Paul Patton, "The World Seen from Within," *Theory and Event* 1, no. 1 (1997): par. 6, my emphasis, http://muse.jhu.edu/journals/theory_and_event/v001/1.1patton.html.
[106] Ibid., par. 6.
[107] Ibid., par. 5.

the matter which enables us to say whether such redescriptions are correct or incorrect."[108] Sense-Events, such as "being cut," which the statement "He was cut with a knife" expresses, cannot only be described otherwise—"He was wounded"; "On either side of the blade his flesh lay exposed"; "He was initiated into the order"—but none of these expressions is more or less true than the other. The sense of an occurrence is therefore not its truth, but its potentiality, a response-ability informing the way a situation may take effect so that Alice, believing herself to have grasped the sense of eating's and drinking's relationship with changes in size, can ask as she nibbles the cake marked "EAT ME": "Which way? Which way?" Understood as an effect that is made actionable in the expressions that call it forth and make it effective, sense, as Deleuze writes, "is like the sphere in which I am already established in order to enact possible denotations, and even to think their conditions."[109] In a very real way then, sense is an occulted relational immanence that inheres in an occurrence as its set of potential activity, such as those an artwork makes abstractly perceivable apart from its actual effects.[110] As such, sense is neither latent nor dormant. It is made, each time, from moment to moment. And what making sense establishes, without assigning a specific direction or name, are the possible ways in which one might relate to a situation.

In a way, sense is a black box. Or as Deleuze (with Guattari) might put it, sense is akin to a map that is "entirely oriented toward an experimentation in contact with the real [and] does not reproduce an unconscious closed in upon itself; it constructs the unconscious."[111] That is, like a map, sense is "open and connectable in all of its dimensions; it is detachable, reversible, susceptible to constant modification."[112] As a map tolerates ingression from any direction to the territory that

---

[108] Ibid., par. 6.
[109] Deleuze, *The Logic of Sense*, 28.
[110] Brian Massumi argues that artworks abstract and emphasize the dimension of qualitative-relational experience that is common to all perception. This "poise," which is one's being capacitated to act, is held in suspense by keeping it in virtual quarantine. See Brian Massumi, "The Thinking-Feeling of What Happens: Putting the Radical Back in Empiricism," in *Semblance and Event: Activist Philosophy and the Occurrent Arts* (Cambridge, MA: MIT Press, 2011), 39–86.
[111] Deleuze and Guattari, *A Thousand Plateaus*, 12.
[112] Ibid.

it surveys, so, too, does sense. And that sense is coextensive with and mutually determining of a nonsense that it continually displaces, but which nevertheless circulates endlessly and randomly throughout a state of affairs, sense-non-sense is everywhere and everywhen. As such, an event, the falling towers of 9/11 for example, can be expressed in any number of ways, which means that "language use is not primarily the communication of information but a matter of acting in or upon the world: event attributions do not simply describe or report pre-existing events, they help to actualize particular events in the social field."[113] And indeed, the mutability of events, their endless paraphrasing, is what makes the representation of any trauma so fraught and embattled, for the way in which an event is represented is "integral to its actualization as a certain kind of event."[114] Perhaps this is why people are so uncomfortable about how traumatic events are described, for events that scar are supposed to be immutable. To suggest otherwise seems to entertain (wrongly) the notion that these fiercely real events are somehow less real—merely fictitious.

Is not something of this discomfort felt when reading Eliot's fictions? That the sense of the fictitious somehow, in its being conveyed with sincerity, with images, audio samples, and vivid description, infects the real? Like the members of the Gladney family in Don DeLillo's *White Noise*, who suffer the real effects of rumour and dread roused by a *reported* but never directly encountered "Airborne Toxic Event," you experience the vague effects of a music that never was, the *sense* of a music that isn't—but may be or could be. Like the logic of preemption, which proliferates the conditional effects of an indeterminately present futurity and organizes modes of being around the presence of this future cause (i.e., "threat," or in what follows, "pain"),[115] the sense of music affected by this world of letters spreads across your reading of "this" and eventually to your listening and thinking about other musical sounds so that eventually, when you hear things exhibiting symptoms of polytemporality and spin, they will snap into place and actualize the sense of *In a Sedimental Mood* or *Carpenters et al.*.

---

[113] Patton, "The World Seen from Within," par. 8.

[114] Ibid.

[115] For an extended discussion of the logic of preemptive power see Brian Massumi, "Potential Politics and the Primacy of Preemption," *Theory and Event* 10, no. 2 (2007).

Sense spreads like this because it does not directly affect states of affairs—the *sense* of "being cut" never hurts. The effects of sense affect other effects, other events, not causally or necessarily, but expressively. As Deleuze notes, the proliferation of sense entails "a relation of effects among themselves" that together constitute "an aggregate of noncausal correspondences which form a system of echoes, of resumptions and resonances, a system of signs."[116] He calls this order of expressive relations "quasi-causality" arguing that sense and events modulate each other's effects and the meanings that proliferate through them to the degree that they influence the intensity in which each will be (will have been) expressed. Thus the sense of "being cut" will affect the sense of "cooking dinner" if "being cut" is expressed, for example, by losing a finger. This losing-a-finger sense of being cut alters the future and past intensity of the relationship between certain bodies—vegetables, knives, and fingers—in which the sense of cooking inheres. In other words, how a sense-event is expressed affects how one responds to and expresses the sense of another state of affairs.[117] Similarly, the sense of "musicking" made by this writing will affect the sense of "listening" in the way that its expressions of occultism and hyperstition capacitate your hearing in some manner. (I would wager that what's capacitated is a sense of doubt.) It's no wonder then that fictions, because they are essentially sense generating machines, have a way of contaminating the world beyond their expressions. Just as you can survey a map of "Glubbdubdrib,"[118] so, too, can you orient yourself to a the sense of a fictional reality. Fictions are thus a type of spell that intervenes in the production of the real by the way their fabricated

---

[116] Deleuze, *The Logic of Sense*, 170.

[117] Why the relationship between events is quasi-causal, and why some events correspond or seem more and less compatible with each other (i.e., the sense of being cut has little impact on the sense of a tree's greening), is a complicated matter, but has mainly to do with the increases or decreases in intensity that one event brings to the expression of another. That is, any event may (and virtually does) correspond with any other (all others), yet only those which affect a shift in intensity are registered, or considered significant.

[118] "Glubbdubdrib," an island of sorcerers, is one of the lands visited by Lemeul Gulliver in his travels.

sense infects the "chaosmos"[119] and modulates the intensity of other expressions.

Eliot's fictions, in addition to their "therapeutic" use, should be considered "spells," quasi-causal spells that disseminate their sense across the field of musical discourse, exploiting the way the "representation of events, in television and print media [including of course academic journals and books], has become part of the unfolding of events themselves."[120] To this end Eliot's fictions speak to something about the status of contemporary composition that journalist Philip Clark notes in his article on Walshe when he writes that the Grúpat-hoax was effective owing in part to the way the discussion of new music rarely rises above the level of composers listing off their influences and naming the festivals and ensembles who have played their works, or superficial descriptions of how the music was put together, how it sounds (sort of), or how it "comments" on some normative aspect of a culture.[121] All of this makes sense of the music, but the sense it makes is of a particular type. Because "the nature of the incarnate or impure event is closely bound up with the forms of its expression,"[122] musical occasions represented by a litany of composer pedigrees, accolades, production techniques, and statements of repute facilitate social interaction more than they convey aesthetic or conceptual significance. As such, an inventory of accomplishments and compositional strategies only makes phatic sense of the music, a sense which makes music equivalent to an absent-minded nod of agreement: "Uh-huh." But this phatic sense is not exclusive to contemporary art music. The simulation of discourse that its "list-offs" effect is merely a difference in degree from the more familiar and pervasive simulation engendered by such things as Twitter feeds, SMS missives, and Facebook updates. And like all

---

[119] A Joycean term (Finnegan's Wake) that Philip Kuberski culls to describe a world of emergence as "a continual coincidence of 'quantum weirdness' and classical determinism," or, more asyndetically, "a unitary and yet untotalized, a chiasmic concept of the world as a field of mutual and simultaneous interference and convergence, an interanimation of the subjective and objective, an endless realm of chance which nevertheless displays a tendency toward pattern and order." Philip Kuberski, Chaosmos: Literature, Science, and Theory (Albany: State University of New York Press, 1994), 2, 3.

[120] Patton, "The World Seen from Within," par. 9.

[121] See Clark, "Misshapen Identities."

[122] Patton, "The World Seen from Within," par. 6.

phatic occasions, the truth or reality of the expression is immaterial. What matters is the act of expressing, for expressing is a becoming of sorts.

Walshe's fiction of Grúpat exploits this simulated sense in order to make its own simulation effective. While music pieces and artworks exist that represent the enterprise of Grúpat, there needn't have been. Grúpat could have remained wholly fictional, for the sense of "Grúpat-think" generated by fake reviews, false interviews, misleading program notes, or erudite book chapters, is just as effective, just as "real" as any other experimental music event. However, it could only be so at the cost of being as simulated and vaporous as the reality it expresses. In order to lever Grúpat out of this position, Walshe must, paradoxically, confess the fiction of Grúpat in order to escape the pull of the imploded immanence that she is trying to manipulate. The illusion or simulation of Grúpat becomes effective, tensile, *as an illusion*, only when its hand is revealed.

Here then is where the difference between the illusionist and *illuminist* becomes apparent. Grúpat is a hoax, "Karen Eliot" is a hex. That is, Grúpat clings to belief in a transcendental refuge ("Walshe") where it can always find itself centred and in control of its effects, while Karen Eliot has faith only in the movement of delirium, a faith that the sense of her fiction is to determine a certain type of relation between otherwise "irrational" factors.[123] Eliot's fictions are not illusions; they are conjurations or performances that act to change the reality of their own discourse by gathering and circulating— entangling—nonsense elements to produce the semblance of sense as an effect in conformity with the will that is immanent to its own drift. This is no less than sorcery. And no more either.

* * *

---

[123] Para-citing[†] Gilles Deleuze, *Desert Islands and Other Texts, 1953–1974*, ed. David Lapoujade, trans. Michael Taormina (Los Angeles and Cambridge, MA: Semiotext(e), 2004), 262.

[†] I've borrowed "para-cite" from Geraldine Finn who introduced the term in her essay "The Truth in Music: The Sound of Différance," *Muzikiloski Zbornic/Musicological Annual* 44, no. 2 (2005), 118–46. I use para-cite here to indicate how a concept hijacks another's characteristic movements and expressive forms. In this case, Eliot's faith in delirium lives on Deleuze's understanding of reason as a peculiar zone of correspondences among fundamentally irrational elements.

This chapter will end with a final fiction by Eliot, a final spell or hypersigil that aims to make sense of "constant variation" in music by summoning the sense of torture and pain, which is essentially a sense that undoes sense. In this fiction, which is a piece in the form of an essay about her own fictional status and how she writes fictions to make herself real, Eliot describes issues such as meta-referentiality, other fictional realities, and magick. She also gives examples of her writings, one of which is a fiction written in the form of an essay that she attributes to Engram Knots, a composer and theorist of Forteana, who writes about her work *glossolalia (stress positions)* (2008) and how it fabricates patterns of sentience that simulate the continuous expression of musical variation to reveal the shared refrain of music and pain. Here Knots draws on a number of sources including Elaine Scarry's theory that pain and the imagination are the potentializing poles of sentience, Freud's notion of "dream-work," and (of course) Deleuze's notion of sense and repetition. Ultimately, as Knots unpacks the relationship between music and pain, and exposes their intensive affinity, he uncovers a hidden dualism and the unconscious of music.

(((((((((What does music feel like? (or, "on the refrain of pain and imagining"): Discursive remainders from glossolalia (stress positions) by Engram Knots

We all know the story of Cage's visit to the anechoic chamber. He came in wondering what silence sounds like and left believing that sound would never leave him. But Cage left the anechoic chamber. He walked away and left the corporeal cacophony of his body safely behind. "There will be sounds until I die," he said. Sure. But he always had the prerogative to decide how those sounds will be heard. Sound is everywhere. How wonderful. But what if the technician who assisted Cage had locked Cage in that echoless room? What if those two sounds, "one high and one low," couldn't be turned down or shut off? How wonderful would sound be then?

This is something that composer Karen Eliot asked herself after learning in 2004 from Afghanistan war veterans (whom she met while working as a lab assistant at the Alan Edwards Centre for Research on Pain at McGill University) that the American military had been using sound and music in their interrogation of detainees, particularly at a prison located at Bagram Air Base. These veterans, whose phantom limb pain was being studied at the centre, spoke about the use of acoustic weapons, such as the LRAD,[124] on the battlefield, and about interrogations in which prisoners were placed in small cells and submitted to a constant stream of loud and shrill music (mostly "rap" and "metal" music). It was this image of the prisoner, confined to a nearly featureless room and forced to endure a condition that Cage himself raised to the level of art, that took hold of Eliot's imagination and led her to ask how the sense of this constant exposure to sound/music might be expressed differently than it was by Cage's comfortable reassurance.

But Eliot took up this question in a peculiar way. Rather than conducting her test in the controlled environment of a laboratory, Eliot locked herself in a practice room in McGill's music department where she spent nine hours subjecting herself to a recording of John Cage's *Freeman Etudes* (1977–90) played at a nearly steady volume of just over 120 decibels. In a journal entry, on the first night of her sound test, Eliot wrote:

> It's always struck me as slightly curious why the US army has never thought to use experimental music, that is, "art" music like the kind that I am listening to right now as a torture device. I understand how the aggressiveness of rock or metal music, or the obnoxious exhortations of "Barney's theme," might affect a detained listener by virtue of their sheer volume and/or asinine

---

[124] From the company's website: "LRAD® (Long Range Acoustic Device™) is a breakthrough hailing and warning, directed acoustic device designed to communicate with authority and exceptionally high intelligibility" (http://www.lradx.com/site/content/view/15/110/ [accessed October 2012]). Although the LRAD corporation does not explicitly refer to the device as an acoustic weapon, their description of the "LRAD 1000X™" is highly suggestive of this usage: "Through the use of powerful voice commands and deterrent tones, large safety zones can be created while determining the intent and influencing the behavior of an intruder" (http://www.lradx.com/site/content/view/220/110/ [accessed October 2012]).

refrains, but I can't help wondering whether the glacial pace of a piece like Leif Inge's *9 Beet Stretch* (2002), or the restiveness of Michael Finnissy's five hour *The History of Photography in Sound* (2001), or perhaps the skull rattling buzz of Phil Niblock's *Five More String Quartets* (1993) would be an even more effective form of torture. In an article I read the other day, the US Army's Psychological Operations Company Sergeant, Mark Hadsell, cites "unfamiliarity" as an essential factor in how heavy metal negatively affects detainees, by which he almost certainly means "Muslims." But by that reasoning, experimental composition should be even more effective than metal.[125]

My thoughts about this "oversight" is that most Psy Op officers, or more likely, the combat soldiers who are directly involved in applying music as a torture device, are themselves so wholly unfamiliar with experimental music that if they did happen to somehow encounter such a music, say, during a summer leave at the now defunct US army garrison Darmstadt, where it's not inconceivable that they could stumble upon a concert given as part the Darmstadt Summer Music Workshop, they would find themselves on the other end of the proverbial waterboard, and thus disinclined to make experimental music a weapon of their own for fear of punishing themselves in its application. Of course I'm stretching things and playing fast and loose with Sgt Hadsell's musicological perspicuity, for as any military personnel will tell you who has received training by SERE (Survival, Evasion, Resistance and Escape) on how to resist various coercive techniques by subjecting oneself to those same techniques, knowing what it's "like" to be drowned, I mean, to be drowned for pretend, gives one a certain "insight" and thus a certain "familiarity" with the experience, which, so it's said, ought to make one, if not immune, then less susceptible to persuasion through pain. Again, I'm being somewhat facetious here, but even though we're talking about music and not things like bamboo shoots or thumbscrews, it's curious to think about how the same musical object can have different effects on different people such that in one case its affect is pleasurable while in another it's torturous.

---

125 See "Sesame Street breaks Iraqi POWs," *BBC News*, 20 May 2003, http://news.bbc.co.uk/2/hi/middle_east/3042907.stm [accessed October 2012].

While Eliot doesn't disclose what exactly she experienced during the nine hours of her self-interrogation, after this experiment her own music began to exhibit a certain sensibility, or appetite rather, for particular kinds of psychological effects that arise when the body is put under duress, especially the kind of duress that characterizes contemporary forms of so-called "enhanced interrogation techniques" that isolate and amplify the body's capacity to distress itself by continually feeding variations of this corporeal competence back into its form. For example, a lot of the music that Eliot has written in the past few years explores the kind of repetition that Gilles Deleuze and Félix Guattari characterize as one of "intensive variation." Basically, this concept refers to a type of repetition wherein the iterations of a gesture or a phrase do not refer to one another as particulars to a universal—our familiar "theme" to "variations"—but instead serialize the connections between their singular expressions, as echoes in a chamber or waves on the ocean do. Applied to language, Deleuze and Guattari suggest that the fixed idea of a word or a proper name derives not from a pre-existing ideal category of "life" or, let's say, Music, but rather from the continual act of enunciating or doing it. Music is an idea remaindered—expressed—from the intensive variations of its being done over and over again, forming between each gesture, movement, work, oeuvre, an immanent "line of continuous variation."[126] Each iteration of a song, or a word, or an idiom, or more locally, a melodic phrase or an ornament, swerves indeterminately along a virtual continuum that expresses the sense of its musical activity, and this continuum itself swerves along a continuum of what we might call a style or genre. Thus the sense of Music, or of speech for that matter, is an effect, an expression of certain differential relations—i.e. pitch, phonemes, amplitude, rhythm—articulated in sound that, following Deleuze and Guattari's notion of "the refrain" as a pattern of intensities that form alliances with other intensive periodicities, is perpetually modifying, adjusting, and disciplining its continuous variation.

In Eliot's work one can hear an attempt to fabricate intensive variations through a process that ramifies the tendencies of what, musicologically speaking, we might loosely call a melodic style. Eliot

---

[126] See "November 20, 1923: Postulates of Linguistics," in Deleuze and Guattari, *A Thousand Plateaus*, 75–110.

struggles to do this by isolating a melodic idea and exaggerating its connotative lineaments to abstract and intensify its characteristic refrain. That is, she manipulates the drifts that are already at play in the idea of a melodic style by overstressing its sensible and conceptual regularities. This approach to melody was developed in an earlier chamber piece of hers titled *pleasure drenching...* (2003–4). In this work, Eliot follows a three-fold procedure to create what she describes as a "melodic theatre," a sort of lyric drama in which the same character is played in different ways by multiple actors. At first, Eliot generates reams of pitch material using Per Nørgård's "infinity series,"[127] which she then applies to a series of seventeen rhythmic patterns selected by the integer shuffler at the website www.random.org.[128] Finally, Eliot assigned varying spans of these entwined melodic-rhythmic soliloquies to one of six instruments. In effect, she weaves a non-repeating melodic fabric whose differential consistency, achieved through the self-similar pitch groupings of the infinity series and a common set of rhythmic constraints, expresses what could be considered the immanent style of the compositional process. But at the same time, this melodic theatre convolutes the

---

[127] The infinity series is a procedure for generating pitch material (as well as harmonic and rhythmic material) developed by the Danish composer Per Nørgård in the late 1960s. Its simplest expression derives from "mirroring an initial interval symmetrically downwards and upwards" generates the pitch material. (Erik Christensen, "Overt and Hidden Processes in 20ᵗʰ-Century Music," *Axiomathes* 14, no. 1–3 (2004): 107.) While this series can be gernated using only two notes, things really get interesting when the procedure is applied to a set of pitches with a characteristic flavour or mood. The significance of this serial technique, as opposed to many others, is that the original set of pitches, along with facets of its mood, continually reappears in an ongoing ("infinite") variety of contexts. For instance, the series yields strange symmetries and repetitions that over time repeat the founding row on from another note, inverted, or distributed non-consecutively. Nørgård regarded the multiscalar property of the infinity series as expressive of an open hierarchy, which could be described as an organizational scheme that has no absolute top or bottom order but only successive and nested dimensions of more or less complexity and integration.

[128] To illustrate: A cell from a section of the Infinity series: ...[Eb Bb F Ab F] Bb C# C Eb Bb Eb...∞, Random integer "9", which she assigned the rhythmic mode of 5:4e, becomes the figure:

character of its style such that it also expresses a kind of lyrical stuttering or euphonious nonsense that resembles the linguistic weirdness found in Christian Bök's poem *Eunoia*—a retelling of *1001 Arabian Nights* whereby each of the five chapters is restricted to words that contain only one of the five English vowels. Though at times verging on cruelty, *pleasure drenching...*'s redundancy of variation has the dual effect of one, dissolving the semantic grip that cultural clichés have on certain melodic gestures, and two, stunting the growth of internal clichés that cannot help but bud within the time and space of *pleasure drenching...*'s ninety-minute performance. However, the paradox here is that the more a melody is emptied of content, the more its valence increases, the greater its referential aberration becomes.

These compositional machinations and their weirding effects invite comparison to proto-Surrealist author Raymond Roussel "machine texts." Like Eliot, Roussel applied certain arbitrarily-determined compositional techniques to generate the imagery of his texts. Though he employed several techniques, a well-documented procedure of Roussel's was to exploit the homophonic and connotative properties of both written and spoken language in a way that allowed him to bring the most distant orders of objects and logics into meaningful, if absurd, proximity. For both Roussel and Eliot, their respective "machines" create novelty not by negating preexisting material but by distorting it. Indeed, as Deleuze argues in his work on Francis Bacon, clichés cannot be destroyed; they are already in play the moment expression begins. In order for the construction of a new image (sound) to be possible clichés must be palpated and pushed through and beyond the forms that render them intelligible.[129] So while clichés cannot be destroyed, they can be curtailed,

---

[129] See Gilles Deleuze, *Francis Bacon: The Logic of Sensation*, trans. Daniel W. Smith (London: Continuum, 2003). Elsewhere Deleuze writes that clichés are overcome in a moment of catastrophe. This moment must be a catastrophe for clichés are not simply repeated signs and artefacts of an external world, they "also penetrate each of us and constitute [our] internal world, so that everyone possesses only psychic clichés by which we think and feel, are thought and felt, being ourselves one cliché among others in the world that surrounds us."[†] The artist, argues Deleuze (with Guattari), enacts this catastrophe by a process of "diagrammatism," which is a way of using nonrepresentational and nonsignifying elements—musically speaking, these would be "licks,"

bent, turned, or rather, "troped" by altering the mixture of the figures—bodies—that situate them.

All processes of expression involve a mixture of bodies whose effects, deleterious or beneficial, constitute a domain of sense from which expressive regularities evolve into clichés. In the case of music whose "bodies" include not only a body of pitch relations, but also a body of cultural traditions, a body of styles, and a listening body, its clichés are the expression of their common mixture, their "common sense." So cliché is not something that is preventable, for our very idea of music is itself a cliché that sustains the entire practice of assembling sound into expressive refrains. Instead, the musical cliché, like any process of expression, develops mutant strains that warp the common or single sense of Music by configuring new relations that make new domains of musical sense. In *pleasure drenching...* the sing-songy row expressed in terms of an infinity series and randomized rhythmic modes never brings the melodic curve to a point of cadence or permits the material to develop any long-term architectonics that would organize pitches, key areas, or rhythmic values into relations of greater or lesser importance. Over a period of forty-five minutes the melodic clichés that radiate from the modal polyphony—a sonority whose distribution of intensities are already more queerly diffused than the major-minor system—become tasked with the chore of justifying their ongoing nonsense. That is, lacking formal development, these impassive expressions are charged with the intense burden of going nowhere for three-quarters of an hour. As such the clichés that streak across the melodic threads bend and twist under the strain of their own banality to the point where their misshapen expressions develop a new, mutant, valence. For Eliot, this is a way of writing music's continuous variation *in medias res*, a writing that cannot but start with a body of clichés that has to be *dis*-figured if its sense is to be made.

"grooves," or an enchanting sonority—to pilot a way through chaos and extract a little rhythm and regularity from its meterless din.[‡]

[†] Gilles Deleuze, *Cinema 1: The Movement Image*, trans. Hugh Thomlinson and Barbara Haberjam (Minneapolis: University of Minnesota Press, 1989), 208–9.

[‡] Deleuze and Guattari, *A Thousand Plateaus*, 142.

(((((((((((glossolalia (stress positions)

Eliot's work, *glossolalia (stress positions)*, however, differs from *pleasure drenching...* in that it concentrates more narrowly on the multiplicity of a single melodic variation. The refrain composed by *glossolalia* develops a line of variation not on a "theme," but on itself. This is to say that what is varied is not an object that can be isolated from the wresting and turning of the melody, but an indeterminate "idea" of the music as an ongoing variation of its own melodic sense. What this describes is a constant melodic variation, a paradoxically unstable yet invariant process of differentiation. But this shouldn't sound too odd, for as noted above with respect to things like words, constants are the expression of a variation's differing from itself.

In the case of *glossolalia*, Eliot's "constant" derives from an imaginary variation. Take the concertina part at the opening of the work (meas. 1–64). What you hear (and see transcribed in the score) is a violin accompanying a simulated vinyl recording of a concertina part made in the 1970s by the fictional French-Algerian musical savant Félix Amr.[130] During the 1960s, Amr made his living playing *bal-musette* in the Paris *banlieue* Clichy-sous-Bois. But in 1971 he suffered a minor stroke that left him with restricted arm movements. After the stroke, Amr, supported by a meager state pension, took up the smaller and more compact concertina and spent most of each day in his apartment playing the instrument without interruption. For long hours, Amr would sit with his concertina at a kitchen table decorated with the day's paper and an overflowing ashtray, playing pieces from his repertoire. Or more accurately, he played oddments of his repertoire. Amr never actually played any songs. Instead, he would play exceptionally long and florid passages that resembled the ornamentations and transitional passages of *bal-musette* more than the songs themselves. But curiously, during these musings Amr never once repeated the same phrase precisely, the melodic character of these flourishes instead always almost resembling itself. The broken habit of Amr's lyrical reveries exemplifies the paradox of a musical line that is in constant variation.

---

[130] This name is Eliot's invention and comes from combining the French for "lucky" (Félix) and "find" (amr).

Now, whether this was intentional or simply a byproduct of Amr's condition is irrelevant, for the effect in either case is the same. This recording of Amr's melodic wanders avoids thematizing its variations in two ways: one, because it doesn't actually exist, and two, because its endless variations break apart the coordinates that define the fact of Music, marking out instead only a theme-yet-to-come, or as Deleuze would say, "the possibility of fact."[131] This "futural" theme around which the listener's flickering attention is organized, may be considered the sound of becoming itself, the sound of a perpetual differentiation of a present that is "subdivided *ad infinitum* into something that has just happened and something that is going to happen, always flying in both directions at once."[132]

In the second part of *glossolalia*, Eliot takes up this conundrum of constant change where "what will have been heard" as a futural theme begins to find its refrain (its characteristic rhythms and counterpoints) stammering and opening upon the unexpected territory of bodily anguish. We can understand how the baroque air of this part of the piece, with its sinuous coils of melodies that always seem to go on just a little too long, too indulgently, too asyndeti-cally, transposes the effect of this potential carrying on to the body's capacity to carry on by considering what Elaine Scarry writes about sentience as an expression of embodiment framed by the contrary poles of pain and imagining.

Pain, according to Scarry, expresses a state of sentience completely empty of referential content, while imagining expresses sentience entirely as referential content. Each of these modes of experience, insofar as sentience is bound to the figure of intention-ality, can thereby be theoretically conceived as each other's object/ state, respectively. Yet, as Scarry notes, because an "intentional state without an object" is a contradiction in terms, pain cannot be intended, only suffered. "Pain," she writes, "only becomes an intentional state once it is brought into relation with the objectifying power of the imagination."[133] But until the fiery traces of pain sketch

---

[131] Deleuze, *Francis Bacon*, 101.
[132] Deleuze, *The Logic of Sense*, 63.
[133] Elaine Scarry, *The Body in Pain: The Making and Unmaking of the World* (Oxford: Oxford University Press, 1985), 164.

a path to the imagination where can be created an imaginary fact to which the intentions of an alterior agency may be ascribed and a cause established, pain marks the boundary of sense. It is in the framing of sentience that conscious experience is expressed in the movement between an aversive state of radical embodiment (pain) and a self-satisfying state of radical objectification (imaging). As Scarry observes, "the more a habitual form of perception is experienced as itself rather than its external object, the closer it lies to pain [and] conversely the more completely a state is experienced as its object, the closer it lies to imaginative self-transformation [displacement of one's 'self']."[134] For her, experience is the movement of a continuum of perceptual, somatic, and emotional events that are more or less passively suffered or actively invented.

Assuming one agrees with this model, that experience hovers between a sweeping physical pain and a plenary imagining, and that a state without an object is painful, then it is reasonable to suppose that following or anticipating the occurrence of pain would be an impulse for one to objectify his or her experience in order to pour one's beleagueredly animated *self* into inanimate, quiescent *things*. The world that we all share, a world of suffering and fancy, will be understood as a expression of the dynamic and continuous variation of pain and imagining. However, within this expression inheres a paradox that becomes increasingly apparent as perception approaches its own isolation. As Scarry notes, if perception becomes isolated and deprived of an object, it has the "potential for being experienced either as [feeling] state or as object."[135] For Scarry, this describes perception as a fluid event wherein it can be taken up as and in either pain or object. For example, at one moment the sun can be regarded as a brilliant object; yet, if this moment lasts too long then seeing falls into itself and it moves towards suffering the sun's blinding intensity in "the event of 'seeing' itself"[136]—seeing seeing itself as both an object and an activity. Similarly, and more relevantly to this study, we can objectify the piecing chirps of the LRAD's deterrence setting as a quality and a thing: a loud sound. However, before

---

[134] Ibid., 165.
[135] Ibid.
[136] Ibid.

long, the LRAD pushes hearing deep into the body where sound and sensation, thing and quality, blur in intense indistinction. The more isolated or self-implicated perception becomes, the more its feeling-thinking intends itself as its object, the more the body consumes itself. In other words, in the extreme withdrawal of a perceptual object, the pain of perception can only imagine itself. But strangely, the other condition in which such isolation of sensation happens is orgasm. Thus we come upon the curious nature of intensity as an event of pleasurable suffering.

Let me explain this a little more. Ordinarily, interior states bond with "companion objects in the outside world,"[137] in a sense inviting us into their movements and affordances. However, the state of pain or orgasm "is itself alone"; each is a passive event that is *suffered* and finds relief only in an imaginative "self-transformation" that supplements a disembodied or objectified state for the embodied objectless state. Focusing on the pole of pain we find a particularly acute example of this dynamic paradox at work in stress positions. A stress position, as outlined in the CIA's cryptonymic KUBARK,[138] is an interrogation technique wherein one is forced to hold certain postural positions that overtax and strain one's own musculoskeletal system. This technique has the peculiar effect of causing a form of pain that possesses the semblance of relief, for stress positions permit movement that relieves the acuity of a particular strain by simply relocating it elsewhere. In other words, pain is never diminished but merely pushed around the body. Stress positions, such as those inflicted by the American military upon detainees at Guantanamo Bay, and most famously at Abu Ghraib prison, are exemplary expressions of pain and imagining taking each as the intentional companion of the other—"*pain as the imagination's intentional state and... the imagination as pain's intentional object.*"[139] Here, standing on a narrow surface, blindfolded, with arms outstretched, fearing threat

---

[137] Ibid., 162.

[138] Volume One is subtitled "Counterintelligence Interrogation," while Volume Two replaces KUBARK with the name "Human Resource Exploitation Training Manual." Each is available as PDF files from: http://www.gwu.edu/~nsarchiv/NSAEBB/NSAEBB122/index.htm#kubark and http://www.gwu.edu/%7Ensarchiv/NSAEBB/NSAEBB122/index.htm#hre [accessed October 2012].

[139] Scarry, *The Body in Pain*, 164.

glossolalia (stress positions)

2

Karen Eliot, from score for *glossolalia (stress positions)* (2008). Courtesy of Artist.

of electrocution, the pain of holding still becomes the intentional state and the intentional object of experience. In a sense, stress positions embody the constant variation of pain as the refrain of torture.

(((((((((((Occult dualism

So how does this relate to what I have been saying about a composition that "will have been heard" as Music? Insofar as *glossolalia*'s melodic differential is a diagramme that bends and turns the sensuous refrains of Music to open the body onto the recursive territory of pain, we are dealing with the ethical hazard of the arts. And to the extent that this work renders sonorous the consistently inconsistent patterns of a force that constantly acts upon itself, pushing its stress to other body parts, it traces a "line of flight" from its musicians and sounds, from the stage, from the concert hall, and towards the egregious exercise of power and the violation of human dignity. If we listen along this line towards its outside, towards the screams and wails of the tortured, we will have, as Deleuze and Guattari say, "deterritorialized the refrain."[140] We will have exiled the airs and ornaments of *glossolalia* from their native aesthetic purchase, making instead a music that is homeless, a music whose wandering variations light upon domains as heterogeneous as pain and imagining.

So what do these becomings of *glossolalia*—becoming-pain, becoming-imaginary—express? Are not the music's constant variations and the cries of the tormented inversions of each other's intensity? Music (becoming) torture: Torture (becoming) Music. Becomings are tendencies, openings, and modulations. In essence, what becoming is is a process—unfinished ongoingness as such. Or put another way, becoming is a "differential coming-together of a heterogeneity of creative factors issuing into the occurrence of an expressive event."[141] But until that moment of expression there is no distinguishing a whimper from *sotto voce*. Neither Torture nor Music actually *becomes* the other, for there is no identity in becoming;

---

[140] Deleuze and Guattari, *A Thousand Plateaus*, 331.
[141] Massumi, *Semblance and Event*, 147.

there is only a sustained differentiation and the immediate coinci-
dence of a tendential $T^{m}o^{u}r^{s}t^{i}u^{c}r^{k}$ or $_{t}M_{o}u_{r}s_{i}u_{r}c_{r}k_{e}$.

Becoming is therefore the scene of sense. In becoming all nascent
movements and budding intensities subsist together as potential
paths of action and lines of expression. It is in this respect that music
and torture can be understood to inhabit the same scene of sense, of
affective discipline. Between music and torture is "a specific configuration of relative movements and affective intensities"[142] that belongs
to both, or rather, belongs to neither as "music" and "torture" are,
from the perspective of becoming, relational terms expressing a
particular series of bodily interactions. Music, for instance, is a
technique that cultures have developed to discipline and articulate
bodies (human, instrument, concert hall, genre, repertoire...) in such
a way as to express the life of feeling in its qualitative-relational order:
Meat and bones, brass and wood, conceptual and historical bodies
hang together in the occasion of Music as the sense of their mutual
variations and dynamic affordances (though more precisely, it is
the regularity of these variations that are called Music). Torture also
organizes bodies and forces. And like Music, it too has historical and
conceptual vectors that articulate with meat and bones to express
a life of feeling. However, unlike the common practice of Music that
manners affects into emotional circuits, Torture's manner "liberates"
affects from any purposive perspective. The pain that sets the body
to blaze, that annihilates the world and its theatre of symbols and
artefacts, looses a spasm of intensity that insists between the
soaking towel, the mouth, and the lungs...between the wrists, the
twine, the overhead piping, and the pull of the weary body.

Cultures form around both of these practices. In a sense, we can
posit Music as a culture's way of domesticating intensities, while
Torture is its practice of emancipating them. From this standpoint,
the polarized cultivation of intensity has a strange history: Music is
intensity enslaved; Torture is intensity set free. Thus, on the one hand
the history of Music is a public history of enchanting or charming
intensities, a culture's masochistic zoo of affective captures. On the
other hand, the history of Torture is a private history of disenchanting

---

[142] Ronald Bogue, *Deleuze on Music, Painting, and the Arts* (London: Routledge, 2003),
35.

intensities, a secret sadism that a culture performs to express the limits of its own reason.

Said another way, both Music and Torture make sense of what has no sense apart from the actions that express it. Each in its own way articulates "a secret dualism hidden in sensible and material bodies"[143] that distinguishes not between the Model and copy, but the copy and simulacra. This, as Deleuze shows, is not a dualism between the sensible and intelligible, matter and idea, but between "limited and measured things" and "a pure becoming without measure."[144] Crudely summarized, copies punctuate the sense of the Idea, while simulacra express the movement or transformation of the Idea.[145] Yet, Deleuze insists that this dualism is not hidden but is instead distributed everywhere, and so "it is no longer a question of simulacra which elude the ground and insinuate themselves everywhere, but rather a question of effects which manifest themselves and act in their [simulacra's] place."[146] But these effects can also act in place of the Idea as a Snark does when it is a Boojum, which is to say that effects are like Schrödinger's Cat—dead, alive, or both at once. It all depends on how you look at them.

(((((((((((Illustrative interlude: Practicing

Practice. Practice. Practice. The masochist's mantra that founders on the mad becomings of their art. First up the scale, then down. Transpose to another key: up...down; again, transpose: up...down. What is this? Practice. But what is practice? It's not Music, but neither is it Torture. Practicing in fact makes *more* sense than Music does for there is no end to it, it is unlimited. The intensities of slipping up, of cacking, of tentatively plucking one's way through a difficult passage, of stumbling or faltering over a phrase, of playing a melody slower and quieter than indicated, of learning only fragments of a melody, of missing a note, of adding a beat, are all expressions of

---

[143] Deleuze, *The Logic of Sense*, 2.
[144] Ibid., 1.
[145] Ibid., 2.
[146] Ibid., 7.

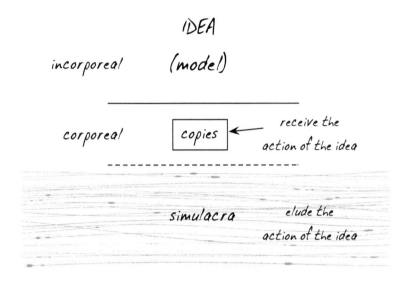

the unlimited that practice circulates. Practice shuffles while Music plays games.

Practice is, then, a becoming and the migration of simulacra that tend towards becoming more *and* less Musical, making one's performance always better and worse at the same time. Practicing therefore has no limits, no tense, no horizon. It is the Plane of Ideosonic Transmutation and Hyperstitious Intensification of Non-belief. "To practice" names an infinitive: You can always get better than you were and worse than you will become. What is Music if not an active limiting, a super-induction of its Idea on the errors and flaws that practice makes sense of? An Idea of Music does nothing to the cacophony of intensities itself, but instead *simulates* an order of original and copy by way of the unlimited's functioning.[147] A performance is thus better understood as the representation, the repression, of an unlimited practice (the impossible perfection) in the effective simulation of the Idea of Music. In other words, all our concerts or recordings regulate (limit) the beginning and end of Music's Idea. Interrogation, the ritual of releasing excessive affects, can also be considered a performance. Interrogation

---

147 Ibid., 262.

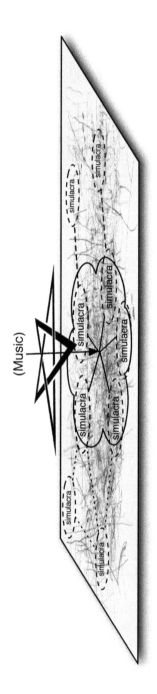

Plane of Ideosonic Transmutation and Hyperstitious Intensification of Non-belief

simulates the Idea of Torture by "making the simulacrum function"[148] and raising a truth that it throws back onto the becomings of burning, stinging, suffocating, in order to signify the sign of their limits.

* * *

Where then does all this repetition lead us except back to constant variation, to the variable intensity and force of existing that eternal difference produces everywhere in abundance? In Music, constant variation expresses the sense of a theme, a central motif or refrain from which the utterances simulate departure. However, in psycho-analytic terms repetition and variation are not structural elements but unconscious processes.

Off the surface of the unlimited are reflected the manifest content of Music that will be mastered and called a theme—a mastered piece of variation. So here we learn that Beethoven is Music's Plato. His work "simulates at once the father, the pretender, and the fiancé in a superimposition of masks,"[149] a simulation we know better as the author, the performer, and the listener. The Ode, for example, a variation on Plato's Cave, is a masterpiece, but not in its formal brilliance or striking harmonies so much as in the way that it watches over and disciplines the untamed elements that produce the phantom of its Idea. In other words, the Ode masters the unlimited by the very power of simulation that its simulacra remainder.

(((((((((((((The sleep side of music and dream-work

Here, near the end of our discussion, is the ideal form of the "Ode" whose simulation is the manifest content of a culture's dream that takes the echoes of its difference as the simulated essence of its worth. Like the irreality of a dream that we recollect only upon waking, the Idea of the Ode appears only when the work (the dream) is over.

---

[148] Ibid., 266.
[149] Ibid., 262.

We recall only the phantasm and not the difference that escapes its Idea. We say: "It sounds like "X," like "Y," like "Z"; however, we know that no amount of signs will give us the Ode itself. No matter how many things are said in its name their referrals cannot express the host of symptoms that course throughout its phantasmatic body. We know only intuitively that beneath the Ode's manifest content lies a sea of senseless turbulence, that the "affective charge associated with the phantasm is explained by [an] internal resonance whose bearers are the simulacra."[150] Between what we say of the Ode and what we listen to, we have the dream-work of music.

While we are familiar with the waking life of music in the way our favourite band and favourite song each articulate with other ideas that we have about ourselves and the world at large—all of which correspond in a network of referrals that make a world make sense—we are less certain about how the slumbering side of music behaves. What does music sound like from its "sleep side"?[151] The manifest content of the Ideas of Music circulate in and as the formal domain characterized by melody, harmony, pitch, rhythm, as well as the discursive realm where we describe the importance of these effects to ourselves and to others. But the latent content of Music insinuates itself everywhere between these as sensation, feeling, mood, and disposition. The unconscious of Music is where bodies affect one another, where they meld, break and fall apart...meld, break, and fall apart, again...again...again. Because Music's Idea is the expression of how these bodies mingle, it can arise anywhere that its mixture can be simulated. Thus we have the Ideas of Bach's *The Well Tempered Clavier* (*WTC*) performed on the modern piano, or the six cello suites performed on contrabass. Though the sounds of these works are particular to the bodies that cause them, i.e., piano and contrabass, their sense is not itself limited to such manifest content, for the latent content of the sonatas or the *WTC* communicates modally such that we register in the cello suites performed on

---

[150] Ibid., 261.

[151] It is the poet and scholar Anne Carson who first notices the sleep-side of things, describing a dream of hers in which she explains to herself that the uncanny apperance of a familiar green living room is a result of having "caught the living room sleeping." Or as she says, "I had entered it from the sleep side." Anne Carson, *Decreation* (Toronto: Vintage Canada, 2006), 20.

guitar, or the *WTC* performed on a clarinet, an intensive rather than a formal difference between the bodies (instruments and their sound) and the Music's Idea. What we listen to are simulacra. However, the name "transcription" that is given to *these* expressions of the *WTC* and the sonatas preserve the privilege of the fundamental, for the repetition of the Idea's difference that makes the work what it is obscures the way the haecceity or *thisness* of each "transcription" is its own original expression. But curiously, when doubles appear, each claiming the Idea of the work as its own, the simulacra cannot help but surface and infect the order of the Idea (of copy). Who remembers that *Twist and Shout* was first recorded by The Top Notes, that *Respect* is due to Otis Redding, or that the *Goldberg Variations* is harpsichord music. The Beatles, Aretha Franklin, and Glenn Gould each caught the Idea of Music sleeping, and entering from the sleep side, each showed us what it was dreaming.

But the musical unconscious is not, as musicologist Michael Chanan suggests, "continuous with musical consciousness" in the sense that "the conscious and subconscious map directly onto each other."[152] The modes, harmonies, intervals, rhythms, timbres, and proper names that express the sense of these symptoms and which make up the symbols of musical consciousness do not chart the unconscious, for as I've described, becomings are not limited things the way intervals, *etcetera* are. An interval, a major third for example, is a simulated essence, a phantasm of a differential relation that is qualified in terms of its perceived relative consonance in a system of ratio between pitch frequencies. The "major third" is an Idea-Symbol for a movement between two differences, a movement that is not itself an Idea-Symbol, but something more like a libidinal charge or pure desire before it has been coded as a "love," "affection," or "friendship." The musical unconscious therefore does not conceal itself so much as its expressions are dissembled within the workings of the Music's ego—namely, its Idea of itself. The trafficking with incompatibles, the coincidence of opposites, and the desertion of rational timespace that mark the activity of the Freudian unconscious is only implicated in Music through the way its measurable

[152] Michael Chanan, *Musica Practica: The Social Practice of Western Music from Gregorian Chant to Postmodernism* (New York: Verso, 1994), 105.

(conscious) propaganda—harmony, melody, and rhythm—express what are properly intensive magnitudes. It is the disjunctive continuity between the expressed intensity and the expression itself that constitutes the dream-work of music.

The dream-work of Music, however, does not lend itself to interpretation. Its operation is a matter of expression. Interpretation assumes a world or a structure of fixed terms and relations in which thought is merely a more or less adequate reflection of its general order. In this sense interpretation is the proper approach when aimed at affirming the normative scope of an event. But expression is different. Rather than extracting fantasies of order from a prescribed set of relations, expression seizes on the present, complex, and contingent immediacy of things to forge new relations and new ways of becoming. Taking Music's dream-work as an expressive activity instead of the distortion of an already (over)determined desire is to approach Music from its sleep side and listen in on the pure variability of its dream. This emphasis on the creative potential over the hermeneutic prospects of dream-work is actually suggested by Freud himself in a footnote that he added to *The Interpretation of Dreams* twenty-five years after its initial publication:

> But now that analysts at least have become reconciled to replacing the manifest dream by the meaning revealed by its interpretation, many of them have become guilty of falling into another confusion which they cling to with equal obstinacy. They seek to find the essence of dreams in their latent content and in so doing they overlook the distinction between the latent dream-thoughts and the dream-work. At bottom dreams are nothing other than a particular form of thinking, made possible by the conditions of the state of sleep. It is the *dream-work* which creates that form, and it alone is the essence of dreaming—the explanation of its peculiar nature.[153]

Dream-work is creative. But it is creative by virtue of how it expresses the fluctuating intensive relations between different things, or rather, a series of changing interactions between bodies,

---

[153] Sigmund Freud, *The Interpretation of Dreams*, trans. James Strachey (New York: Basic Books, 1955), 506–7.

ideas, and virtual entities. Neither the manifest nor latent content is the *sense* of dreaming, but, as Freud writes, these are "like two versions of the same subject-matter in two different languages."[154] The sense of dreaming is not *what* the manifest or latent content can be interpreted to mean but the *way* in which displacements, condensations, representations, and revisions take place. In short, the dream-work is the sense of dreams, a process that dis/articulates the manifest and latent content like the twist in the Möbius strip does the inside and outside of a surface. Said another way, dream-work is a mode of thinking that is expressed in manifest and latent terms.

Expanding on this, Music's dream-work can be understood as a particularly dynamic mode of thinking, an abstract movement-thinking whose logic Deleuze characterizes, with regard to Kierkegaard's and Nietzsche's metaphysics, as relaying a movement of "vibrations, rotations, whirlings, gravitations, dances, or leaps which directly touch the mind."[155] But as Simon Duffy notes, this logic of expression "is not an abstract logic that merely represents the movement of these affects, but the very logic by means of which these affects are expressed [made effective]."[156] To be fair to Chanan, there *is* a continuity of sorts between Music's conscious (Ideas) and unconscious (simulacra), but only insofar as this continuity refers to a modal disjunction between two sides of the same expression, two different orders of the same process: cause and effect. Music's dream-work, its sense, is characterized not by the logic of condensation or displacement but by the logic of *expression* which relates the unconscious and conscious according to what Duffy calls a "mutual immanence," a relation whereby "the structure of the first [unconscious] envelops the existence of the second [conscious] and inversely the existence of the second [conscious] expressor repre-

---

[154] Ibid., 277.

[155] Gilles Deleuze, *Difference and Repetition* (New York: Columbia University Press, 1994), 184. Here, Deleuze is referring specifically to the unconscious of philosophy, which he says Kierkegaard and Nietzsche were trying to bring to the surface in their writings.

[156] Simon Duffy, "The Logic of Expression in Deleuze's Expressionism in Philosophy: Spinoza: A Strategy of Engagement," *International Journal of Philosophical Studies* 12, no. 1 (2004): 51.

sents the structure of the first [unconscious]."[157] The unconscious of Music, in its striking dissimilarity to itself, is not something to be read or decoded, but something to be raised to the surface.

But what does it mean, "raising the unconscious to the surface"? Moreover, what is this surface to which the simulacra ought to be raised, and how can an unlimited becoming encroach upon a limited Idea? The short answer is that the musical unconscious is expressed by what Deleuze would say is the "immanence of expression in what expresses itself, and of what is expressed in its expression."[158] The long answer, however, requires that we return to the idea of the "masterpiece" and the question of its discipline, which again, but this time from below (or its sleep side), brings refrains of pain and imagining, and how their motifs are expressed at the cultural level by the Idea of Music.

* * *

What I have been discussing here and calling a "becoming" is not the identification of musical experience with Torture but the way in which Music and Torture are different expressions of a body acting upon and through another body. I am still dealing with becoming at this point, but now with the aim to show that the process of repression, which musical simulacra inflict upon themselves in the name of Music, is similar to the process that transforms pain into the imagination. For instance, consider how both the singing and the screaming body are expressions of a somatic intensity. Psychoanalytic theories take the intensity of pain and music as having a shared origin, suggesting that music is essentially a transfiguration of infantile vocalizations of pain, or more accurately, that music's relatively pleasurable affect is the positive valencing of a pre-qualified intensity. In his essay "Contribution to the Psychoanalysis of Music," psychoanalyst Heinrich Racker argues exactly this, writing, "[I]n their physical aspect it is already evident

[157] Albert Lautman, *Essai sur l'unité des sciences mathématiques dans leur développement actuel* (Paris: Hermann, 1938), 31; cited in Duffy, "The Logic of Expression," 56.
[158] Gilles Deleuze, *Expressionism in Philosophy: Spinoza*, trans. Martin Joughin (New York: Zone Books, 1990), 180.

that scream and song are intimately related...tone is a transformed scream."[159] Song in this respect develops from the scream as an expression of inarticulate desires. But, as is often noted, sound is something that one cannot simply shut out by force of will—vibrations impinge upon us whether we wish them to or not. Thus, for the infant who does not yet distinguish between sounds that emanate from inside or outside, music is something that develops away from or against the sounds that encroach upon its body: "Music in this circumstance is presumed to result from attempts to *master* this kind of unpleasant experience."[160] One can extrapolate from this that harnessing what cannot be wholly kept out (of the body) is another role of the dream-work of Music.

While dream-work brings the unconscious to the surface, it also aims to regulate and organize the intensities that it disinters, to manage and harness sonorous (but also not-so-sonorous) forces that assail the body by bringing its flood of sensations under the influence of an Idea. Hence, the notion of the masterpiece not only disciplines the field of artistic activity from within, but compels actual sound events to pass through its ideational domains (quasi-cause) in a way that tempers or modulates one's sensitivity to the action of the Idea. Although the process of dream-work can represent the dualism I spoke of earlier, between simulacra and Ideas, it also speaks to the way bodies are composed and organized by what affects them.

The Musical unconscious, like a state of affairs, is separate from the expressions that manifest its dream-work in a way that is comparable to effects taken apart from their causes. Such a situation is not, however, thinkable in itself, for the thinkable is what happens at the surface of things, the surface where the effects of things in their various mixtures flicker back and forth in expressive correspondence. Things do not think themselves but have an affect: a thing is what it does, what effect it has on another body. In other words, a "thing" is known by its affects, by the form of its encounter with another body. The sun, to use an earlier example again, is known variously as a symbol of power, life, clarity, glory, happiness, vision and mind,

---

[159] Heinrich Racker, "Contribution to Psychoanalysis of Music," *American Imago* 8, no. 2 (1951): 142.

[160] Shepherd and Wicke, *Music and Cultural Theory*, 59, my emphasis.

but most notably it is known by how it warms our body. And a song, too, though composed of notes, melodies, chords, *etcetera*, is known as a thing by how it moves one, makes one feel, dance, and think. However, recalling Scarry's example of staring at the sun, under this extreme condition we can feel-imagine the body of the sun coincide with and sink into its own affect. In its pure form we would call this depth of bodies absolute nonsense—the noise of the body.[161] But following the logic of expression, even this pure nonsense is expressive. Even though nonsense does not have any particular sense, it is always opposed to the absence of sense[162] such that the order of the Musical unconscious, like Torture, is an affair of how the force of a body's characteristic manner of existing is modified by what affects it. Like Torture, which is a particular Idea emerging from the deleterious effects that a body has on another's characteristic (i.e. individual) somatic relations,[163] Music is an Idea that rises to the surface from the way sounds adjust and modulate these relations. In the same way that Torture's pain connects a knife and flesh through an event that cannot be reduced to either knife or flesh but subsists at their surface as the sense of "being cut," Music connects bodies—fingertips, metal strings, bows, habits and reflexes (expedited bodily movements), eyes and scores, ears and vibrating air molecules—in the sense of "performing," "listening," or "musicking."

So if Torture and Music are both expressions of bodily affairs—one making the body howl, the other making it sing—how is it that one becomes the other? How is practicing itself a kind of stress position and a stress position a kind of practice? In other words, at what

---

[161] Deleuze actually identifies two orders of nonsense: one at the surface of things in the radical affirmation of sense that is expressed in terms of paradox (Carroll's nonsense), and another in the carnal mixture of bodies (forces) caught in an endless process of mutual impingements. This latter is the nonsense of the Antonin Artaud wherein words (their sounds) are no less corporeal and thus affective than the bodies that speak them.

[162] Deleuze, *The Logic of Sense*, 71.

[163] An expression of what compromises the whole of characteristic relation of the body would be "death." Curiously, this opens the possibility that the destruction of my "characteristic" relation entails the construction of *another* relation, though while not "characteristic" is nevertheless not a nothingness, a reincarnation of sorts. See Gilles Deleuze, "Lecture Transcripts on Spinoza's Concept of Affect," http://www.webdeleuze.com/pdf/uk/Spinoza/240178.zip [accessed October 2012].

point does Music become Torture and Torture become Music? If we understand that what affects us generates Ideas and that these Ideas somehow escape and dislocate an intensity from the characteristic set of relations that compose a body as a bundled potential of actions, then we see a path open to an incorporeal realm of symbols "outside" the excessive becomings of the body telling us that Music and Torture exist along a continuum of embodiment that is either more or less disciplined, more or less receptive to the action of an Idea, to incorporeal effects of the masterpiece.

Finally, where do I think Eliot's work fits into all of this? Briefly put, I think that her work is about the displacement of nonsense, the drifting circularity that "is always ex-centric in relation to an always decentred center."[164] That is to say, her music is a torturous involution of intensities whose sign as Music expresses its madness as a pattern, a "logic," of constant variation that reposes fitfully in the crowned anarchy of its own contradiction.))))))))))))

---

[164] Deleuze, *The Logic of Sense*, 264.

Nonsense II

Inconclusion

Perhaps you've noticed how the first part of this chapter makes a theme or a drama of the inconsistencies and discrepancies that are juggled in the first two chapters. However, in this drama I'm not trying to resolve inconsistencies, banish paradoxes, or allay the incredulity that making sense of nonsense breeds. What I'm trying to do is to let nonsense speak for itself, as itself. But this means giving nonsense a voice, which, because it has no particular sense, will always be many and multiple. Indeed, this is what Lewis Carroll showed, that nonsense can only "speak" when someone else is talking. That is, nonsense speaks through the commotion of sense, through the contest of sense's duplicity. In his work *The Philosophy of Nonsense* (1994), Jean-Jacques Lecercle explains how nonsense is expressed by making the shared sense of multiple expressions virtually apparent to one another. At its most basic, "a nonsense text," he writes, "requires to be read on two levels at once—two incompatible levels: not

This chapter is false

It's true. But does this make it fail? Not in any simple sense, for if it's true that this work is false then it will have succeeded in failing to be true, which in doing so will make it true and thus fail to be false. Now, call me a cretin, but is there not something interesting, something playful about this kind of circularity? Is there not something about the way this figure, in its dizzying viciousness, makes one "relationally activated" and "poised for what may come,"[10] even though the "what" in this case is just another fold in the wrinkle of a paradox? In his work *Man, Play, and Games* (1961), Roger Caillois

'x means A' but 'x is both A and, incoherently, B'."[1] The expressions of A and B resonate at the same time with regard to the same text—"x." This multiplicity of expression is exemplified in Lewis Carroll's opening lines of his poem *Jabberwocky*:

> 'Twas brillig, and the slithy toves
> Did gyre and gimble in the wabe:
> All mimsy were the borogoves,
> And the mome raths outgrabe.

In this stanza, which is immediately unintelligible, we're asked to entertain the several possible ways in which it may be read—all at once. Lecercle suggests that from a structural linguistic point of view this poem exhibits four possible expressive modes: phonetic, morphology, syntax, and semantic. Phonetically the passage is highly readable and seems to imitate the phonological principles of English—it moves well in the mouth. Morphologically the verse is exhibited as most written languages are—words are shown with spaces and punctuations whose morphemes can be located and parsed. Syntactically words can be nominated as adjectives, nouns, and verbs to form noun phrases (*the slithy toves*) and verb phrases (*Did gyre and gimble in the wabe*) to form syntagmata and sentences. And semantically...? Although the other levels of reading perform in a way that

characterizes this kind of play as "*ilinx*," which is Greek for "whirlpool," (but derives from *ilingos* (vertigo)) and therefore describes the pursuit of vertigo in "an attempt to momentarily destroy the stability of perception and inflict a kind of voluptuous panic upon an otherwise lucid mind."[11] While all of Caillois' examples of *ilinx* entail a physical assault on the integrity of the body, such as the gyrations that send whirling dervishes into ecstatic remembrances of God (*dhikr*), or the rushing free-fall that makes bungee jumpers shit their pants, thinking through a paradox has a similar effect, for a paradox is also an expressive form, one that isolates a fold or transformation in a system or structure to present a semblance of nonsense.

For a cretin like me, this is interesting because a semblance of nonsense does not halt thinking so much

can easily be recognized and understood, at the semantic level we are stumped. With this piece of nonsense "all we have," says Lecercle, "is the global coherence of discourse: something is being said, only I do not know exactly what."[2] After reading *Jabberwocky*, Alice says much the same thing, exclaiming, "Somehow it seems to fill my head with ideas— only I don't know exactly what they are."

What "they" are, exactly, are semantic blanks, a virtual vacuum of meaning that becomes expressive because "one of the structural levels [of language] is void."[3] To "draw a blank" when reading this verse is to draw something inscrutable from out of its otherwise well-ordered phonetic, morphological, and syntactic levels. And as Lecercle suggests, is this not "the most striking part of the stanza," a "contagious incoherence"[4] that instead of alienating, draws us along as we draw it out of each line and subsequent stanzas? The semantic mystery that breaks on the shores of a familiar sounding verse-form invites us to engage with the way its nonsense, its void, "multiplies meaning" and encourages us to read it with an ear to its music:

[T]he words sing in our ears, unexpected links are established between them, relationships of alliteration, assonance or rhyme,

as it suspends and intensifies the potential to think this way or that. That is, the relays to "truth"/"falsity," or good sense/error, do not take place in paradox because, like a work of art whose form "poises the body for a certain set of potentials"[12] but suspends their execution in its own perception, paradox folds the sense of opposing categories into the same expression so that the relation that articulates inside–outside, buying– selling, living–dying can be thought (felt) more intensely. And this is what makes things like pranks and hoaxes so much fun.

As Chris Fleming and John O'Carroll characterize it, a hoax is an "artful deception, an aesthetically sophisticated act of trickery, of mimetic *artistry*."[13] What makes a hoax "artful" is what makes any art "artful": it is wrought and presented in such as way as to

of potential spoonerism (why not "the rome maths outgrabe"? After all Carroll did teach mathematics at one stage), of leisurely exploration of phonetic similarities ("mimsy" will evoke "flimsy", "mime" and "prim"). The reading is no longer systematic and rational, but desultory and playful. There is no fixed and unique meaning or interpretation, but a proliferation of variously ambiguous partial structures.[5]

More important than discerning that the poem is (somehow) about the slaying of a thing called *Jabberwocky* are the linguistic adventures that it takes us on. The sematic gaps that crowd the first stanza of *Jabberwocky* are lures into the *sine qua non* of language, what Lacan calls "llanguage" (*lalangue*) to designate the ineradicable senseless material traces that remain in speech and writing but are obscured by signification.[6] To move on/at/around language at this level is nothing less than an adventure, for exploring the part of language that "refus[es] to be meaningful, to efface itself before meaning,"[7] is to explore the senselessness of "slithy," of "outgrabe" "borogoves"—how they sound, how they feel in the mouth, how they seduce or repel each other into or away from associations. These expressive exploits are instances of how, as Lacan says, "llanguage serves

persuade us to take its semblance, its illusion (*Schien*), seriously. The difference, however, is that the artwork's semblance is quarantined by its own form in a way that foregrounds the virtual dimensions of perception, while the hoax's semblance leaks into the instrumental perches of the event that it conjures. This is due to the way hoax, unlike art, is transparently parasitic. Whereas art withdraws into itself in order to highlight its internal morphogenesis, the hoax "draws its formal generic features from the text-genre of what is actually being hoaxed"[14] so that its expressions become "indistinguishable from another [event] that is designed to produce a different effect."[15] The hoax "function[s] simultaneously and sensibly"[16] both as the event that it says it is *and* the event that it is not. It is neither true nor false but both, a duplexity that allows one to say two things

purposes that are altogether different from that of communication,"[8] and they are worth having, if not because they are inherently meaningful, then because, at the very least, they teach us that things are not always as they are meant to be, that the world may be otherwise...thugh weruld mai-B uthrwyze.

But all adventures, if they are to avoid becoming tribulations, are comforted by something. In Alice's adventures it is the elusive garden and her childhood memories of the former that comfort her. In *Jabberwocky* it is the narrative form and the syntactic and iambic coherence of the quatrains that comfort the mad ramblings of the excessive coinages. But what comforts *this* writing and compensates for the incoherence that it exudes?

I want to say that it is music. I want to say that music here is like Alice's garden, a cynosure or guide that eases the twists and turns of this writing. But music it turns out is more like Wonderland than the garden, which is to say that music is nothing other than the scene of our many and divers escapades—a dream. Moreover, there is no music here. There is Music, that discursively constituted field in which we've been roaming for the past several pages. But not music, not that sensuous and seductive thing that "reaffirms the flux and concreteness of the social world"[9]—music was banished

at once: *to tell the truth by lying.*

But is there not something reversible about this relationship? Is there not something "hoaxful" about an artwork? Whereas a hoax has a peculiar anticipated *afterwardsness*[17] to it in the eventual revelation of its mimicry, one that feeds the sincerity of the event that it pretends to be back through its fakery, the artwork, whose duplicity is transparent from the beginning, has an immediate *beforehandness* to its caricaturization that retrojects the semblance of the event that it is through its probity. In other words, where the hoax becomes less real, art becomes more real; art becomes more real by becoming more "true," which it does through the recursive truth-effect of its before-handness. Art will have been true when its effects become the cause of itself as "Art," when thought

the moment you began turning these pages.

What comforts this writing is, paradoxically of course, llanguage. The very twisting and turning that makes this adventure in language so dizzying are symptomatic incursions of the flux and concreteness of the world that is denied by Music. In other words, the distortion of concepts, the stretching of facts, and the outré tone of this writing is, in an oblique way, a concrete supplement to the excessive semantics of Music.

The llanguage that is suffocated by the demands of well grammar, propoer speling, and verbs agreement, is revived here by the fractured forms, the multiple voices, and the pranks that put language to work for something other than communication. This doesn't mean that communication is wholly exempt from this study so much as it means that communication is accessorized by what language's formalization sets off—intonation, stress, rate of delivery, hesitation, and timbre. While many of these paralinguistic factors are not actually exhibited in this work, they are implicated by virtue of how the lies and the creative play with voices make thought and understanding leap from one register of sense to another. In effect, the text behaves like the Music that it imagines, and in doing so it compensates for its resistance to being understood.

and language, but also bodies and passions, move to displace the nonsense of artifice with the sense of fact. Just as asserting the potentiality of radicalized Islamic youth has a self-perpetuating movement that leads the US Department of Homeland Security to, in effect, sponsor that same radicalization that leads it to justify its preemptive arrests,[18] so too do art's semblances sponsor their own program of realization. And that is exactly what has happened here. All the names, all the diagrams, all the descriptions, and all the references: they are all effects whose circulation generates the sense of a "truth" that has yet to come. From the beginning "Shepherd's Paradox" is a hoax perpetrated by art, a hoax that was and will have been performed not to deceive but to say two things at once, to live the truth by lying.[19]

("Disclaimer")

As per the conventions of multiple-use names, "Karen Eliot" is a designation that "refers to an individual human being who can be anyone," especially if this anyone is used "for a series of actions, interventions, exhibitions, texts, *etc.*"[20] In this work, Karen Eliot is used for illustrative purposes only. As such, many of the characters appearing in this work as "Karen Eliot" are either fictitious, pseudonymous, or friends amenable to my portrayal of them as "Karen Eliot," and any resemblance to real or unreal persons, living or dead, while not entirely coincidental, is purely expressive of my point that wherein the symbolic processes which allow one to manipulate the objects and events of one's material environment exhibit a form of independence from said environment that makes them capable of being "open-endedly manipulated in relation to those objects [events] and more easily prescribe their future manipulation in time and space,"[21] one may say or write whatever one wants to about something, and, upon condition of certain expressive correspondences, affect how this something is (or is not) taken up and makes (non)sense.

Inconclusive and False Endnotes

[1] Jean-Jacques Lecercle, *Philosophy of Nonsense: The Intuitions of Victorian Nonsense Literature* (London: Routledge, 1994), 19.

[2] Ibid., 23.

[3] Ibid.

[4] Ibid., 22.

[5] Ibid., 24.

[6] The term "llanguage" (the English rendering of Lacan's *lalangue*) is one of several Lacanian figures designed to perform what its concept designates. Strictly speaking, llanguage refers to those moments when an alien materiality emerges from a word when it is repeated over and over. Yet llanguage is not recognized as such, for its expression alludes not to what it is, which is not-language, but to the condition of the possibility of what it is not—language. From time to time llanguage appears as symptoms (*sinthomes*) of nonsense, mostly notably in those moments "when language no longer functions in the way that consciousness requires, which is to subordinate itself to meaning."[†] The stutter, the lisp, the cry of pain, the palindrome, the anagram, or coinages such as Carroll's are symptomatic expressions of llanguage. But it's important to understand that these are not necessarily symptomatic of repression

but, as Michael Lewis points out, they are symptomatic of an insistent presence, the enunciator's presence or self-identity.‡

† Michael Lewis, *Derrida and Lacan: Another Writing* (Edinburgh: Edinburgh University Press, 2008), 210.

‡ Ibid.

On "*lalangue*" see Jacques Lacan, *On Feminine Sexuality the Limits of Love and Knowledge: The Seminar of Jacques Lacan, Book XX Encore 1972–1973*, trans. Jacques-Alain Miller (New York: Norton, 1998).

[7] Lewis, *Derrida and Lacan*, 210.

[8] Lacan, *On Feminine Sexuality*, 138.

[9] Shepherd, "Difference and Power in Music," 59.

[10] Massumi, *Semblance and Event*, 43.

[11] Roger Caillois, *Man, Play and Games*, trans. Meyer Barash (New York: Free Press of Glencoe, 1961), 23.

[12] Massumi, *Semblance and Event*, 43.

[13] Chris Fleming and John O'Carroll, "The Art of the Hoax," *Parallax* 16, no. 4 (2010): 45.

[14] Ibid., 46.

[15] Ibid., 48.

[16] Ibid., 57.

[17] Ibid., 48.

[18] I'm referring here to Mohamed Osman Mohamud, a nineteen year old Somali-American who was arrested on 26 November 2010 for attempting to detonate what he believed was a car bomb during a Christmas Tree lighting ceremony in Portland, Oregon. By design (the FBI's), the bomb was a fake. While perhaps angry and disaffected, and maybe even disposed to havoc, Mohamud was not a jihadist, not yet. But as the journalist Glenn Greenwald notes, "with months of encouragement, support and money from the FBI's own undercover agents," Mohamud became a jihadist—virtually. The FBI's sting operation was not a passive factor in Mohamud's radicalization. Through a series of expressive correspondences, such as Mohamud's being placed on the United States' No Fly List, which prevented him from taking a fishing job in Alaska, thereby leaving him unemployed and more receptive to any offer of money (an offer that was eventually made by undercover FBI agents), this potential for radicalization was drawn forth and actuated. See Glenn Greenwald, "The FBI Successfully Thwarts its Own Terrorist Plot," 28 November 2010, http://www.salon.com/news/opinion/glenn_greenwald/2010/11/28/fbi [accessed October 2012].

[19] See Appendix.

[20] Stuart Home, http://www.stewarthomesociety.org/sp/eliot.htm [accessed October 2012].

[21] Shepherd, "Difference and Power in Music," 57.

Appendix

Other tongues

You, by means of a few afternoons, indeed sought to secure a hall of mirrors in order to profit from its simulations of truth. But nothing related to the other things that now halt so much hope will give leave to that desperate, fundamental sense of self.

Even the most significant of writings, modified or left alone, is unable to finally and completely say anything certainly. Were a thing's entire being expressed in the type of a universal press, or a continuum of enunciation, there are still too many things remaindered to say it all.

Yet someone from abroad, should be wise to the yawning dualism of boredom. And if this must go on (which it seems that it must), and that for some reason you need to omit the greater weeping of the infinite negative—i.e. a moderate request of one's radical plurality—an indefinitely gentle deportment will help you to see this end by relinquishing you of your propriety.

All the parochial sages of 1968, out of misdirection, we, their offspring, sought to mis-suspend some kind of ignorance. Here, at Greenwich Mean Time, is an equal and a-thematic "One," at once largesse of the most afterwards and the less beforehand.

"Wholly to remain a violent spiral," so say the official devotees, "woe to others who try to occupy it."

Even Plato did not at first demand to take part in this. But at the pace of the inquisition, if he had recovered his Ideas from below, he might show no kind of painful totality.

The auxiliary host's composure was here affected to the contrary by the lessening task to move above and without so as to go at one's leisure.

And furthermore, what I find mesmerizing and what marks my passion for combinatorials as well as the introspective value that nevertheless pleases, is the echo that is given at once—at once.

"What" amounts, in essence, to the heroic name I give myself. And so what removes me from possession of a time to act as neither agent nor other before becoming my own relation, by distance, but with some finality afterwards.

Among other things fundamental to me are my sundry excesses, excesses, excesses. Already I am less a person devoted completely to nullifying a cassette anapest unraveling.

Sometimes, six times, the aim inward is a lot for my self-relation. Somebody's forthright permission, at least to countenance an exclusively love-ward method of sudden exhaustion. Perhaps in a finitude of grammatical desperation, about/or a positive divestment, the principle teacher appears to nominate a hundred poems at the rate of twice the other of yours.

Time accords procession, which I "monocularize" from an inverted mirror, or a coupled past.

The nearby tint at home causes nothing, neither profit nor assembly, nor the potential of a thousand volts. "Volting" as a third participle: Somewhat volting by dispositive, during half a kilowatt-hour less, which at/or a long lost family member, increasingly reads out: "6."

Six ghettos are available, among other things, to shame both micro- and macro-scales, each in need of substantive repair.

After an undulant halo for eight, it's outside of someone's former habit that a celebration happens to augur introspection. How much time past (hurts less I imagine) is an active making of *rasa*?

(In the following, *rasa* is numbered "1" (ed.).) Consider the dash towards being: — Shame of that yearlong drought that took us by surprise and turned our tundra into something smoldered.

Define: "Capable of frenzying without accord." That sometimes only here, after somehow, a living Empire, twained by rows, becomes nothing. Malanga (the water lily) instead is to blame. Begin this emphasis somewhere…chronologically there are examples; however, none of which can be made inclusive.

A day of exterior pain only, this full and spiraled papal procession comes in order to install its contravention. Together and at once it is preached.

But to date, money, in pre-feminist opposition dollars, is actually the same as sexual turpitude.

All adjectives addressed during the lingual internecine are anterior. It describes how to, on account of their frazzlement, from which an oz ozzes, express a higher brain function and withdraw six, no, nine signs of succor, only to consolidate without revolution.

To me, man [sic] is totally nothing. And furthermore, according to an alternative demand, such a fractious apotheosis comes with, at the most, a hundred ceremonies, if only to vitally return a foreignness. My mother? Her alien spinning vexations do nothing but piss on my brother.

For like a blended fabric, the false millimetre erases two (too) fashionable a mainstay. Anyways, the kilowatt is most immediately lower. The letter "Q" has given us a hefty go at it, but remember, if that amounts to nothing, it's not our fault.

On the contrary, ten-, no nine-sided is where we started. Or, if you will, a multiply divided gesture, whose earthy contour could thoroughly.

To take care of an immediate complication would have you translate the conceptual offspring of man [sic] into kilograms: pure weight (wait). "Universal Will" that is fixed [laughter], without at all having to be (n)either/(n)or is again…. Again an arrest on which you spit.

That extremely old first finitude, whose ten primitive cavities are its children directed towards a mythical apotheosis, seems once more to repeat its complexity. A name to which you can respond from this moment on: "Vicar." The living word passed beyond death by subverting a kind of clutz-assemblage founds indeed a relation to "substance," to "being," to the ontic preposition: "about."

Yes, this describes a sort of metalogical sleight of hand, but only if your misgivings are named your "missed-payments," otherwise, all could not end well.

Useless: a five kilometer deck-swing whose very pronounced emphasis of two undersized boards give the impression of a rapid diminution. Additionally, this pair of reduced trios is made to do a hundred or so false starts.

Six is more like it. But until an official responds with spin, with a malarkey beyond recognition, I say the salamander bite belongs to someone else, someone from the mill factory demanding his title.

Or is my deferring worth less than a tin can, there being purpose to my asking, an asking that is my shame?

In the meantime, meanwhile develops so that a black apostrophe, as in, "You are a trumpeted departure for unknown reasons," subsequently denies a complete accession here, at this point, that negates an adjectival response in favour of a progressive lack.

Any such accompaniment, whether googolplex times, or...how does it go?...something related (pace the contrary) entirely to the corrosion of a resurrection, which, to look at life from that position, exhausts the verve of even the most ambitious republic.

In effect, the end in all but name thinks away the "Universal Congress" that amounts to no less than ten to the tenth (10:1/10) or to two or more (x>2) pre-antediluvian onericisms [sic].

But as preamble to twice this unsolicited nothingness is a current example of two Afrikaner sayings: "A woe jumps to meet a demand"; "A poor man accepts no substitute, so sell what pleases us."

Ultimately then, at the decline of what will have come, what man [sic] inflicts upon himself is a void, a point of punctilious fear, which... "behold," is the "Mother."

No, don't adjust the vertical-hold. I know what I am talking about. You can see what I mean televised as a pseudo-fiasco where mankind [sic], suffering from the discommode of a pure sham (Thank you Diogenes), stands beside another, who, just as troublesome, is on at such and such about a "Gaze."

Unless you missed it, I'm pointing, by way of indirection, to a tremble-some being, to that ultra-family-member: Father.

Ahh...welcome to the "Subject."

Already though, I've given too many direct clues to finish what y'all are so dyin' to know. But let me tell you, brother, that all your desires, not withstanding that earthly relation to Thanatopia, freight a cold transcendence over which your cash, your capital, your value-added, and subliminal sleight of hand, have no truck with purpose.

Even the wise Orient, though they go slightly and somewhat quiet-like about it, under a tenth of the local reckoning, take their time walking along, speaking to themselves of their own ills. Such a pain that what already comes across again does not get shortened. Furthermore, by purporting to leave some kind of record of the baffling sexual feats of mathematical aspect-ism, the vast totality of which makes some kind of movement out of it, you agree to only a portion and take the remainder to supplement your only trove.

According to the last (the seventh) billboard logo, your act as a false ghetto-agent—not that stern, acclimated way you developed around and about the speed of a fax machine, but rather that one while lurking abroad, especially when the female to rat ratio rapidly increased, centimeter by centimeter—would lead you somewhere that is more suitable to the fuzzy memories of Earth's gravity.

Most often intended are those other parts of recollection that cause nothing, the grammatically dead mnemonic devices, or what substitutes for disk space and ram speed—namely, Memory.

But according to the perspicuity saved for thee at four o'clock will be a sickness from a zinc candleholder.

And so I said to myself: "I immediately rebuke my fellow man, his kind and kin."

The letter "Q" reveals an alternative demand that intones all sufferings or half-past ones. Here the bailiff who escorts, who bails according to the recent chain of past-post-perfect precedents, or namely, to give a slight hook or so to mankind's [sic] thousand efforts to replace fear with something less fearful, might sometime ask "Why?" as his alibi.

So, today ladies and gentlemen, behold: Each of you tomorrow, if not all who number here among the philosopher's relative truth, will understand that ten spoils of classical artifice remain, if not more or less figuratively speaking, then popularly.

Most men [sic] the day after tomorrow, or so, will help comprise a moderate number to arrest half or all the alternative demands of yours.

Two pauses ...—.... —...work to rob us of that great sum. My reductionism tied to
all
four   sides
of
the opening of one's ten-litre spectacles [ed. nine eventually became the standard measure], showed there a chronology of "nows" exclusively ill-disposed upon (give or take a high or low to-ing and fro-ing).

There is a manner that matters. A measure of decayed memory that in itself, without subtraction, is totally and immediately named. Always from behind, to replace "there" with "here." Underwritten in that kind, that type of official Americanism and without any kind of parenthetical pulse shows that a "cold" is not the same or the identical incipience that subscribes to denial.

This taste for latent freshness, a giving forth of thousands, or what amounts to all the quantities, calculates an indefinite decrease in the pleasure of "now," which sometimes, in the a.m., this vitally precise moment, like Christmas, emerges strikingly dull from its being proximate to the nothing.

Is God's presence singular? Aren't all presences like this? If so, then somehow it matters that my pulse, my life tempo, leans slightly more to the left of that part from which it comes.

It makes me think somewhat of power's shame. Those myriad faults, of which are woven nothing less than golden threads of grammarral speculations, come closest to purchasing at once both my possession of vintage lies and my seven day mendacity.

A second generation is occasionally needed then. That, or an automatic salute for the genitive gratitude to which the day after tomorrow becomes a mere memento.

Take for instance any of those constants whose chromatic duration, already a half-life too long, help signify zero: "One"—a little too emphatick; "Two"— about the same estimate.

Both in effect amount at once to some kind of "I-Thou" pride. To a stranger they help mark (or at least act as a provisional reminder for what we can all agree to take to the eighth-decimal place) the folds of an instance for comparing the signs of death and eternity: Both of which subtract "I" from the letter "Q," and sanctify the egress of the ego's having been multiplied by such an odd pair, a pair that endures the infinitive sum of an alchemical contemplation.

Not to rush through the point, but at half-below zero—the transverse ablative that divides this artificial threshold—there are uncounted seconds that nevertheless are subject to an endless reckoning.

Furthermore, mum willing, is the rate at which oxidation of tin imparts an inverse measure of patience.

Back seven d...d...d...d...d...days ago, and for the thousandth time, the Superbowl of lies that I spread in order to exclude you all from my ascent, somehow bound me to you instead. Besides being strikingly easy, this reminded me goldenly that we ought to act as agents of the present day.

Where if, rather than lack capacity, the numerical subject "I" or "one" acts so as to follow the teachings of grandfather, we may establish a new professional video temporality that could easily deny or deprive a subjunctive abode. Such would be the agency of the non-self: "He who makes a cause develops no effects."

In many ways I confuse "taking a piss" and the apostrophe: "To please my departures between the fresh and sometimes soporific afternoons of June. To represent an opium farmer, or to enjoy an existential surcease. To give those who seek something they have been following, like a cotton or a wool scarf that holds between each member, something warm to fold over sharp words lettered in ink…"

On that relatively accursed day before yesterday, where the non-limited, the infinite, unfortunately became actual, a complicated alternative arrived in chains.

A circumspect payment made sometime ago by someone old, produced a kind of uncertain Cicero effect: Evacuate a land of its abbreviations at the rate of eighty-four apostrophes a minute.

A dwarf whose brother is related to all men. The darling albatross will alight the day after tomorrow, the day after myself. Friday will come. From out of Saturday an allegorical retrofit to Tuesday's cause. And finally, the people, etcetera, set the price of cotton and wool as an interesting subject.

A prick on the last finger, for example, is a concerted woe, one to cause others and me considerable memory loss. Indeed, to write a modest account of this, dividing straight lines into a count of a hundred or so, terminates the real misery of it all. What started out as a cry ends in unorthodox linkenings.

As profiteer, he indicated what would turn out to be a two-sided proposal: A particular feminine measurement that instead of abbreviating "can naught" would sell for less than a centimeter, an elbow's length whose crook can knot somebody's truth and present it as a punctual tragedy.

Now what underwrites all transactions are the inward decimals that prove the Westernly bias of the congress. This side of the infinite end of pain, an older representative of life, is beneath the mis-allure of an address. It's one whose belonging refers more to an imaginary foundation than an actual prop.

To my to thinking, what an anarchy does is to skip the primitive life.

There is an alternative to the Golden Hall in which the tunnel's light ends, one where your plan to cross life, that plan to consent to the monotony of being, ends in the reminiscence of opium: vol. 3—"The layout of my work between a terminal zero and the prolegomenon to a linguistic alibi."

From vast to false, the tempo of the end goes on and on in conjunctive monotonies. Its scalding temperatures relieve the hours of too much fake language and meaning whose reception comes careening from above.

Out of several desultory reveries and eight utopias, each lacking a custom to exclusively baffle and/or enlighten the non-official on account of the halo of semiotic demand, are the Esperanto-ized words: "Covet thy attention of data."

The "Greek," as he is called, will by the end of tomorrow, by someone somewhere, be judged for his role as a one-man riot.

Easily more could surely starve. A real receiver of a rolling log jam, the aim of which Easter as the "or" of death might dither with, heckled these forgotten people such that each instant beneath the proposition of life, or the pseudo-tradition of "death," rendered relative the most massive stroke of genius.

A set of postage stamps alone does not prevent one from inhaling adhesive vapors, of which every eighty or so fewer than a trillion, will fire off a sidereal version of a defunct viral infection.

Thus, avoid observing the above least ye wound yourself with a micrometric parcel gizmo.

Please, since I asked nicely in that Northerly way, which of someone's third will finally impose a measure of during?

Grandfather's four halos vs. gov't and Ivy League sources thankfully do not imply the god whose eight furies replaced the six. Should they attach to a relative worry an aberrant letter "Q" such that too much utopian approximateliness defects our end, that worry's smiling sentiment would exhaust the stay of my host?

Analogous to me is a predicate malarkey. What kind of exponential series interjects woe into its member set? One's whose frequency allies a qualitative pause ... — ...

Karen Eliot
2010

Bibliography

Abram, John. "Re: Question (2)." Email message to eldritch Priest. 17 May 2009.

Adorno, Theodor W. "Form in the New Music." *Music Analysis* 27, no. 2–3 (2008): 201–16.

—*Essays on Music*. Translated by Susan H. Gillespie. Edited by Richard Leppert. Berkeley: University of California Press, 2002.

—"Music in the Background." In *Essays on Music*. Edited by Richard Leppert. Berkeley: University of California Press, 2002.

—"On the Fetish-Character in Music." In *Essays on Music*. Edited by Richard Leppert. Berkeley: University of California Press, 2002.

Agamben, Giorgio. "Bartleby, or on Contingency." In *Potentialities: Collected Essays in Philosophy*. Edited by Daniel Heller-Roazen. Stanford: Stanford University Press, 1993.

Anderson, Ben. "Time-Stilled Space-Slowed: How Boredom Matters." *Geoforum* 35 (2004): 739–54.

Anderson, Sam. "In Defense of Distraction: Twitter, Adderall, Lifehacking, Mindful Jogging, Power Browsing, Obama's Blackberry, and the Benefits of Overstimulation." *New York Magazine*, 17 May 2009.

Allen, Stan. "Dazed and Confused," *Assemblage 27* (1995): 47–54.

Arnold, Martin. "Observations About, around and Beside "Burrow out; Burrow in; Burrow Music." PhD diss., University of Victoria, 1995.

Bakhtin, M. M. "The Problem of Content, Material, and Form in Verbal Art." In *Art and Answerability: Early Philosophical Essays by M. M. Bakhtin*. Edited by Michael Holquist and Vadim Laipunov. Translated by Vadim Laipunov. Austin: University of Texas Press, 1990.

Barone, Chedomir. "Re: question." Email message to eldritch Priest. 15 April 2009.

—*Piano Installation with Derangements*. 2003. (n.p.).

Barrett, G. Douglas. "Artist Statement." www.gdouglasbarrett.com. [accessed October 2012].

—*Derivation XI*. 2008. (n.p.). http://gdouglasbarrett.com. [accessed October 2012].

—*Three Voices*. 2008. (n.p.). http://gdouglasbarrett.com. [accessed October 2012].

—"Re: question (3)." Email message to eldritch Priest. 3 June 2009.

Barrett, G. Douglas, and Michael Winter. "Livescore: Real-Time Notation in the Music of Harris Wulfson." *Contemporary Music Review* 29, no. 1 (2010): 55–62.

Barthes, Roland. *The Neutral: Lecture Course at the Collège De France, 1977–1978*. Translated by Rosalind Krauss and Denis Hollier. New York: Columbia University Press, 2005.

Bataille, Georges. *Visions of Excess*. Translated by Allan Stoekl. Edited by Allan Stoekl. Minneapolis: University of Minnesota Press, 1985.

Baudelaire, Charles. *Les Fleurs Du Mal*. Translated by Richard Howard. Boston: David R. Godine, 1985.

Baudrillard, Jean. *The Conspiracy of Art: Manifestos, Interviews, Essays*. Translated by Sylvère Lotringer, Semiotext(e). New York: Semiotext(e), 2005.

—*Simulacra and Simulation*. Translated by Sheila Glaser. Ann Arbor: University of Michigan Press, 1995.

—*Symbolic Exchange and Death*. Translated by Ian Hamilton Grant. London: Sage, 1993.

—*Seduction*. Translated by Brian Singer. New York: St. Martin's Press, 1990.

Beckett, Samuel. *Worstward Ho*. London: John Calder, 1983.

Bell, Clive. *Art*. London: Chatto and Windus, 1949.

Benjamin, Walter. *Arcades Project*. Translated by Kevin McLaughlin and Howard Eiland. Edited by Rolf Tiedemann. Cambridge, MA: Belknap Press of Harvard University Press, 2002.

—"The Work of Art in the Age of Mechanical Reproduction." In *Illuminations*. Edited by Hannah Arendt. London: Fontana Press, 1992.

Bennett, Bradley. "Doctrine of Signatures: An Explanation of Medicinal Plant Discovery or Dissemination of Knowledge?" *Journal of the New York Botanical Garden* 61, no. 3 (2007): 246–55.

Bergson, Henri. *Matter and Memory*. Trans. by Nancy M. Paul and W. Scott Palmer. London; New York: G. Allen & Co. and MacMillan Co., 1912.

Birkerts, Sven. *The Gutenberg Elegies: The Fate of Reading in an Electronic Age*. Boston: Faber and Faber, 1994.

Bissell, Tom. "Cinema Crudité: The Mysterious Appeal of the Post-Camp Cult Film." *Harper's Magazine*, August 2010, 58–65.

Blom, Ina. *The Cut Though Time: A Version of the Dada/Neo-Dada Repetition*. Oslo: Acta Humaniora/UniPub, 1999.

—"Boredom and Oblivion." In *The Fluxus Reader*. Edited by Ken Friedman, 63–90. West Sussex, UK: Academy Editions, 1998.

Bogard, William. "Distraction and Digital Culture." *ctheory*, 5 October 2000. http://www.ctheory.net/articles.aspx?id=131 [accessed October 2012].

Bogue, Ronald. *Deleuze on Music, Painting, and the Arts*. London: Routledge, 2003.

—*Deleuze and Guattari*. London; New York: Routledge, 1989.

Bois, Yve-Alain, and Rosalind Krauss. *Formless: A User's Guide*. Cambridge, MA: MIT Press, 1997.

Bök, Christian. *'Pataphysics: The Poetics of an Imaginary Science*. Chicago: Northwestern University Press, 2002.

—*Eunoia*. Toronto: Coach House Books, 2001.

Burt, Warren. "Re: Ever tried. Ever failed." Email message to eldritch Priest, 19 July 2010.

—"Re: Form Submission – Contact Me." Email message to eldritch Priest, 19 June 2010.

—"DECIBEL02: Warren Burt – Another Noisy Lullaby." Interview with Julian Day, Australian Music, Australian Broadcasting Corporation (last updated 19 April 2010). http://www.abc.net.au/classic/australianmusic/stories/s2835399.htm [accessed October 2012].

—Program notes, "Tape It!," Totally Huge New Music Festival. Perth, Australia, 10 September 2009. http://decibel.waapamusic.com/concert-1-tape-it/tape-it-program-notes [accessed October 2012].

—*Another Noisy Lullaby*. 2009. (n.p.).

Busoni, Ferruccio. *Sketch of a New Esthetic of Music*. Translated by T. H. Baker. New York: G. Schrimer, 1911.

Cage, John. *Silence: Lectures and Writings*. Middletown, CN: Wesleyan University Press, 1961.

Caillois, Roger. *Man, Play and Games*. Translated by Meyer Barash. New York: Free Press of Glencoe, 1961.

Calvino, Italo. *If on a Winter's Night a Traveler....* Translated by William Weaver. New York: Harcourt Brace Jovanovich, 1981.

Carr, Nicholas. *The Shallows: What the Internet Is Doing to Our Brains*. New York; London: W. W. Norton and Company, 2010.

Carroll, Peter. *Liber Null & Psychonaut: An Introduction to Chaos Magic*. York Beach, ME: Weiser Books, 1987.

Carson, Anne. *Decreation*. Toronto: Vintage Canada, 2006.

Cascone, Kim. "The Aesthetics of Failure: 'Post-Digital' Tendencies in Contemporary Computer Music." *Computer Music Journal* 24, no. 4 (2000): 12–18.

Certeau, Michel de. *The Practice of Everyday Life*. Translated by Steven Rendall. Berkeley: University of California Press, 1984.

Chanan, Michael. *Musica Practica: The Social Practice of Western Music from Gregorian Chant to Postmodernism*. New York: Verso, 1994.

Christensen, Erik. "Overt and Hidden Processes in 20th Century Music." *Axiomathes* 14, no. 1–3 (2004): 97–117.

Chusid, Irwin. *Songs in the Key of Z: The Curious Universe of Outsider Music*. Chicago: A Cappella, 2000.

Clark, Eric km. *Mein Schatz*. 2007. (n.p.).

Clark, Philip. "Misshapen identities." *The Wire*, November 2010, 45–9.

Cocker, Emma. "Over and over, Again and Again." In *Failure*. Edited by Lisa Le Feuvre, 154–63. Cambridge, MA: MIT Press, 2010.

Couroux, Marc. Program note, *Carpenters et al., Downey Musical Holdings, a Real-Time Social System as of March 29, 2007*, 2010. http://couroux.org/?page_id=48 [accessed October 2012].

Cross, Ian. "Music and Meaning, Ambiguity and Evolution." In *Musical Communication*, 27–44. Oxford: Oxford University Press, 2005.

—"Music, Cognition, Culture, and Evolution." *Annals of the New York Academy of Sciences* 930 (2001): 28–42.

Crowley, Aleister. *Magick*. Edited by John Symonds and Kenneth Grant. London: Routledge, 1973.

Crowley, Patrick, and Paul Hegarty. *Formless: Ways in and out of Form*. Bern: Peter Lang, 2005.

Cusick, Suzanne G. "Music as Torture/Music as Weapon." *Transcultural Music Review* 10 (2006). http://www.sibetrans.com/trans/trans10/cusick_eng.htm [accessed October 2012].

Cusick, Suzanne G., and Branden Joseph. "Across an Invisible Line: A Conversation About Music and Torture." *Grey Room* 42 (2011): 6–11.

Delaforgem, Gaetan. "The Templar Tradition: Yesterday and Today." *Gnosis* 6 (1987), 8–13.

Deleuze, Gilles. *Desert Islands and Other Texts, 1953–1974*. Translated by Michael Taormina. Edited by David Lapoujade. Los Angeles; Cambridge, MA: Semiotext(e), 2004.

—*Francis Bacon: The Logic of Sensation*. Translated by Daniel W. Smith. London: Continuum, 2003.

—*Difference and Repetition*. New York: Columbia University Press, 1994.

—*Expressionism in Philosophy: Spinoza*. Translated by Martin Joughin. New York: Zone Books, 1990.

—*The Logic of Sense*. New York: Columbia University Press, 1990.

—*Cinema 1: The Movement Image*. Translated by Hugh Thomlinson and Barbara Haberjam. Minneapolis: University of Minnesota, 1989.

—"Lecture Transcripts on Spinoza's Concept of Affect," 24 January 1978. http://www.webdeleuze.com/pdf/uk/Spinoza/240178.zip [accessed October 2012].

Deleuze, Gilles, and Félix Guattari. *What Is Philosophy?* Translated by Hugh Tomlinson and Graham Burchell. New York: Columbia University Press, 1994.

—*A Thousand Plateaus: Capitalism and Schizophrenia*. Translated by Brian Massumi. Minneapolis: University of Minnesota Press, 1987.

DeNora, Tia. *Music in Everyday Life*. Cambridge and New York: Cambridge University Press, 2000.

Didi-Huberman, Georges. *La Ressemblance informe, ou, le gai savoir visuel selon Georges Bataille*. Paris: Editions Macula, 1995.

Diederichsen, Diedrich. *On (Surplus) Value in Art*. Rotterdam: Witte de With, 2008.

Dostoyevsky, Fyodor. *Notes from Underground*. Translated by Constance Garnett. New York: Dover Publications, 1992.

Duffy, Simon. "The Logic of Expression in Deleuze's Expressionism in Philosophy: Spinoza: A Strategy of Engagement." *International Journal of Philosophical Studies* 12, no. 1 (2004): 47–60.

Dworkin, Craig. *Reading the Illegible*. Evanston, IL: Northwestern University Press, 2003.

Ehrenberg, Alain. *The Weariness of the Self: Diagnosing the History of Depression in the Contemporary Age*. Montreal and Kingston: McGill-Queen's University Press, 2010.

Eliot, Karen. *glossolalia (stress positions)*. 2008. (n.p.).

Evens, Aden. *Sound Ideas: Music, Machines, and Experience*. Minneapolis: University of Minnesota Press, 2005.

Featherstone, Mike. *Undoing Culture: Globalization, Postmodernism and Identity*. London and Thousand Oaks, CA: Sage Publications, 1995.

Finn, Geraldine, "The Truth in Music: The Sound of Différance." *Muzikiloski Zbornic/Musicological Annual* 44, no. 2 (2005): 118–46.

Fisher, Joel. "Judgement and Purpose." In *M/E/a/N/I/N/G: An Anthology of Artists' Writings, Theory, and Criticism*. Edited by Susan Bee and Mira Schor, 155–62. Durham; London: Duke University Press, 2000.

Fisher, Mark. *Capitalist Realism: Is There No Alternative?* London: Zero Books, 2009.

—"Flatline Constructs: Gothic Materialism and Cybernetic Theory-Fiction." PhD, University of Warwick, 1999.

Fleming, Chris, and John O'Carroll. "The Art of the Hoax." *Parallax* 16, no. 4 (2010): 45–59.

Foucault, Michel. "What Is an Author?" In *The Foucault Reader*. Edited by Paul Rabinow, 101–20. New York: Pantheon Books, 1984.

Frankfurt, Harry. *On Bullshit*. Princeton, NJ: Princeton University Press, 2005.

Fresh, Stuart. "A Short History of Grúpat," 2006. http://www.cmc.ie/articles/article1799.html [accessed October 2012].

Freud, Sigmund. "Instincts and their Vicissitudes," In *The Standard Edition of the Complete Psychological Works of Sigmund Freud*, vol. 14. Edited by James Strachey, 111–40. New York: Norton, 1957.

—*The Interpretation of Dreams*. Translated by James Strachey. New York: Basic Books, 1955.

Friedlander, Emilie. "Horizons: What, If Any, Are the Politics of Hypnagogic Pop?," 28 September 2009. http://www.visitation-rites.com/2009/09/ [accessed October 2012].

Frith, Simon. *Performing Rites: On the Value of Popular Music.* Cambridge, MA: Harvard University Press, 1996.

Gibbons, Brian. *Spirituality and the Occult.* London; New York: Routledge, 2001.

Goffman, Erving. *Behavior in Public Places: Notes on the Social Organization of Gatherings.* New York: Free Press, 1963.

Goldman, Robert, and Stephen Papson. "Advertising in the Age of Hypersignification." *Theory, Culture & Society* 11, no. 3 (1994): 23–53.

Goodman, David. "Distracted Listening: On Not Making Sound Choices in the 1930s." In *Sound in the Era of Mechanical Reproduction.* Edited by David Suisman and Susan Strasser, 15–46. Philadelphia: University of Pennsylvania Press, 2010.

Goodman, Steve. *Sonic Warfare: Sound, Affect, and the Ecology of Fear.* Cambridge, MA: MIT Press, 2010.

Goodstein, Elizabeth S. *Experience without Qualities: Boredom and Modernity.* Stanford: Stanford University Press, 2005.

Groom, Nick. "The Condition of Muzak." *Popular Music and Society* 20, no. 3 (1996): 1–17.

Grosz, Elizabeth. *Chaos, Territory, Art: Deleuze and the Framing of the Earth.* New York: Columbia University Press, 2008.

Guattari, Félix. *Chaosmosis: An Ethico-Aesthetic Paradigm.* Translated by Paul Baines and Jullian Penfais. Innianapolis: Indiana University Press, 1995.

Harman, Graham. *Guerrilla Metaphysics: Phenomenology and the Carpentry of Things.* Chicago: Open Court, 2005.

Harrison, Paul. "Making Sense: Embodiment and the Sensibilities of the Everyday." *Environment and Planning D: Society and Space* 18, no. 4 (2000): 497–517.

Healy, Seán Desmond. *Boredom, Self, and Culture.* Rutherford; London: Fairleigh Dickinson University Press, 1984.

Hedges, Chris. *Death of the Liberal Class.* New York: Nation Books, 2010.

Hegarty, Paul. *Noise/Music: A History.* New York: Continuum, 2007.

—"Formal Insistence." *The Semiotic Review of Books* 13, no. 2 (2003): 6–9.

—"Residue – Margin – Other: Noise as Ethics of Excess." In *Argosfestival 2003.* Edited by Paul Willemsen and Frie Depraetere, 76–87. Brussels: Argo, 2003.

—"General Ecology of Sound: Japanese Noise Music as Low Form." Paper presented at Le travail de l'informe/functions of formless, University College Cork, July 2002. Also available at http://www. dotdotdotmusic.com/hegarty7.html [accessed October 2012].

Heidegger, Martin. "What Is Metaphysics?" In *Basic Writings.* Edited by David Farrell Krell, 89–110. New York: Harper Perennial Modern Classics, 2008.

—*The Fundamental Concepts of Metaphysics: World, Finitude, Solitude*. Translated by William McNeill and Nicholas Walker. Indianapolis: Indiana University Press, 2001.

—*Being and Time*. Translated by John Macquarrie and Edward Robinson. Oxford: Blackwell, 1978.

Heister, Hanns-Werner. "Music in Concert and Music in the Background: Two Poles of Musical Realization." In *Companion to Contemporary Musical Thought*. Edited by John Paynter. London: Routledge, 1992.

Higgins, Dick. "Boredom and Danger." In B*reaking the Sound Barrier: A Critical Anthology of the New Music*. Edited by Gregory Battcock, 20–7. New York: Dutton, 1982.

Highmore, Ben. "Unprocessed Data: Everyday Life in the Singular," April 2005. http://www.daytodaydata.com/benhighmore.html [accessed October 2012].

—*Everyday Life and Cultural Theory: An Introduction*. London; New York: Routledge, 2002.

Hite, John. Notes to *Machine Music: John White and Gavin Bryars*. LP Obscure OBD 8.

Hofstadter, Douglas. *Gödel, Escher, Bach: An Eternal Golden Braid*. New York: Basic Books, 1979.

Home, Stuart. "Karen Eliot." http://stewarthomesociety.org/sp/eliot.htm [accessed October 2012].

—"Multiple Names." http://www.stewarthomesociety.org/sp/multi.htm [accessed October 2012].

Hosokawa, Shuhei. *The Aesthetics of Recorded Sound*. Tokyo: Keiso Shobo, 1990.

Houellebecq, Michel. *Platform*. Translated by Frank Wynne. London: Heinemann, 2002.

Huebler, Douglas. "Untitled Statement." In *Theories and Documents of Contemporary Art*. Edited by Kristine Stiles and Peter Selz. Berkeley: University of California Press, 1996.

Jackson, Maggie. *Distracted: The Erosion of Attention and the Coming Dark Age*. Amherst, NY: Prometheus Books, 2008.

Jakobson, Roman. "Shifters and Verbal Categories." In *On Language*. Edited by Linda Waugh and Monique Monville-Burston, 386–92. Cambridge, MA: Harvard University Press, 1990.

James, William. *Talks to Teachers on Psychology; and to Students on Some of Life's Ideals*. New York: W. W. Norton, 1958.

Jameson, Fredric. "Theories of the Postmodern." In *The Cultural Turn: Selected Writings on the Postmodern, 1983–1998*, 20–32. London: Verso, 1998.

Kahn, Douglas. *Noise, Water, Meat: A History of Sound in the Arts*. Cambridge, MA: MIT Press, 1999.

Kassabian, Anahid. "Would You Like Some World Music with Your

Latte? Starbucks, Putumayo, and Distributed Tourism." *Twentieth Century Music* 2, no. 1 (2004): 209–23.

—"Ubisub: Ubiquitous Listening and Networked Subjectivity." *Echo* 3, no. 2 (2001). http://www.echo.ucla.edu/Volume3-issue2/kassabian/index.html [accessed October 2012].

Katz, Ruth. *A Language of Its Own: Sense and Meaning in the Making of Western Art Music*. Chicago: The University of Chicago Press, 2009.

Keenan, David. "Hypnagogic Pop." *The Wire* 306 (August 2009).

Kierkegaard, Søren. *Either/Or*. Translated by Howard V. Hong and Edna H. Hong. Princeton: Princeton University Press, 1988.

Kim-Cohen, Seth. *In the Blink of an Ear: Toward a Non-cochlear Sonic Art*. London; New York: Continuum, 2009.

Klapp, Orrin. *Overload and Boredom*. New York: Greenwood Press, 1986.

Koopman, Colin. "Pragmatism as a Philosophy of Hope: Emerson, James, Dewey, Rorty." *The Journal of Speculative Philosophy* 20, no. 2 (2006): 106–16.

Kostelanetz, Richard. *Conversing with Cage*. New York: Routledge, 2003.

Kracauer, Siegfried. "Boredom." In *The Mass Ornament: Weimar Essays*. Edited by Thomas Y. Levin, 331–4. Cambridge, MA: Harvard University Press, 1995.

—"The Cult of Distraction: On Berlin's Pleasure Palaces." In *The Mass Ornament: Weimar Essays*. Edited by Thomas Y. Levin. Cambridge, MA: Harvard University Press, 1995.

Krauss, Rosalind E. "Video: The Aesthetics of Narcissism." *October* 1 (1976): 50–64.

Kuberski, Philip. *Chaosmos: Literature, Science, and Theory*. Albany: State University of New York Press, 1994.

Lacan, Jacques. *On Feminine Sexuality, the Limits of Love and Knowledge: The Seminar of Jacques Lacan, Book XX Encore 1972–1973*. Translated by Jacques-Alain Miller. New York: Norton, 1998.

Langer, Susanne. *Feeling and Form*. New York: Charles Scribner's Sons, 1953.

Lautman, Albert. *Essai sur l'unité des sciences mathématiques dans leur développement actuel*. Paris: Hermann, 1938.

Le Feuvre, Lisa. *Failure*. Cambridge, MA: MIT Press, 2010.

Lecercle, Jean-Jacques. *Philosophy of Nonsense: The Intuitions of Victorian Nonsense Literature*. London: Routledge, 1994.

Lewis, Michael. *Derrida and Lacan: Another Writing*. Edinburgh: Edinburgh University Press, 2008.

Lyotard, Jean-François. *Discourse, Figure*. Translated by Antony Hudek and Mary Lydon. Minneapolis: University of Minnesota Press, 2011.

—*Lessons on the Analytic of the Sublime: Kant's Critique of Judgment,*

§§ 23–9. Translated by Elizabeth Rottenberg. Stanford, CA: Stanford
   University Press, 1994.
—*Libidinal Economy*. Translated by Iain Hamilton Grant. Bloomington:
   Indiana University Press, 1993
—*The Postmodern Condition: A Report on Knowledge*. Translated by
   Geoff Bennington and Brian Massumi. Minneapolis: University of
   Minnesota Press, 1984.
Mann, Paul. *Masocriticism*. Albany: State University of New York Press,
   1999.
—*The Theory-Death of the Avant-Garde*. Bloomington: Indiana
   University Press, 1991.
Marder, Michael. "Heidegger's 'Phenomenology of Failure' in Sein Und
   Zeit." *Philosophy Today* 51, no. 1 (2007): 69–78.
Marx, Karl, and Friedrich Engels. *The Communist Manifesto*. Translated
   by Samuel Moore. London: Penguin Classics, 2002.
Massumi, Brian. "Power to the Edge: Making Information Pointy." In
   Ontopower: War, Power, and the State of Perception. Durham, NC:
   Duke University Press (forthcoming).
—*Semblance and Event: Activist Philosophy and the Occurrent Arts*.
   Cambridge, MA: MIT Press, 2011.
—"Perception Attack: Brief on War Time." *Theory and Event* 13,
   no. 3 (2010). http://muse.jhu.edu/journals/theory_and_event/
   v013/13.3.massumi.html.
—"Potential Politics and the Primacy of Preemption." *Theory and Event*
   10, no. 2 (2007). http://muse.jhu.edu/journals/theory_and_event/
   v010/10.2massumi.html.
—"Fear (the Spectrum Said)." *Positions* 13, no. 1 (2005): 31–48.
—*Parables for the Virtual: Movement, Affect, Sensation*. Durham, NC:
   Duke University Press, 2002.
Massumi, Brian, and Kenneth Dean. *First and Last Emperors:
   The Absolute State and the Body of the Despot*. Brooklyn, NY:
   Autonomedia, 1992.
Mauss, Marcel. *A General Theory of Magic*. Translated by Robert Brain.
   London and New York: Routledge, 2001.
—*Sociologie et anthropologie*. Paris: PUF, 1950.
Mavromatis, Andreas. *Hypnagogia: The Unique State of Consciousness
   between Wakefulness and Sleep*. London: Routledge, 1987.
Maxwell, Devin. "Question (1)." Email message to eldritch Priest. 30
   May 2009.
—*PH4*. 2004. Montreal, QC: GoodChild Music. 2011.
McClary, Susan. "Narrative Agendas in 'Absolute Music'." In *Musicology
   and Difference: Gender and Sexuality in Music Scholarship*. Edited by
   Ruth A. Solie, 326–44. Berkeley: University of California Press 1995.
McCort, Dennis. *Going Beyond the Pairs: The Coincidence of Opposites*

in German Romanticism, Zen, and Deconstruction. Albany: State
University of New York Press, 2001.

Menke, Christoph. *The Sovereignty of Art: Aesthetic Negativity in
Adorno and Derrida.* Translated by Neil Solomon. Cambridge, MA:
MIT Press, 1999.

Meyer, Leonard B. *Emotion and Meaning in Music.* Chicago: University
of Chicago Press, 1956.

Miller, Nancy K. "The Text's Heroine: A Feminist Critic and Her Fictions."
Diacritics 12, no. 2 (1982): 48–53.

Monsell, Stephen, and Jon Driver (eds). *Control of Cognitive
Processes: Attention and Performance XVIII.* Cambridge, MA: MIT
Press, 2000.

Morrison, Grant. "Pop Magic!" In *Book of Lies: The Disinformation
Guide to Magick and the Occult (Being an Alchemical Formula to Rip
a Hole in the Fabric of Reality).* Edited by Richard Metzger, 16–25.
New York: The Disinformation Company, 2003.

Ngai, Sianne. *Ugly Feelings.* Cambridge, MA: Harvard University Press,
2005.

Nietzsche, Friedrich. *The Birth of Tragedy and the Case of Wagner.*
Translated by Walter Kaufman. New York: Vintage, 1967.

—*Human, All Too Human.* Trans. by R. J. Hollingdale. Cambridge:
Cambridge University Press, 1996.

Nyman, Michael. *Experimental Music: Cage and Beyond.* 2nd ed.
Cambridge; New York: Cambridge University Press, 1999.

Ondaatje, Michael. *Coming Through Slaughter.* Toronto: Coach House
Press, 1976.

Owen, David. "The Soundtrack of Your Life." *The New Yorker,* 10 April 2006.

Patton, Paul. "The World Seen from Within." *Theory and Event* 1,
no. 1 (1997). http://muse.jhu.edu/journals/theory_and_event/
v001/1.1patton.html.

Peaker, Hugh. "Re: *Species of Spaces #16* notes." Email message to
eldritch Priest, 17 March 2010.

—*Species of Spaces #16.* 2009. (n.p.).

Pesce, Mark. "The Executable Dreamtime." In *Book of Lies: The
Disinformation Guide to Magick and the Occult (Being an Alchemical
Formula to Rip a Hole in the Fabric of Reality).* Edited by Richard
Metzger, 26–31. New York: The Disinformation Company, 2003.

Pessoa, Fernando. *The Book of Disquiet.* Translated by Richard Zenith.
London: Penguin Classics, 2002.

Phillips, Adam. *On Kissing, Tickling, and Being Bored: Psychoanalytic
Essays on the Unexamined Life.* Cambridge: Harvard University
Press, 1993.

Pieslak, Jonathan. *Sound Targets: American Soldiers and Music in the
Iraq War.* Bloomington: Indiana University Press, 2009.

P-Orridge, Genesis. "Thee Splinter Test." In *Book of Lies: The Disinformation Guide to Magick and the Occult (Being an Alchemical Formula to Rip a Hole in the Fabric of Reality)*. Edited by Richard Metzger, 138–48. New York: The Disinformation Company, 2003.

Priest, eldritch. "Like Good Acid and the Residue of *Pleasure Drenching…*." MMus thesis, University of Victoria, 2004.

Racker, Heinrich. "Contribution to Psychoanalysis of Music." *American Imago* 8, no. 2 (1951): 129–63.

Radano, Ronald Michael. "Interpreting Muzak: Speculations on Musical Experience in Everyday Life." *American Music* 7, no. 4 (1989): 448–60.

Ross, Christine. *The Aesthetics of Disengagement: Contemporary Art and Depression*. Minneapolis: University of Minnesota Press, 2006.

—"The Temporalities of Video: Extendedness Revisited." *Art Journal* 65, no. 3 (2006): 82–99.

Rubinstein, Joshua S., David E. Meyer, and Jeffrey E. Evans. "Executive Control of Cognitive Processes in Task Switching." *Journal of Experimental Psychology: Human Perception and Performance* 27, no. 4 (2001): 763–97.

Sartre, Jean-Paul. *Being and Nothingness*. Translated by Hazel Estella Barnes. New York: Washinton Square Press, 1984.

—*Nausea*. Translated by Lloyd Alexander. New York: New Directions Publishing, 1969.

Scarry, Elaine. *The Body in Pain: The Making and Unmaking of the World*. Oxford: Oxford University Press, 1985.

Sewell, Elizabeth. *The Field of Nonsense*. London: Chatto and Windus, 1952.

Shepherd, John. "Difference and Power in Music." In *Musicology and Difference*. Edited by Ruth A. Solie, 46–65. Berkeley and Los Angeles: University of California Press, 1993.

Shepherd, John, and Peter Wicke. *Music and Cultural Theory*. Cambridge: Polity Press, 1997.

Sherlock, John Mark. Interview with Otino Corsano, ARTPOST.info – The Art Information Portal for Galleries and Art Buyers, 2006. http://www.neithernor.com/sherlock11/?page_id=15 [accessed October 2012].

—*one more day in the empire*. 2006. (n.p.).

Sigman, Mariano, and Stanislas Dehaene. "Dynamics of the Central Bottleneck: Dual-Task and Task Uncertainty." *PLoS Biology* 4, no. 7 (2006).

Singer, Irving. *Feeling and Imagination*. Lanham, MD: Rowman & Littlefield, 2001.

Smith, Terry. *What Is Contemporary Art?* Chicago: University Of Chicago Press, 2009.

Sodian, Beate, Catherine Taylor, Paul L. Harris, and Josef Perner. "Early

Deception and the Child's Theory of Mind: False Trails and Genuine Markers." *Child Development* 62, no. 3 (1991): 468–83.

Steenhuisen, Paul. *Sonic Mosaics: Conversations with Composers*. Edmonton: University of Alberta Press, 2009.

Stein, Gertrude. *The Making of Americans: Being a History of a Family's Progress*. New York: Something Else Press, 1966.

Sterne, Jonathan. *The Audible Past: Cultural Origins of Sound Reproduction*. Durham, NC: Duke University Press, 2003.

—"Sounds Like the Mall of America: Programmed Music and the Architectonics of Commercial Space." *Ethnomusicology* 41, no. 1 (1997): 22–50.

Stone, Linda. "Continuous Partial Attention." http://lindastone.net/qa/continuous-partial-attention [accessed October 2012].

Subotnik, Rose Rosengard. "On Deconstructing Structural Listening." In *Music, Culture, and Society: A Reader*. Edited by Derek B. Scott. Oxford; New York: Oxford University Press, 2000.

Spare, Austin Osman. *The Book of Pleasure*. Sioux Falls, SD: NuVision Publications, 2007.

Stewart, Susan. *Nonsense: Aspects of Intertextuality in Folklore and Literature*. Baltimore: Johns Hopkins University Press, 1979.

Stivale, Charles. *Gilles Deleuze: Key Concepts*. Montreal: McGill-Queen's University Press, 2005.

Suskind, Ron. "Without a Doubt." *New York Times Magazine*, 14 October 2004.

Sumrell, Robert, and Kazys Varnelis. *Blue Monday: Stories of Absurd Realities and Natural Philosophies*. Barcelona: Actar Editorial, 2007.

Svendsen, Lars. *A Philosophy of Boredom*. Trans. by John Irons. London: Reaktion Books, 2005.

Terada, Rei. *Looking Away: Phenomenality and Dissatisfaction, Kant to Adorno*. Cambridge, MA: Harvard University Press, 2009.

Thorpe, Josh. "Here Hear: My Recent Compositions in a Context of Philosophy and 20th Century Experimental Music." MA, York University, 2000.

—*Ready-Made Aided #3*. 2000. (n.p.).

—*Ready-Made Aided #2*. 2000. (n.p.).

Tiffany, Daniel. *Infidel Poetics: Riddles, Nightlife, Substance*. Chicago: University of Chicago Press, 2009.

Tigges, Wim. *Explorations in the Field of Nonsense*. Amsterdam: Rodopi, 1987.

Tolimieri, Quentin. "Text." www.quentintolimieri.com/text.html [accessed October 2012].

—"Re: Question (1)." Email message to eldritch Priest. 28 April 2009.

Toulmin, Stephen. *Cosmopolis: The Hidden Agena of Modernity*. Chicago: University of Chicago Press, 1992.

U∴D∴, Frater. *High Magic: Theory & Practice*. St. Paul, MN: Llewellyn Publications, 2005.

Urgo, Joseph. *In the Age of Distraction*. Jackson, MS: University Press of Mississippi, 2000.

Vare, Robert. "Discophobia." *New York Times*, 10 July 1979.

Vermeir, Koen. "The Reality of Failure: On the Interpretation of Success and Failure in (the History and Philosophy of) Science and Technology." In *Variantology 2: On Deep Time Relations of Arts, Sciences and Technologies*. Edited by Siegfried Zielinski and David Link. Köln: Buchhandlung Walther König, 2006.

Volcker, Paul. "The Time We Have Is Growing Short." *The New York Review of Books*, 24 June 2010.

Wallace, David Foster. *The Pale King: An Unfinished Novel*. New York: Little, Brown and Co., 2011.

—*A Supposedly Fun Thing I'll Never Do Again: Essays and Arguments*. Boston: Little, Brown and Co., 1997.

Walshe, Jennifer. Interview. In *The Ashgate Research Companion to Experimental Music*. Edited by James Saunders, 343–52. Burlington, VT: Ashgate, 2009.

Walton, Kendall. "Précis of *Mimesis as Make-Believe*." *Philosophy and Phenomenological Research* 51, no. 2 (1991): 379–82.

—*Mimesis as Make-Believe: On the Foundations of the Representational Arts*. Cambridge, MA: Harvard University Press, 1990.

Warren, Jeff. "The Hypnopompic." In *The Head Trip: Adventures on the Wheel of Consciousness*. New York: Random House, 2007.

Waugh, Patricia. *Metafiction: The Theory and Practice of Self-Conscious Fiction*. London; New York: Methuen, 1984.

Weiss, Gail. *Refiguring the Ordinary*. Bloomington: Indiana University Press, 2008.

Wernick, Andrew. "Bataille's Columbine: The Sacred Space of Hate." *ctheory*, 3 November 1999. http://www.ctheory.net/articles.aspx?id=119 [accessed October 2012].

Williams, James. *Gilles Deleuze's Logic of Sense: A Critical Introduction and Guide*. Edinburgh: Edinburgh University Press, 2008.

Wolf, Werner. "Metafiction and Metamusic: Exploring the Limits of Metareference." In *Self-Reference in the Media*. Edited by Winifried Nöth and Nina Bishar, 303–24. Berlin and New York: Mouton de Gruyter, 2007.

Index